Living and loving with cancer

Fanahan McSweeney

Typesetting & design
Quill Print and Design
Tel: (01) 4922413

A Quill Print publication

Contents

To Jean, Andy, and Fanahan Beag

Introduction by Ger Canning

The book you are about to read is a work of fact, not fiction. Every detail is precise, recorded as it happened. Being the inner thoughts and perceptions of a young man battling with cancer, it was never intended for publication. In fact when close friends, including myself, were allowed glimpses of the manuscript, the writer strenuously resisted their urgings that he have it published. It began only as a personal diary of a bizarre sequence of events. It ended up, however, as a staggering account of one man's battle for the ultimate prize, life itself.

Fanahan McSweeney has spent a lifetime in athletics, but he was no ordinary athlete. In 1972 he represented Ireland at the Munich Olympic Games, where but for injury he would most certainly have contested the 400 metres final.

Television sports broadcaster Brendan O'Reilly describes Fanahan as a 'genius in everything he ever did'. The late Dr Pat O'Callaghan, a double Olympic champion, regarded the Grange/Fermoy clubman as 'one of the greatest natural talents this country has ever produced'.

Fanahan was reared in the environs of Castletownroche, County Cork. In his early years he excelled as a hurler, winning a county intermediate medal at just 16 years of age and playing for the Cork minors in the mid-Sixties. But it was as a sprinter of real class that he was to fully blossom. In 1968 he shattered the national record for 220 yards with a scintillating time of 21.1 seconds on grass. Over the next few years he added to that mark national records at 100 yards, 200 metres, 440 yards, and 400 metres. He was national champion eleven times and was unbeaten over 12 years at the Cork City Sports.

In 1969 Brendan O'Reilly, himself a former international high-jumper, helped Fanahan secure an athletics scholarship to McNeese State University, Lake Charles, Louisiana. While at college, Fanahan won two US national indoor (USTFF) titles, in 1970 and 1971. He competed in the World Student

Games in Turin and the European Championships in Helsinki, as well as the Munich Olympics. In Munich he had the curious distinction of hinting to the outside world the presence of Arab terrorists in the Olympic village - only hours before fuller details emerged of the massacre of Israeli athletes.

When Fanahan arrived at McNeese in the late Sixties, convention had it that students went to the USA for a 'good time'; study was of secondary importance. Fanahan was quickly disillusioned. The war in Vietnam inculcated a doctrine of 'survival by degrees'. In other words, the successful undergraduate could avoid the draft (or at least postpone it) by intense application to study.

As well as graduating with a degree in civil engineering, Fanahan maintained exquisite form on the track. Indeed, he was selected as a member of the 'Outstanding College Athletes of America' on four consecutive occasions, 'in recognition of outstanding ability, accomplishment, and service'.

On the indoor circuit, Fanahan became an instant hit. He gave the crowds what they came to see: a captivating white sprinter beating all-comers. Inevitably, psychology was a factor. Warming up for a race in his early years in the States, he was approached by a black opponent with a strange question: 'Whatsa ma number, man?' Fanahan looked at his back and told him, wondering why the query. 'Cos you're gonna be seein' it all de way to de finish line.' Needless to relate, the Irishman duly prevailed.

In February 1970, at the Astrodome in Houston, Texas, Fanahan set European indoor records for 440 yards and 400 metres. The time clocked was a magnificent 46.3 seconds. Fanahan had beaten the previous European marks of 47.8 for 440yds and 47.0 for 400m.

Of his four national senior records, the 200m mark remained unbeaten for 14 years; the 400m time was unbroken for 16 years; and the 220yds and 440yds marks remain unsurpassed at the time of writing. What greater testimony could there be to his enduring place in the international athletics firmament.

Fanahan's most recent accolade came in 1991, when sportswriters and TV pundits in the Cajun/French-speaking areas of the southern states voted for their Cajun Sportsman of the Century: he was the unanimous choice in track and field (athletics). Veteran television sportscaster Ray Valdetero said, 'The athlete that held college records in South Louisiana from the 100 yards to the mile is the unanimous choice for Athlete of the Century, even though McSweeney himself is not a native Cajun.'

Tales of Fanahan's prowess are legion. One day, while working in Limerick, he hitch-hiked to a meet in Quin, County Clare. On arriving at the track, his first port of call was the trophy table - to see what prizes were on offer and so choose his events with some discrimination. Our hero cleared the boards, including the trophies for 'Athlete of the Meeting' and 'Best all-round Club'. He put all his booty into a big, black bag, flung it over his shoulder, and headed out the road to thumb home. The lucky motorist who obliged the trophy-winner was well recompensed: Fanahan told him to look in the bag and take a clock, a silver tray, or indeed anything he fancied.

In an era when Irish athletics produced few stars and failed to make an impact internationally, Fanahan McSweeney kept the flag flying with a string of impressive wins. Indeed he won 48 consecutive international 400m races.

Indoors in the States he had few peers. Unfortunately, indoor running takes a heavy toll on the body. Injury became a constant companion; recurring aches and pains dogged his footsteps around the track. Recuperation often entailed having to walk up flights of stairs backward. At times, sciatic and lumbar rigidity could only be alleviated by the bizarre expedient of lying face down and having a teammate walk across his back.

Away from athletics, Ireland's premier quarter-miler set his fertile brain to work and was granted a worldwide patent for inventing a heating system designed to keep home fires burning more efficiently. An estimated 80 percent of all heat from a coal fire goes up the chimney. Fanahan's invention captured this escaping heat by surrounding the flue with a stainless-steel casing. Electric fans pushed the heat throughout the house. Simple yet ingenious.

The book you are about to read touches a raw nerve. The most universally feared piece of information for all mortals comprises three short words: 'You have cancer.' This is the harrowing, courageous, and witty story of how one brilliant athlete and wonderful human being coped - and is still coping - with those dreadful words and their aftermath.

Many of us have been fortunate to meet people who have enriched our lives by their presence and friendship. To me, such a person is the author of this book. Long Life and Good Health, Fanahan!

Tribute by Eamonn Coghlan

I first met Fanahan McSweeney in 1974, when I was selected to run for Ireland in my first senior international, in Bielefeld, West Germany. Fanahan was then a seasoned international who always seemed to be the only winner on the Irish team.

We immediately hit it off. He took me under his wing, and rather than sit around nervously the night before the competition, we went out on the town. We stayed out very late - and were sternly reprimanded by team management when we got back. Ironically, as the next two days of competition unfolded, we were the only two Irish winners. Fanahan won the 400m; I won the 1500m.

Though I might have been considered a bit of a troublemaker, Fanahan was anything but. He is a born motivator with a great attitude and a rare ability to think, analyse, construct, and project in a positive way. That is why I always listened to and respected his views.

Four men in particular influenced my athletics career: my father, Bill; my coach at Villanova, Jumbo Elliott; my mentor and coach in Ireland, Gerry Farnan; and my friend Fanahan McSweeney.

The first three instilled in me the self-belief and confidence to pursue my goals. They taught me to work hard through discipline, honesty, and willpower - and never to quit.

Fanahan, for his part, showed me much of the true meaning of life and living. 'Do unto others as you would have others do unto you' seemed to be his philosophy. As we competed together I used to observe his behaviour. He never had a bad word to say about anyone. He analysed and advised - but he was always constructive. Whenever I was running badly, he had a wonderful ability to rekindle my spirit to winning ways.

Fanahan was also the greatest single influence - outside my immediate family - on my decision to return to live in Ireland with my family. He saw through the superficiality of life in America. In 1980, when I was thinking of buying a plot of land in Dublin, it was Fanahan who assessed it and advised me to proceed with the purchase.

Fanahan then accepted the challenge of building the house. While still battling the 'big C' he travelled the 320-mile round trip between Cork and Dublin every week for almost two years until the job was finished. He told me once that the project helped him forget his problem. But how could he forget? He had to stop for rest many times on those trips, so severe was the pain in his back. Only for Fanahan, my family and I would probably still be living abroad.

Even during Fanahan's worst moments, he always appears incredibly happy-go-lucky. You would never suspect he was dealing all the time with colossal adversity. Suffering from cancer is the ultimate test of attitude. Just as in his running days, Fanahan has the heart, the courage, and the will - the three traits that define a warrior - to take up the challenge and not be afraid.

Fanahan has fought relentlessly against his illness - but the cancer itself is unrelenting. When it reappeared and a second vertebra collapsed, Fanahan set me a new goal: "Why not attempt to be the first man over 40 to break four minutes for the mile?" he asked. At his urging I was inspired to attack - and break - one of the greatest barriers in running.

Though Fanahan McSweeney may never again be able to reproduce the track speed that brought him national and international records, he can still put together a mean round of golf. Some time ago we played a round at Silver Springs, his local course. While he shot par or better at every hole I struggled to beat bogey. His advice to me? 'Just get a six-inch rectangular rod fused to your spine. It will stiffen your back, slow down your swing, and do wonders for your game!'

While Fanahan continues to run the 'race of life', his ability to deal with reality has a profound effect on those of us privileged to know him. We don't know what it's like to live with cancer until we are personally faced with it. Losing a race, losing a football final, having a business fail, suffering physical injury can be devastating - but they are minor setbacks compared with cancer.

Of course, all setbacks are relative - and only tragic to those who allow the adversity to get them down. Overcoming adversity is what life thrives on; it is food for life. And while Fanahan has had no choice but to live with his cancer, there are great lessons to be learnt from the way he has confronted the pain, the misery, the questions, and the joys. His story shows us the true meaning of life.

Acknowledgments

Never for one moment when I was scripting the contents of this book did I truthfully intend anyone to read any part of it. In the beginning this prose exercise helped to pass many almost unbearable moments in hospital, and having begun, I found it something of a therapy which eased my incarceration.

When the cancer reappeared and I had to spend many more months in bed - some of them in my own house - I resumed my private epistle on my word processor. Eventually, I typed my initial notes onto the same machine.

My health improved, and one day while golfing with a friend - TV sports personality Ger Canning - I happened to tell him of my writing and typing exercise. 'I'd like to read it', was his instant reply. I assured him that my personal thoughts and perceptions during the most terrifying days of my life would be both depressing and uninteresting and that absolutely no-one would ever read one word of the text.

Ger persisted, however. He called to my home and eventually persuaded me to let him borrow the 250-or-so ill-typed pages of computer printout. I was taken aback when he phoned me the following day and told me he had finished the entire 'book' at four-thirty in the morning - the first time he had ever read a book in one sitting. He had also contacted the television studios and was pretty certain that a TV documentary would be filmed within a few weeks.

But fate intervened and my health problems returned. Still Ger persisted, and a mutual friend, solicitor Michael Joyce, sent a copy to publisher Frank Greally, himself a former international runner. Frank's skill and persistence in co-ordinating the mammoth task of compiling the book amazed me. Sub-editor and athletics fanatic Richard Gallagher was roped in to check for textual errors.

Fate, too, kindly intervened when Frank Greally decided to contact one of Ireland's most internationally respected companies - Waterford Crystal - to sponsor the project. Without their assistance the manuscript would never have reached the bookshelves.

I owe thanks to several others whose professional skills helped bring the book to publication: to Peter Staunton, Charlie Neville, and Alec Tuohy for their help on the design; to Annette Quirke for her contribution to typesetting and layout; to Martin Joyce for his eagle-eyed proofreading; to Gerry Kennelly of Newsfax, Tralee, for an abundance of advice and technological assistance; and to Martin Brett and his colleagues in Kilkenny People Printing for bringing everything together in the finished product.

A special thanks too must be given to my innumerable and very positive friends who have been a constant source of comfort. To the many priests, ministers, nuns, and lay missionaries of orthodox and unorthodox sects who did their utmost to guide me inside the Pearly Gates - though unsuccessfully, I am glad to confirm. To all the fine doctors and nurses whose endeavours just had to be God-given vocation. To Eamonn Coghlan and Maura Connolly, who unselfishly helped in many ways. And, finally, to my wife, Jean, who gave me two delightful and healthy boys, Andy and Fanahan Beag, and who continues to be my greatest reason for living.

Fanahan McSweeney, October 1994

1 Bolt from the blue

The first day of the rest of my life began just like many another. That October Bank Holiday Monday of 1985 was full of glorious promise. The tiny fishing village of Roundstone, in Connemara, lay bright and clean in the Autumn sunlight; the waters of the Atlantic sparkled under a vast blue sky; the sea air was cool and sharp and salty.

The only blot on the landscape was that a few of us had partied too well the night before. Someone had suggested putting the coracle to sea. The fresh air and the pulling on the oars, we were assured, would be just the tonic for tender heads and delicate tummies. And so we began wrestling the cumbersome vessel down the shingle.

'Come on, fellows! Wake up! Pull, pull, or we'll never shift her!' I planted my heels firmly against a rock and heaved. Instantly, a thunderous explosion knocked me onto the boat. I slid to the ground. A burning wave of heat engulfed me. Then I lost consciousness.

I woke up to find myself draped across the bonnet of a car that was being driven very slowly down the main street of the still-dormant village.

'Lie still, Fanahan. You've hurt your back. We'll find a doctor to examine you.'

An ageing, unkempt GP was eventually hunted down - incredibly, in a nearby pub. 'Move the toes of this foot,' he said. 'Good. Now the other. Now see if you can move this leg. Now the other. Good - the spinal cord is okay. Put him lying on a hard, smooth surface and let him get some rest.' He wrote a prescription for painkillers.

'How much do I owe you, Doc?' one of my companions asked.

'Oh, a pint later on in the pub.'

Back at our rented chalet, I was very gently lifted from the car bonnet and carried inside. Soon the tablets arrived, and my friends were free to resume their interrupted sea-voyage. They had no reason to doubt - no more had I - that a little rest and medication would cure me.

I dozed fitfully. When I awoke, the chalet radio was giving out live commentary of the Dublin City Marathon.

'Who's Number 305 in the leading bunch?' asked one commentator.

'I don't recognise him,' came the reply. 'Let me check - Andrew Sheahan - Fr Andrew Sheahan from the Drimnagh parish. This is some surprise.'

My heart missed several beats. Fr Andy was a lifelong pal. We had been born in the same village of Castletownroche, Co. Cork. I had introduced him to running only six months previously. Now here he was, as crazy as ever, leading the charge after eight miles of a world-class marathon.

Later that evening I was helped into my car and driven home to Cork. The pain had almost totally gone, but I was scarcely able to walk. The following day, however, I had improved dramatically. I called Fr Andy's number.

'Andy, did I hear your name mentioned on the radio yesterday?'

'Oh, my God! Don't mention radio or marathons. I have never come closer to dying in all my life. I took your advice and ran the way I felt. I got totally taken in by the hype at the beginning of the race and stayed with the leaders until the eight-mile mark. Then the bear jumped on my back - no, the whole zoo descended on me - and the last eighteen miles were hell. I got sick, got blisters, fell, ran into the back of a stationary car, and almost everyone in the whole marathon passed me in the last few miles. Oh Lord, every inch of me hurts so much! My legs, my feet, my shoulders - I think even my hair is sore.'

I just laughed and laughed. 'Andy, why in the name of the Lord did you take off running at a suicide pace like that? Surely you did not expect to win? You haven't done a tiny fraction of the number of miles the top guys would have done.'

'It all began up at my old pal Pat Whelan's house last Sunday night - may God have mercy on his blessed soul! I had intended hitting the pillow at about 9 o'clock, but I got a message saying that old Pat was on his last legs. So I drove all the ways to his tiny house at the top of the Wicklow Mountains, and believe me, I had possibly the most marvellous and fulfilling experience of my priestly life. I was all alone in that little two-roomed cottage with Pat and his old sister Molly, and I can tell you, I witnessed the happiest death imaginable. Molly and I almost walked through the Gates of

Heaven with old Pat. It was something else.

'Of course Molly opened a vintage bottle of best Hennessy cognac for the holy priest, and sure enough, before the sun rose the bottle was empty. By then it was too late to go to bed, so I finally returned to the presbytery, where I forced myself to partake in a wee dram of the hair of the dog that bit me, and when I reached the start of the marathon I had not a pain or an ache in the whole world. For the first half of the marathon I felt just as good, and then all hell broke loose. I cursed old Pat every step of the way to the finish, but it did not do him the slightest bit of harm - he was well ensconced in Heaven by then.'

It was several weeks before I could walk unimpeded. Then, three months later, another accident befell me. I was awkwardly disengaging a heavily-laden trailer of firewood from my car when once again a disc seemed to slip in my spine. I collapsed semi-conscious to the ground. Fortunately, I was outside my own house and managed to drag myself on my face and hands inside the front door.

I lay panic-stricken in the hallway. The first thing I was conscious of was an inordinate amount of perspiration on the floor in front of my eyes. I tried to move, but was a jelly-like paraplegic. Some time later, I found myself prostrate on the floor of my upstairs bedroom - not remembering how I had ascended the stairway. After some time, my mind began to clear. I reached for the telephone by my bed and phoned a friend who lived near-by.

'Deirdre, I think I've broken my back. Please get some painkillers and phone Victor next-door and send him in - I can't get into bed.'

Victor ran halfway up the stairs, then stopped and called up, 'Are you alright, boy?' As I tried to respond, he apprehensively peeped in the door. 'Some young fellow told me you had a heart-attack about an hour ago out on your front lawn. Sure I thought he was only joking.'

Victor carefully raised me from the floor and put me lying on the dressed bed. 'Will I take off your shoes?'

'No - just leave me lie still like this for a while. Young Deirdre Cooke is bringing me painkillers later on. By then this bloody disc or whatever it is in my back will probably have shifted back into place,' I groaned.

Within half-an-hour Deirdre ran through the unlatched front door with several bottles and packets of pills. 'What happened, Mac? Are you alright? Will I call a doctor?' she said in one breath.

'It's the old story of the disc problem in my spine - the legacy from my running and hurling days. There's no need to call a doctor; I'll be fine again in a few days. Anyway, if a doctor saw me like this, I'd be taken to hospital and put in traction for weeks. I doubt I'd like that very much.'

'How about a stiff hot whiskey? I bet that would take the pain away,' she suggested.

Deirdre went downstairs to prepare the hot toddy, while I asked Victor to grab my left ankle and put gentle tension on my leg, in the hope of relieving pressure on the spinal disc. Victor began exerting a very tentative strain on the leg. 'Pull a little harder,' I urged.

'God, I'm afraid to! I could easily paralyse you - I never did anything like this before,' he said, shaking his head and doing very little in his timidity to ease my discomfort.

Deirdre made several hot whiskeys and joined me in most of them. 'What are you going to do when you need to go to the bathroom?' she asked.

'I never thought about that,' I said.

Deirdre disappeared downstairs, checked the fridge and rubbish-bin, and arrived back with an empty two-litre milk container and four plastic pint bottles: 'These will surely keep you going until tomorrow.' I smiled for the first time in several hours.

Later that night, I phoned my youngest brother in the USA. Terry had recently qualified as a doctor. He urged me to go to hospital and have my back X-rayed. I still recall his parting admonition: 'Pain is your friend. It's your body telling you something is wrong. So have it checked immediately.'

But by now the combination of painkillers and whiskey was having the desired effect, and the doctrinaire advice from my baby brother began to sound like so much over-reaction. And while it occurred to me even then that a relapse could prove disastrous, the prospect of immediate imprisonment in hospital was entirely unpalatable. Tomorrow, surely, would be a brighter day!

It took me some time to master the milk-bottle technique, but when I did, it worked like a dream. Soon, my liquid barbiturates weaved their magic, and I was sleeping like the proverbial baby.

The following morning I was awakened by my friendly next-door neighbour, Marie Kenneally. 'How are you this morning?' she shouted up cheerfully as she opened the front door. 'Deirdre gave me the key last night, so I thought I'd bring you in a little breakfast.' She proceeded to whip up a splendid meal, while all the time insisting that I need have no worry about food. 'It's as easy for me to feed seven mouths as it is six. You just relax and get better.'

I told her I was feeling much better - but I was not too convinced myself. The tablets had made the pain tolerable, but I felt as if I would be unable to alight from the bed for at least a few days. Just before Marie left, she smiled at me for several moments, then burst out laughing: 'Sorry, but I couldn't help noticing the four soldiers on the floor behind your bed. Let me empty them for you.'

I almost died with embarrassment. 'Thanks, Marie, but one of the boys will do that later this evening.'

'Don't you worry one little bit,' she laughed again. 'Seeing as I have four children almost reared, something like this is just routine.' Very quickly the four 'soldiers' were emptied, washed, and returned.

The following day my other next-door neighbour, Breda, insisted on helping Marie by feeding me on alternate days. Within a few days I forced myself to make the short trip to the bathroom. It was the slowest and most stressful short journey of my life, but one of the most satisfying in the successful accomplishment of its purpose. Subsequent trips gradually became easier. Fortune was slowly swinging my way. I was enjoying a standard of cuisine much higher than anything ever before tasted in my bachelor dwelling-house. Indeed, it occurred to me that, but for the pain and the immobility, life had never been so good.

Two weeks later, the pain in my spine and left leg had subsided sufficiently for me to begin fending for myself. But even as I gradually regained mobility, the taunting nerve pain in my back remained as a constant reminder that something wasn't quite right.

Six months of relative normality passed; it appeared to everyone that I had totally recovered. Only I myself knew I was physically more restricted than ever before. One night I was celebrating the christening of the first child of one of my best pals. Mike O'Reilly and his wife, Anne, had much more food and wine that night than we were able to consume. The singing and story-telling began. Then, for the first time in half-a-year, I began playing my piano accordion. The more I drank, the more I played that heavy instrument.

When I awoke the following morning, I could scarcely sit up in bed. I lay there ruing my musical exertions of the night before and praying silently that this excruciating pain would cease. The problem seemed now more acute than ever - as if a javelin had lodged in the upper regions of my left hip. Meanwhile, a pronounced numbness ran down the side of my leg to my toes.

As a relatively recent convert to the taste of alcohol, I told myself that most of my present difficulties had been self-inflicted by the previous night's carousing. So, with a residue of Dutch courage still in my veins, I phoned my GP and made an appointment.

I got to Dr Harty's surgery early in the afternoon. He informed me that he had booked an X-ray session for the following day and had also made an appointment with a sports-injury specialist.

When I walked into Cork Regional hospital the next day, it was my first time to do so as a patient. But I knew the place intimately; I had worked for five years on its construction as resident engineer. I proceeded immediately to the X-ray department, where I was bombarded by electrons from several different angles. On leaving, I was told Dr Harty would have the results within two days.

The following day I was deeply immersed in the always competitive game of scrabble with my friend Kevin Esmonde. The phone rang.

'To heck with it! If it's important they'll ring again,' I said.

'Oh, it's never wise to let a telephone keep ringing,' Kevin admonished.

Against my better instincts, I hobbled to the receiver - and was slightly startled to hear Dr Harty's voice so soon. 'Fanahan, the news I have for you is not the best. In fact it is not good at all.'

'Is something the matter with my hip?'

'The X-rays have revealed a collapsed vertebra.'

'A collapsed vertebra? My God, that sounds serious! What am I going to do now?'

'I've made an appointment for you with an excellent spinal surgeon, Tony McGuinness, at three o'clock tomorrow evening. The best of luck!'

I took several deep breaths before returning to the scrabble game. 'Kevin, I think I'll have to concede - I'm into hospital tomorrow with a collapsed vertebra,' I said.

For the first time, I realised some sojourn in hospital was inevitable. Up to now, I had always assumed I was just one 'pop' away from total physical restoration by the arcane skills of some chiropractor or osteopath. But Dr Harty's call had revealed my simplistic self-diagnosis for the nonsense it was.

I sat impatiently in a queue of more than 30 patients for more than an hour that following evening, before finally a nurse led me into Mr McGuinness's surgery. A tall, slim, athletic-looking figure was waiting. His steady gaze bespoke unusual self-confidence and authority. Suddenly, the potential gravity of my situation became clear; I felt a flutter of anticipation.

'You have been speaking with Dr Harty. I am having you admitted immediately. Tomorrow morning we will perform a biopsy,' he said without preamble.

I took a deep breath. Somehow, I felt, events were unfolding too rapidly. 'Tell me, Doctor, is a collapsed vertebra as serious as I think it is?'

'I really need the biopsy results before I can give you an informed answer.'

'How long do you think I'll be detained in here?'

'Everything absolutely depends on the biopsy results,' he said uncompromisingly. I thought of going home for my toiletries and some personal effects, but knew it would be futile to even ask. This guy meant business.

Checking into the hospital was a cruelly impersonal and claustrophobic experience - especially since I had no notion how long I would be kept in. I was hustled from one department to another, until finally I arrived at Ward 6 in Wing GB. The large, bright room had six beds, five of which contained severely-injured casualty patients. I sat as unobtrusively as I could on my own bed, hoping to defer for as long as possible the change into hospital apparel. But a sharp-eyed matron insisted I shed my civvies - and all too soon I was a fully-fledged hospital patient. It was a new and altogether frightening experience.

Quickly and efficiently hospital procedures began to take their course. A fasting sign was placed at the end of my bed. An intern briefed me on the preparation for the imminent operation: at seven o'clock in the morning I would be taken to the operating theatre and given a local anaesthetic; then long, thin needles would be inserted into my spine from the side, and some tissue would be extracted.

It struck me that quite an uncomfortable morning lay ahead. I was also beginning to realise I was a patient in a large surgical hospital and not a guest in a five-star hotel. Still, I slept surprisingly well before being awakened along with my five fellow-inmates at 6am sharp.

Pretty student nurse Elma Kenny advised me to take a shower and gave me a bag-like paper dressing-gown. When I emerged from the bathroom she howled with laughter: 'My God, you have it on back to front!'

I rearranged my flimsy covering and waited with some trepidation. Soon, a wheeled stretcher arrived to transport me to the operating theatre. The eerie feeling of being chauffeured along the familiar corridors was made worse by the knowledge that I was well able to walk.

When I arrived in the theatre I caught a glimpse of a surgeon with his bib covered in blood. By now my brow was damp with perspiration and my heart was thumping. The reality of the situation was becoming more painfully obvious by the minute.

After an initial calm, the momentum within the theatre began to build quickly. First one nurse arrived, then another. Almost immediately a young doctor entered with an older nurse, who informed me I was to be placed face downward. All four grabbed me simultaneously and began to turn me. I could have performed this manoeuvre unaided, but they insisted. A fifth medic entered and walked directly to me. 'Hello, I'm Dr Ryder. We'll begin in a few moments.' His voice was pleasant and reassuring. Out through the corner of my eye I noticed he had discarded his soiled attire. My pulse was now on overdrive.

The first needle, which I assumed was the local anaesthetic, entered my back. It hurt - but worse was to come. A few tedious minutes passed - then, suddenly, something javelin-like was plunged into my lower back. I felt like roaring, but managed to contain myself. I found myself getting groggy. The older nurse grabbed me by the wrist. 'Relax - we'll have some ice water for you in a moment.' Soon the touch of a cloth from the ice-bucket was heavenly on my forehead.

From my tortured vantage point I perceived some kind of consternation building up. Something was apparently amiss. This time I got an injection in my right arm. 'Hold still for a moment and you will be okay ...'

I groped for my wrist-watch at the side of the bed. The time was almost midday. Strangely, I was back in my own bed in Ward 6. I felt abnormally blissful. There was neither pain nor ache. What was happening? I began to wonder if I had just had a nightmare.

Just then Nurse Kenny hurried into the ward and asked me how I was feeling. 'I really feel great,' I replied, then began to ponder on my biopsy. 'I thought I was going to be given only a local anaesthetic, but they must have given me the full treatment.'

'Well,' she said thoughtfully, 'I believe they came across a cyst in your spine - but the surgeon will fill you in later this evening.' She then disappeared as if she had urgent business elsewhere.

Left lying on my own, I began speculating on the morning's events. The word 'cyst' was sticking in my mind. Ordinarily, it would have conjured up some innocuous growth, but now it began to sound strangely sinister. One thing was certain: I had been a long time formulating theories about my chronic back problems, but none of my layman's diagnoses had even remotely anticipated a 'cyst'. I decided to wait for the official analysis from Mr McGuinness; there was little choice.

Still on a high from the anaesthetic, I went for a stroll in the corridor. As I ambled along, I met a nurse pushing a mobile medicine cabinet with a handwritten piece of paper thereon. As she passed, I noted that it apparently contained the names of all 40 or so patients in GB Wing, with a brief synopsis of the condition of each. It was then that I discovered how quickly, when scanning a mass of classified information, the eye can home in on essential detail. There, in a forest of indistinguishable letters and figures was my name, McSweeney - and next to it, jumping off the page, one gigantic word: TUMOUR.

2 Look back in happiness

It may be a cliche, but it's true - the best days of our lives are our school-days and early childhood. My memories of being brought up in Castletownroche, a small town of not more than 500 people in rural Ireland, in the Fifties and Sixties, are almost without exception extremely pleasant ones. We may not have been well off by today's standards, but we had that most precious of all possessions, a happy home.

Dad was a small builder. He supplemented the family income by play-ing the accordion with his own ceili band two or more nights a week. But we remained far from affluent; by the time the last of my four brothers arrived, Dad had to convert his ageing jalopy into a chicken coop and pur-chase a motorbike. Mam worked around the clock caring for her five wild young boys in a small three-bedroomed house - which in the early days did not even have running water.

Years later I would learn that my parents came from opposite sides of the proverbial track: Mam from a prosperous land-owning background; Dad from a long line of farm labourers. That, I now believe, was the secret of their great compatibility.

At the turn of the century, Mam's bachelor grand-uncle, who had made a fortune on the Australian railways, wrote inviting one of his three nieces to travel to Australia and inherit his millions. Grandmother's sister took up the challenge - but contracted malaria during the long sea-journey and died soon after arriving Down Under. Eventually, the ancestral fortune was bequeathed in its entirety to the Catholic Church, and the title of Papal Count was bestowed on good old Mr Redding.

The only count on my dad's side of the family was the annual tally of cattle or potato drills or turnips that he and his folks used to do for one or other of the local landlords. When Mam fell in love with her handsome boyfriend, not alone did her parents disapprove - they refused to attend the wedding. Tragically, the next time she was close to either of them was when they were in their coffins.

School dominated those boyhood years. But there was always time for diversion in the form of hunting, fishing, hurling, robbing orchards, or riding Mrs Galvin's donkey, Trigger, when Mrs Galvin's back was turned. For a long time, the local rabbits, hares, and foxes seemed to have the drop on me and my young pals; it became obvious that unless we could ingratiate ourselves with the local expert, Tom Palmer, our hunting would continue to be in vain.

Tom, in a moment of weakness, agreed to take a dozen of us, boys and girls, on one of his expeditions. Most of us were barely school age; our childish enthusiasm was a far cry from the stealth and discipline required of the small-game hunter. After an unproductive day, Tom swore none of us would ever go on safari again. But the bug had bitten; the following Saturday we were all waiting for Tom and his four mongrel dogs. At first he was adamant: there was no chance - we might as well go home. But then he seemed to relent; he would take one of us - the one who would win a race in the nude across the field. Of course, he was joking. And so he was amazed when every one of us threw our clothes on the grass and toed the line. That was the day I won my first footrace.

Being the eldest of five, I developed a precocious sense of responsibility, which may explain why I actually enjoyed and looked forward to school. Maths was my favourite subject. Because I excelled at it, the teacher took me aside first thing every morning for individual tuition. Then he would sit by the fire and read the daily paper from cover to cover while I gathered my dozen-or-so classmates around me and gladly played tutor.

Sport and music were two other passions. The airwaves in our house reverberated to the sound of Irish and Scottish jigs and reels and hornpipes. Mam played no instrument, but I often heard her tell Dad when he arrived home from work that she had heard a new tune on the radio that day. She would then lilt the tune - and within minutes Dad had added a number to his repertoire.

My own musical debut came early. When I was nine years old, the drummer in Dad's band was taken ill, and I was co-opted without ceremony or rehearsal to take his place. That night I found myself perched proudly behind the large drum and surrounded by four or five snare and wire drums as well as cymbals and timber skulls. As the night progressed, my confidence soared - I wielded the sticks with mounting bravura. But my delight turned to disappointment when I suddenly noticed that the packed crowd was dwindling rapidly. 'They're all going home. My timing has scared them off,' I said to one of the band-members. Soon the entire band were roaring with laughter - and I was still perplexed.

Dad also taught me to play the piano accordion. But when the Beatles came into vogue I quickly reverted to drumming and joined a group that guested at the intervals of local shows.

All types of sport interested me, but hurling was my great passion. I was a member of the local under-16, under-18, and under-21 teams and a substitute on the intermediate team - all at the same time. I was picked for the Cork minors and thought I had reached the pinnacle of my sporting life when I walked out onto the hallowed turf of the national stadium, Croke Park. Soon I was playing for the promoted senior team - though still a minor. It was here that I clashed with a hardened opponent twice as strong and mature as myself and incurred the injury that persuaded me to turn my back on the game I loved so much. Since speed was my forte, athletics then became my sole passion.

The unorthodox way I was tutored in primary school gave me an academic head-start. When the big exam, the Primary Cert, arrived, I got 100 percent in mathematics - a first in the history of the school - and almost as much in the other subjects. I thought I just knew it all.

To the delight of my hard-pressed parents, all the secondary schools in the area offered me free scholarships. They plumped for Doneraile Christian Brothers, where I was to spend five very happy years. The daily 15-mile round-trip by bicycle was by far the hardest part of my education there - except for one memorable episode.

I had been almost three years in Doneraile when Bro. Kavanagh, the principal, approached my desk and placed his velvety hand gently against my cheek. This towering figure addressed the class in a mild voice: 'In first year, McSweeney was the best student in this class.' Then, with one vicious swipe, my head was almost separated from my shoulders. 'In second year, McSweeney was in the middle of the class.' Bang! Another sandbag to the side of my head. His voice remained meek and controlled: 'Now, nearing the end of the most important year, with the Inter Cert approaching, McSweeney is the worst in the class.' A final haymaker knocked me just about senseless.

One minute of savage cruelty for three years of idleness was, in retrospect, not such a bad deal; it was also one of the best lessons I ever learned. I scrambled through that exam, but two years later did infinitely better in the Leaving Cert. The reward was the offer of an academic scholarship to University College Cork.

By now, however, my success in under-age athletics was such that I aspired to follow in the footsteps of great men like Jimmy Reardon and Ronnie Delany - on an athletics scholarship to the USA. My parents were none too pleased when I turned down the chance to attend UCC and took up a job with the national airline, Aer Lingus.

The American dream might easily have foundered. I had no coach and no mentor; there was no-one to advise the innocent country lad. Nor had I even done any formal training, unless you count the occasional run with my German shepherd dog, Prince. But then fate stepped in - in the godlike shape of Noel Carroll. I had just joined the local running club, when my idol arrived for an exhibition race at the village sports. I turned up armed only with an autograph book bought specially for the occasion. I stood on the ditch and watched in awe as this majestic, bronzed steed went through his warm-up in the adjoining field. My day was made when, as he jogged toward the newly-laid grass track, he graciously stopped to sign my book.

Hundreds, even thousands, of locals had gathered for the spectacle. But few senior athletes appeared. That was no surprise - they feared humiliation. Before I fully realised what was happening, the meet organiser had handed me a pair of spikes, a singlet, and a pair of shorts - and I was toeing the line in the outside lane. The organiser sidled up to my shoulder and spoke through the side of his mouth: 'Just one lap of the track. Run like hell for as long as you can and make it look good for the crowd. You'll be running ten yards less than Carroll and no-one will ever know.'

I took off like a startled rabbit. In my heart, I felt unworthy to even stand on the same track as my idol, especially as I had not quite reached my seventeenth birthday. All I can remember was an acute sense of loneliness. The crowd was roaring as I rounded the last bend - but I was in a virtual trance, unaware of what was happening. Everyone could see what was unfolding - except me. I had come to see my hero, but was all confused. Just as the line arrived, Noel passed. Everything was a blur. The superstar patted me on the shoulder and said something. Later, an excited clubmate said to me, 'You know you both broke 50 seconds in a field where cows were grazing yesterday.'

I returned home and fetched my canine friend, Prince. We walked the fields at the rear of my house as I tried to comprehend what had happened an hour earlier. Then, like a cloudburst, hot tears poured down my cheeks. Finally, the cause of my mixed-up emotions dawned on me: my hero was my hero no more - with a little training in America I would claw back those ten yards and much more.

Later that year, Brendan O'Reilly, television personality and former international high-jumper, saw me racing, drew me aside, and volunteered some advice: 'If you go to an American university and have some of the rawness ironed out of your running style, I feel there is considerable room for improvement.' Brendan had himself been through university in the States; he undertook to negotiate a scholarship for me.

Soon after Christmas, Brendan phoned saying I had offers of about a dozen scholarships. He had narrowed it down to the three most scholastically reputable. When I noticed that a certain Bob Hayes was head track coach at McNeese State University, my final choice was easy. Hayes, a living legend, had been Olympic 100m champion and world record-holder. Within days I was on my way to Lake Charles, Louisiana, USA.

I was about to encounter a tremendous culture shock. The intense heat and humidity were the first things to alarm me. Then there was the inhuman timetable: classes began at eight in the morning, but by then the dozen or so track athletes had already run twice around the perimeter of a nearby golf course. My professor warned me that no-one on track scholarship had ever graduated in civil engineering - because there simply weren't enough hours in the day. He insisted I enrol in some other faculty; I was equally adamant I wanted nothing else. I knew, of course, that my academic quest would not be easy, but I relished the challenge.

The second day on campus, I asked my Texan roommate when I was going to meet the great black sprinter Bob Hayes. Roy smiled and, in his lazy southern drawl, told me I had already met Bob several times: 'He's that white guy from Kansas that collected you at the airport - the one with the weird accent.'

In early 1969 the Vietnam War still raged, and since those who passed all their prescribed subjects got a college deferment, the pressure on the male students was intense; virtually everyone studied four, five, or more hours every night.

For me there were other, even heavier, pressures. True, the progressive assessment system was much more demanding than I had ever anticipated; but at least my fate here was entirely in my own hands. Running was my problem. The old hip injury flared up the first day I began formal training. I tried to train every day, but I was spending more and more time in the sports medical department. It soon became obvious that my entire athletics future was in the balance. In desperation, I went to a specialist hospital in Texas. Examination - a myelogram spinal fusion, to be precise - revealed 'nerve damage emanating from the fifth lumbar vertebra and radiating down both legs'. No explanation for this mysterious condition was offered. Nor did I receive any specific treatment - except that it was agreed I need not compete in races during my first college year.

That first year was marred by other sadnesses. I studied hard and enjoyed a certain sense of achievement in attaining good examination results. But one of my fellow students, a millionaire's son, preferred parties to books, and when he did not attain the required grades found himself on an aeroplane to Vietnam. The spring semester had just begun when we got the news: Bruce had been handed a parcel by a little Vietnamese girl - the parcel exploded, and both Bruce and the little girl were killed instantly. The arrival home of his coffin, draped with the Stars and Stripes, marked an abrupt end to the limited social life of the campus.

My running aspirations were dented almost to the point of quitting. What kept me going was the Monday workout. Having fully rested over the weekend, I would find myself briefly on a par with the most senior members of the track team.

By Tuesday, however, my left leg would have deadened - and the frustrating battle with pain would begin all over again. When the spring semester ended, and all my exam grades were safely secured, I spent a month in Houston with my room-mate. Working as a janitor, pushing the mop and the bucket of soapy water to earn my air-ticket home, was a welcome break from the rigours of study and training, and when Roy told me he was competing in a local track-meet, I went along and was allowed enter the 440 yards. I finished seventh of eight - but shaved a tenth of a second off both the Irish national and McNeese records. Only for that race, I might never have returned to college in the USA.

After a relaxing summer vacation in Ireland, including an easy win in the national senior championship, I returned to America with a new approach to running: little or no training, and plenty of rest for my mysterious injury. Soon after Christmas, the US national indoor championships were held in the brand new Houston Astrodome (dubbed the eighth wonder of the world because of its colossal size). I easily qualified for the 440-yard final.

I doubt if anyone before or since has lined up for a US 440 final without starting blocks. But I did. The reason was simple: I had never used this universal aid to sprinting, partly because I was still a relative novice, but principally because I feared that starting from the crouch might aggravate my injury. And so, when the starter had issued the order 'On your marks!' and noticed that I was still on my feet, he wanted to know why. He ordered the other runners to rise.

This was the final of the United States championships. I wasn't about to admit I was a part-time cripple; I invented some excuse about having left my blocks at home. The other competitors, all negroes, were mystified. More than likely, they suspected some psychological ploy.

When the gun sounded, I was slowest off the mark. But to my lasting astonishment, I finished a close second to Fred Newhouse, both of us having bettered the world indoor record of the great Olympic champion, Tommy Smith. My 46.3 knocked a full second-and-a-half off the European record; it also bettered the European record for 400 metres - even though the imperial distance is approximately four metres longer than the metric.

Fred was to go on to even greater things. He would be pipped by Alberto Juantorena of Cuba in the 1976 Montreal Olympics, but would win Olympic gold at the same games by anchoring the USA in the 4 x 400 relay. My 400m European record would survive 14 years. My 440-yard European mark still stands.

After that race, I felt ready to conquer the world. But when I resumed hard training, my injury deteriorated rapidly. Still, youthful enthusiasm, dreams of greatness, and sheer stubbornness led me to persevere. By the time I stepped onto the track at the Munich Olympics two years later, I could compete only with the assistance of cortisone and painkilling injections. And to all the pain, sweat, and tears of training was then added Olympic heartache: I failed by a mere one-hundredth of a second to progress beyond my qualifying heat.

While all of us runners have our egos fed by dreams of gold medals, my brief moment of Olympic fame came outside the arena, in bizarre and tragic circumstances. When my races were run, I decided to forgo the remainder of the games and return to McNeese, where the fall semester had just begun. On the morning of my departure, I rose before six and headed for the cafeteria, intending to climb the 290-metre television tower after breakfast and take some photographs. As I hurried through the Olympic village, my eye was caught by a figure in a balaclava helmet looking out across the village from a balcony. Obviously someone returning, probably drunk, from a fancy dress party - or so I thought. I hurried on, then glanced back. There was something vaguely incongruous. He had something oddly resembling a machine-gun over his shoulder; it was difficult to make out from 100 yards. He looked straight at me - then quickly vanished. Oddly, his body language suggested something other than a party straggler, but the fleeting incident seemed hardly to warrant further speculation.

After breakfast I headed to the TV tower, by the main gate of the village. As I reached the gate, I was surprised to meet possibly 100 television cameras - all pointing at me. Amid the babble of foreign accents, one American caught my attention: 'Anything sinister happening in the Olympic village?'

'Everyone is fast asleep. Today is the athletes' free day,' I told him.

'It's very strange,' he said. 'All telecommunications into the village were severed at two-thirty this morning. There's no official explanation.'

My blood ran cold. I related what I seen less that 30 minutes earlier. Unknowingly, I was giving the world its first inkling of the terrorist massacre of 14 Israeli athletes.

Back in the USA, life in the beautiful, magnolia-bedecked McNeese State University, Louisiana, became idyllic. I had more time to concentrate on my studies. I acclimatised to the hot and humid weather, the hot southern food, and the hot cajun girls. Southern hospitality was the greatest I had ever encountered. I had the good fortune too to be 'adopted' by a sports-loving couple whose own family had all married and left the nest; the Allison household became a home away from home. But though I loved Louisiana and the Southern way of life, Ireland never lost its uniquely gentle, easygoing appeal. Within a few days of graduating I was homeward bound.

Working with the largest firm of consulting engineers in the country was a challenge and a further education. My athletics career continued with a seven-year unbroken sequence of 400m victories in one-day internationals, but the ever-present hip-injury usually prevented progress beyond the second round in major championships.

After less than two years at home, I was fortunate to be appointed resident engineer on the construction of the ultra-modern 650-bed Cork Regional hospital. Five years later, when that project was complete, I was ready to take on the world by setting up my own engineering consultancy.

Soon all my spare energies were channelled into developing and patenting a home-heating system that would retrieve all the useful heat normally lost up a chimney from the domestic fire. Megabucks beckoned - but Fate had other ideas.

3   Fear and trembling

I retreated silently to my bed to try and assess what I had seen. The sight of that one word, 'tumour', had catapulted me into an introverted world I had never even thought existed. I knew it could mean only one thing - CANCER. Not knowing what to say or do, I covered my head quietly with the bedclothes and tried to think.

'Perhaps this is a bad dream - a horrendous nightmare. No, there is no way I have cancer - no, not me. The chances of my getting cancer are less than one in a million. Of course there is no way I could get cancer.' Maybe I really was having a nightmare. 'Go and pinch yourself,' I told myself. 'If it doesn't hurt, then you are definitely sleeping.' I pinched my stomach and immediately realised I was fully awake.

As I lay there hiding, trying to weigh up my chances, tears began to fill my eyes. I told myself not to be silly. The last time I had cried in self-pity I was wearing nappies. If anyone called to visit, they would instantly detect that something was dreadfully amiss. As the tears dried, my problems seemed to diminish. Perhaps I had over-reacted. I had just regained my composure when a girl I recognised as a friend of a friend walked in and handed me a bunch of white flowers.

'Oh, thanks very much!' I said. 'That's the first time in my life ever getting flowers. How are you?' I was so pleasantly surprised by this attractive visitor that for an awkward moment I could not remember her name.

'Jacinta - remember me?'

'Of course I do. Thanks for telling me - I feel so stupid.' She looked so delightful that I temporarily forgot my troubles.

As we talked and laughed, a nurse approached and said a new patient was moving into my bed, and I was going to Ward 1. Jacinta helped me transfer my belongings. When we approached the door, she bid me goodnight: 'I pass the door of the hospital each day on my way home from teaching. I can call to see you again tomorrow evening.'

'I'll look forward very much to that,' I said.

I entered my new ward with trepidation. On the left lay an elderly gentleman in bed; on the right an empty bed beckoned. My new companion was open and friendly. He told me he was a retired surgeon, and though I sensed he would be fascinating to talk to, I had seldom been less in the mood for conversation. With the departure of my pretty friend, an unearthly and claustrophobic aura had once again enveloped me; I began to feel desperately frightened. So having shed my brown dressing-gown, I climbed into bed.

I lay there for a long time, again pondering the seriousness of this foreign substance in my back. As I did, I heard a military-sounding step approach the ward. I looked up from beneath the bedclothes and was startled to see Surgeon McGuinness looking down on me.

'Hi, Doctor. How are you doing?

'Very well, thank you. How are you feeling yourself?'

'Doctor, I believe I have a tumour in my spine,' I said bluntly.

'Who told you? I wasn't aware that you knew.' He was clearly amazed.

'Doctor, please tell me the truth. I have just got to know the truth.' I had taken him completely by surprise. He pondered for a moment.

'Well, to tell you the truth, I had not planned on discussing the matter with you until I had the lab results tomorrow.'

'Look, Doctor, I just cannot wait until tomorrow. You must tell me now.'

'If you want me to be brutally honest, then I will. When I saw the X-rays of the collapsed vertebra, I feared the worst. Eighty-five percent of your fifth lumbar, or L5, vertebra has degenerated. Let me explain: the way the human skeleton is formed makes it impossible for a vertebra to collapse simply from excessive weight or pressure - irrespective of how weak or strong the individual is. So when this morning's biopsy revealed a tumour, I had to conclude, given the disintegration of the vertebra, that it must be malignant. I'm very sorry. I'll be on holiday as and from tomorrow, but I'll call to see you in the morning when I have the results.'

'Doctor, be...before you go, tell me - the fact that it's malignant - does that mean I have no chance? Is it all over? How much time have I got? Can anything be done for me?'

'It's impossible to say, but I should have those answers for you tomorrow,' he said as he departed.

I lay still for some time in the most stupefied trance imaginable. Hundreds and thousands of thoughts rushed through my mind. 'I'm dead! Jesus, I have malignant cancer! I'm going to die! It has to be true - there is no way my vertebra would have collapsed if the cancer wasn't malignant. It must surely have spread to all my bones. My God, there's no way out! I can see it all now - I'm the stiff in the timber overcoat. There is Fr Andy, dressed in black, doing the honours. What am I going to do?'

My mind went into overdrive trying to find a way out. But the facts were inescapable. The thought of dying at this stage of my life was beyond comprehension. I gritted my teeth. 'There is no way I am going to lie down here and watch myself wither away to nothing. I am not brave enough for that. No, that surely is the most difficult route. There has to be a better way.'

For the second time that day I wondered was I dreaming. 'This just can't be true. How could I possibly have cancer? I never smoked, rarely drank - an Olympic athlete who was always health-conscious. Of course, it's a dream. Okay, let's get out of bed, step into the bathroom, look in the mirror - and if I can't see myself, then there's nothing to worry about.'

With perspiration and tears streaming down my face, and my legs shaking, I opened the bathroom door. Directly in front of me was a large mirror - and in the middle of it the most pathetic face I had ever seen.

'Oh, my God,' I thought, 'I'll be dead in a month's time!' I closed the door behind me and fell to my knees. 'What in the name of God am I going to do? This cancer is eating me away by the second - my brain is bursting out through my temples. Oh, I don't want to die!'

My knees grew sore from kneeling on the tiled floor; in a stupor I got up and started back to bed. When I opened the door I was pleased to see a good friend, Maurice Carr, standing by my bed. He looked at me in some astonishment and asked, 'Are you all right?'

'Maurice, I'll put on my dressing gown and we'll go for a walk along the corridor.' I dressed quickly, and we walked from that awful death-room. He courteously ushered me into the corridor, where a cross with the crucified Christ looked down on us from the wall. I stopped and stared at the figure of Jesus. For the first time in my life, I took a really good look at this emaciated, long-haired, former-day hippy and knew I would be meeting him in person within a few short weeks.

'Maurice, let's go to some quiet spot where we can talk. I have to tell you something.' Poor Maurice must have thought I was about to have a mental breakdown. He listened astounded but deeply sympathetic as I related my story. His own father had died from cancer, and Maurice and I had shouldered the coffin together. As we talked, my burden seemed to grow lighter, but ultimately - I kept reminding myself - there was nothing he or anyone else could do. Several times I apologised for troubling him with my tale of woe.

His concern for my welfare was palpable. And considering my state of mind, he might well have been sent by my guardian angel. I remember telling him how tempting it was to end it all there and then. He was aware I had been resident engineer on the construction of this huge six-year-old hospital and knew every square inch, every access and egress, of the structure. Two safety-exit stairways led to the roof of the highest block - and a 100-foot drop that seemed, in those dreadful hours, fatally attractive. He insisted on escorting me back to my ward and seeing me comfortable and secure in bed.

My room-mate, Dr Riordan, had fallen asleep. So when Maurice left, and with sleep for me impossible, I decided to phone a few friends; I had news I felt I had to share. Maybe someone would have some magic formula. I picked out the number of Brendan White, a gentle soul who had himself recently suffered a medical scare. 'Hello Bren, how are you doing?'

'Fine thanks,' replied my pal. 'How are the nurses treating you?'

'The nurses are fantastic - but it's the surgeon I'm interested in.'

'You lucky wretch! Fortune follows you wherever you go. I never suspected that a gorgeous young lady surgeon would be on your case,' he laughed.

'Mr White, you got me all wrong - I had a biopsy performed this morning and a tumour was found. The surgeon told me eighty-five percent of my L5 vertebra has degenerated - so it's malignant. I'm afraid the big C has got me, Bren. That's the end of the disco scene, the end of the golf - the end of everything.'

There was a prolonged silence, then the words, 'Holy shit! That's unbelievable.' I took perverse amusement from Brendan's startled reaction, but as our conversation continued, the reality of my situation came back, and I found myself becoming strangely introverted and overwhelmingly isolated.

I then decided to call my dad. Unfortunately, my mother answered the phone; I chatted casually to her as if nothing had happened. When Dad came to the phone I told him I did not have very good news and would like him to come to the hospital the following morning - but not to tell Mam. I also asked him to get in touch with my great friend Fr Andy in Dublin and have him call to see me as soon as possible.

My dad and Andy were the two people I needed to help me with the final arrangements - my dad with the practical, Andy with the spiritual. Fr Andy, a lifelong friend of our family, was an enigma in every sense. A handsome fellow with a fabulous tenor voice, he was a leading light with the priestly cabaret group *The Holy Show*, which through their weekly performances had amassed over two million pounds for charity. His zany sense of humour coupled with his totally unorthodox approach to his ministry made him unique as a pastor. I was already taking solace from the knowledge that he would be the confessor steering me from this world into the next.

When I returned to the 'death room', my doctor friend was still fast asleep, in preparation for an operation the following morning on an Achilles tendon. I immediately got into bed, covered my head with the bedclothes, and began crying like a baby. Try as I might, I just could not come to terms with the overwhelming vision of soon being six feet under that dirty and heavy clay. At the same time, I knew my fate was inescapable - and that I would continue to speculate and wonder several times every minute for the few painful weeks remaining.

'This room is driving me crazy - I must get out or I'll die!' I thought. I knew that a neighbour, Mary Liz Palmer, was a patient on the fifth floor; I decided to pay her a visit.

Mary Liz was having her own problems. She began by telling me how she was awaiting a liver-biopsy and was terrified they might find cancer.

'Mary Liz,' I said, 'the surgeon told me I have cancer. It looks like my number is up.'

'Let's get out of this ward and go to the TV lounge,' she said. 'No-one will be there at this time of night.'

We stood near a south-facing window, with the wind and rain beating against it like in a Hitchcock movie. 'I can't believe it,' she said. We held each other tightly, both of us sobbing uncontrollably.

I thought again of the quick and easy way out. 'One thing I know for sure,' I blurted, 'is that I am not suicidal.' Mary Liz stopped sobbing and screamed with laughter. I now felt thoroughly confused. Soon, we were again weeping in unison.

I suppose I contemplated suicide, but not very seriously. Many, many times I told myself that the thought of watching my two legs wither away was something I could not face. And yet the idea of abruptly turning my back on all the people and things I held dear, just to minimise my own suffering, was equally repugnant. I was thus on the horns of the ultimate dilemma.

I wasn't long back in bed when a nurse brought me some welcome sleeping tablets; I fell asleep almost instantly. When I awoke the following morning, my very clear and alert mind was temporarily overcome with the thought of having to face a full day of the type of anguish I feared was to be an inescapable part of my brief future. Those few hours of the previous night had been infinitely more stressful than the sum total of my entire 30-plus years before that.

Everything was still. My room-mate was still asleep. I gazed around the ultra-modern ward and felt as if I were barely alive inside an oversized coffin. I decided to peep out the window for what might be the last time and was startled by what I saw. There was a common ash tree - maybe eight feet high. Normally, it would have seemed very ordinary - if I had noticed it at all; now it manifested itself as the most incredible and spectacular creation of God. I gazed at it and marvelled at the mystical genius who had fashioned it. Entranced and misty-eyed, I felt as if I had just arrived in the Garden of Paradise. Then I became frightened. Had I just died? What was happening?

Dr Riordan rustled in his bed and shattered my reverie. I returned to bed and began to wonder if I were losing my reason. Every moment now was like what we are told happens at the instant of a car-crash, when literally millions of thoughts spin with blinding clarity through the mind. Most of these thoughts were looking for an escape route from dying - but there was no escape. Mr McGuinness's practical and logical explanation of the collapse of my vertebra did not allow for even the remotest chance of error. Many thousands of times I told myself I could not die; it just could not happen to me. But it was going to happen - and happen so very soon. I just lay in bed, my head covered with the sheets, not wishing to see anyone ever again except my dad, who would be along soon, and my dear friend Fr Andy.

When Dad arrived, I realised immediately it was going to be just as difficult for him as for me. He shook hands with me and began to cry. I decided
then I had to be strong. His handshake brought back memories of when I
was a teenager and had started to win races. Then he would drink a few pints
of beer to celebrate. Now I was sure he would again drink a few, but for a
different reason.

'It's hard to believe what's happening, Dad.'

'Unbelievable,' he said. 'But God is good - you can never know.'

When very little is left to speculate on, conversation can soon dry up
- even with your own father. To keep the chat flowing I eventually said,
'Dad, where will you plank me - with your side of the family in Malogga,
with Mam's side in Castletownroche, or in the new graveyard on Fatty
Batterberry's farm?'

Dad pounced on the chance to enliven the conversation: 'Okay.
There's no way you're going into that new graveyard. Nobody wants to be
buried there. We know a new graveyard was needed - but who'd want to be
lying down in that swamp? The old parish priest bought the cheapest site in
the entire parish and no-one will go in there. I bet you he won't be buried
there himself. Did you know that when old Marian O'Flynn died last week
the sly PP was sure he had his first customer - and if he could get one, others would follow. He approached Marian's brother, old doddering Liam,
who has lived all his life in the same little cottage as Marian. "Liam," says
he, "I am sorry for your trouble. How would you like a large plot in the new
cemetery - free of charge?"

' "Oh, no thanks, Father," said Liam. "I couldn't let her be buried in
that place. Wouldn't she look very foolish over there all on her own." '

Dad was great: genial and gentlemanly as ever. My final resting place
was forgotten for an hour at least as he recalled events that had happened
when I was just a baby, many of which I had never been told about. I
learned, for example, that an older brother and sister had both died before
birth. He also told me of the old gypsy woman who called to our house
before I was born. While she drank a cup of tea, she told Mam to name me
after the saint of the feast-day on which I would be born - and I would live
long and be both rich and famous.

Sure enough, I was called after St Fanahan, but rich and famous I was
not to be. Certainly, in my athletics days I had entertained thoughts of being

famous, especially when in the Houston Astrodome, Texas, I set European records for 400 metres and 440 yards, the latter of which still stands more than 20 years later. Of course, Munich 1972 was my big chance to become a household name - but then there was the small matter of my perpetually-numb leg, and the fact that Olympic medals never come easily.

As Dad left I warned him not to tell Mam until the latest possible moment. He said he would return the following day and that Fr Andy would probably be down later that day.

Dad's visit had cheered me enormously; I now felt less alone and isolated. I knew he would do everything possible, and spend every penny he had, if he thought there was even the remotest chance of saving me. I knew too that Fr Andy would do the very same.

I speculated as to how Fr Andy would behave on his arrival. I knew he would not do the pious and righteous act with me; too much praying or talking about the next life would not help.

Shortly after dinner - which I could not eat - I heard the melodious tones of Andy's usual greeting: 'Ah-hum-a-ha-chi!' I lifted the bedclothes from my head and there was the bold Fr Sheahan dressed up in a big pair of muddy wellingtons and full shooting gear. I was speechless; surely, I had assumed, the occasion warranted at least the black priestly garb and the white collar. Andy's extraordinary magic was already evident.

'Just down south for a shot at a few duck,' he said eagerly. 'Ah, I had cursed luck over at Loughshouraheen pond. You won't believe what happened. I borrowed Billy Whelan's dog, and he scared the living daylights out of ten fine mallard before I had time to even cock the gun -'

'Andy,' I cut in, 'do you know the news?'

He looked at me as if I had interrupted an extremely important narrative. 'Yeah. You'll be okay,' was his blithe response.

'How in the hell will I be okay when I'll be dead in a month?' I spluttered.

'I tell you - you have nothing to worry about.'

'Andy, if you were in my shoes or my slippers you would not talk like that.'

He laughed heartily. 'Slippers - that's funny. Do you know that since I was ordained a priest, I am preparing indirectly, and I suppose directly too, for the day when I will leave this world? You're lucky - you know you are going. I promise you, I will have you ready. Believe me, I'll have you so pre-pared that you'll go through the Pearly Gates like a scalded cat. St Peter won't even have time to ask you for your passport.'

'Thanks, Andy, but I cannot face that hole in the ground. I don't want to go for at least forty or fifty years. I don't want to go at all.'

'Fanahan, you must be tough; you must really try hard. No doctor has the right to play God - miracles do happen. Anyway, cheer up and let the last half-hour be the hardest. What you may have to go through won't be easy. The only thing I can tell you is that it's best you be prepared. This old world ain't that great anyway. The Good Book tells us that the next world will be infinitely better. It's best that you start looking forward to that big day, right this minute. I'll have the old throat in great shape and I'll sing better that ever before. I'll make it a particularly happy event, and no-one will enjoy it more than yourself up above looking down on all of us.'

'Jesus, Andy, you can't be serious! It's my life you're talking about. It's my body that's going in that hole in the ground. It just can't happen. There is no way I can face death - lingering or otherwise. I can't even begin to comprehend what is happening.'

'Fanahan, the surgeon could be wrong, and I really hope and pray that he is. But again, should he not be, then it is no harm being prepared. Believe me, it will ease your mind a lot. After all, what's forty or fifty years in sev-eral millions. We'll all be together in the blink of an eye anyway.'

'That's easy to say, Andy - even though it's meant with the best will in the world - but when it's happening to yourself it's a different proposition altogether.'

'I realise that of course,' continued my friend. 'And you know that no-one would be more sorry than me to see anything happen to you - but it's best you face up to it right now. You can do it. I know you can.'

'Andy, I wish it were over quickly,' I said abruptly.

'Don't even dare to think like that,' he said sternly. 'Listen to me: as soon as you get up there, get on to Elvis, Jim Reeves, John Lennon, and all the friends we know, and in a very short time we all will be up there with you, and we'll have the hell of a party - I mean the heaven of a party.' He erupted into laughter, then cleverly steered the conversation to the carefree days we had spent on holidays together in many and diverse parts of the world.

All too soon, it was time for him to return home. As he gestured his intention to depart, he took a small golden casket from his coat pocket, removed the lid, and started to pray. He dipped his thumb into the casket and rubbed oils on my forehead. Eventually he said, 'I bet this is the first time you got the last rites. But don't think for a moment that this sacrament is only for people on their last legs. On the contrary, it very often gives special graces which set the patient straight back on the road to recovery. Hang on in there - I just know things will work out fine for you. Don't forget to pray. It's good to keep in touch with the Man Above. I'll pray for you too - you know what they say about sinners' prayers.' Andy laughed, and as he turned to leave added, 'I'll do more than that - I won't drink one drop of alcohol from now until Christmas Day. God bless you!'

Andy's visit helped me enormously - and reminded me of how fortunate I was at a time like this to have a priest as one of my very best friends. The prospect of planning a party with Elvis and company was something to ponder on during the lonelier moments later that night. But the prospect of Andy being a teetotaller for five months was what really tickled me. Now, I felt, we needed two miracles.

Dad could not have been more considerate. The strength of his comprehension and resolve, his paternal understanding and sympathy, helped me greatly. I knew that in the lonelier moments that would surely come, his moral support and Andy's unconventional advice would prove more valuable than diamonds.

A meal was placed at my bed, but food was the last thing on my mind. Matron insisted I eat. 'Why waste good food, Matron, when I'm as good as dead anyway?' I said.

She scolded me roundly for my lack of spirit and threatened dire consequences if I did not make the effort. I decided it would be wise to humour her. Having eaten a little, I felt the better for it. In fact, I was now feeling reasonably well in body, because the medication had significantly reduced the pain in my back. But the mental strain was still unbearable. I thought my brain would burst through my temples at any moment. Since the only two people I wanted to meet had come and gone, the room again began to stifle me, as if I were already inside my coffin.

Just then my room-mate, Dr Riordan, was wheeled in on a stretcher back from the operating theatre. He lay motionless, still under the influence of the anaesthetic. I asked the nurse when Mr McGuinness would be back and was told probably later that night. I told her I did not wish to be disturbed until then; under no circumstances should she admit visitors. She had scarcely left the room when Brendan White, my phone confidant of the previous evening, sneaked into the room. Brendan had recently been a short-term patient in the Regional and well knew hospital procedures. He had hidden in the broom-closet while the nurses wheeled in Dr Riordan, and slipped out when they left. He stood there and just stared at me for what seemed like ages, then asked, 'How are you?'

'Brendan, you'll be murdered when you're found in here. There's a medic in and out every five minutes.'

'Tell them I'm your brother,' he said.

'No, I'll tell them you're my father.' We laughed; our ages had always been a bone of contention between us, until I proved I was six months the younger.

'How are you today?' he asked again with obvious concern. 'Did you get any good news since last night?'

'The only good news is that Fr Andy wants me to seek out Elvis and a few other people when I get to Heaven and to prepare a big party in the sky for you all.'

'That sounds like Fr Andy for sure,' said Brendan.

Even though I had been adamant I did not want to see anyone, I was now delighted to share my thoughts with someone. 'To be absolutely truthful, Brendan, I'm really scared. I cannot believe what is happening. It breaks my heart to think that I'm going to die. I just don't know what I'm going to do. I can tell you that if the Good Lord appeared here this minute, I would make a deal with Him to take both my hands and legs and whatever else He wanted - but to just leave me live.'

It was a tremendous relief to air a few of my myriad thoughts to a receptive ear. I continued to lecture poor Brendan: 'Life only becomes really sweet when it is evident that it is about to end. I remember a psychology course which said that our strongest emotion by far was self-preservation. The example given was an event that occurred in a concentration camp during World War Two. The Gestapo had lined up a row of Jews at the side of a trench into which they were about to be shot. The commander then realised that one row too many had just been shot into another trench about a hundred yards away. The unfortunate Jews about to be shot were given a choice: volunteer to walk the one hundred yards to the other trench, pull a freshly-shot body from that trench, drag that bleeding corpse back into the new trench, and then face the firing squad - or be shot where they stood. Each and every one of those wretched people chose to perform that ignominious assignment - just so that he could remain in this world for a further ten minutes or so.'

I continued my bombastic pontifications to my alarmed friend: 'We should all endeavour to live each ten minutes of our lives as if they were as important as those final ten minutes were to those ill-fated Jews; then life would be much more meaningful and enjoyable. When the chips are really down, every second is so precious.'

I had formulated these philosophical and psychological dogmas only in the past 24 hours - yet I was expounding them with all the zeal of a religious maniac. Certain death surely banishes conjecture and speculation on so many of life's imponderables and furnishes perfectly obvious solutions to seemingly insurmountable and perplexing problems. As I thundered on, a nurse entered, and Brendan exited more quickly than discreetly.

I now began to intensely focus my undivided attention on every syllable and facial movement of every medic who entered the ward, endeavouring to glean information about my condition. Any word or action that deviated from my interpretation of normality alarmed me. My powers of deduction and inference worked overtime. I craved the minutest tell-tale sign. The more I observed, the more confused and overtaxed my mind became. Exhausted, I tried to desist from my fruitless imaginings - but could not.

'My Dear Lord,' I prayed silently, 'what have I ever done to deserve this?' As I awaited His reply, my freshly-sharpened sense of hearing detected the military-style step of Mr McGuinness heading in my direction from the far end of the corridor. He marched into the room - but went straight to my room-mate. I lay in my bed in abject terror awaiting further confirmation of my death sentence, trying to pray but unable to concentrate. I inhaled several silent and nervous deep breaths. Finally, Mr McGuinness turned in my direction: 'I won't have the preliminary test results from the laboratory until the morning. I'll call to see you as soon as they arrive.' He then left the ward as briskly as he had entered.

I lay there motionless, feeling totally exhausted. The previous few seconds of anticipation had drained me beyond belief. These life-and-death situations were threatening to overwhelm me. My fevered imagination continued on overdrive: 'Why has nobody explained my situation to me? Definitely there is no hope and I'm going to hear the words of condemnation from some saintly cleric rather than a doctor. I suppose I am just a piece of decaying or dying meat with no chance of survival.'

I lay there in a mental fever. A nurse advised me to eat the food already served, but my appetite had totally deserted me. I had no desire to read a book or a newspaper, not even the sports pages. Why bother to get interested in something when I wouldn't be around for the final result?

The only person who could now be the bearer of any possible good news was Mr McGuinness, so my options were limited in the extreme. I would just have to sit and await the verdict. There was no possibility of an early night's sleep while my mind frantically conjured up innumerable escape routes. Alas, each one contained at least one fatal flaw, and led me mercilessly back down the lonely road to eternity, a journey I did not wish to travel for many a year.

Unfortunately, Mr McGuinness's logical explanation of my injury - almost in engineering terms - made such very practical sense. Surely, if it was impossible for a human, whether strong or weak, to collapse a vertebra by lifting a heavy weight (and since I had now attained that dubious distinction) then my chances were minuscule or less. I tried to tell myself many times that there was always the possibility that the constant pain I had suffered for most of my life, the apparent legacy of that sporting injury incurred when I was 17, might have been involved. Perhaps the vertebra really had disintegrated under some sort of chronic mechanical pressure. Alas, all the medical logic disagreed. But that fantastical hypothesis was my only hope. I knew all too well I was grasping at straws - but there was precious little else to hold onto. Even though medical staff, friends, and relatives were helping me in every way possible, I was feeling more isolated and frightened by the minute.

My mind flashed back to another crossroads in my life. I stepped onto the track to run the 400 metres at the Munich Olympic Games with seven other aspirants. I gazed around at the vast crowd and the barrage of television cameras and felt for a moment as if I were really dreaming. I thought then about my coach in Ireland, Sean Kyle; I thought about my Louisiana coach, Bob Hayes; I thought about my parents and friends and all those who had encouraged and helped me through thousands of miles of training for this moment. But then, even under the millions of eyes trained on us, I felt strangely alone.

When that race finished, in less than one minute, normality would and did inevitably return. But now, only the uncertainty of the next world was waiting for me. Back then my luck was out; I was beaten by the narrowest of margins - one-hundredth of a second. Now - 'Jesus, why are you doing this to me?'

4 Light in the tunnel

I awoke the following morning at six. Again, I wondered briefly if I had simply suffered a nightmare. Too soon, the truth stared me in the face - another
day older and deeper in 'death'.

I ate lightly; then my super-sensitive ears detected that now-familiar
military step of Mr McGuinness in the distance. He entered the room smartly and immediately pulled the curtain around my bed. The death sentence
was about to be confirmed. My whole world stood still.

He stared directly into my eyes; his voice was dispassionate: 'We have
the preliminary test-results back from the laboratory. They are very much
inconclusive as yet, but it seems apparent at this stage that you have what's
called plasma cytoma. Actually, all the X-rays and tests at first seemed very
much to indicate that you had the more serious multiple myeloma. We are
now sending samples of tissue to a cancer hospital in Edinburgh and will
have more detailed results in two weeks. You will be discharged from here
later this evening. I would be grateful if you would phone me at my private
offices on August 14th at 2 pm.'

'Doctor,' I shouted as he turned to leave the room, 'does this mean I
haven't got cancer at all?'

'No, no,' he said emphatically. 'But it's apparently not the rampant
type malignancy we first anticipated. Plasma cytoma can, however, progress
to the more malignant multiple myeloma.'

'Still, Doctor,' I again asked, 'it seems I have some chance now - what
do you think?'

'We just do not know until we have the full results.'

'I understand that, Doctor,' I persisted. 'But surely there is some slight
chance now.' He said nothing as he pulled back the curtains; but as he left
the room he gave me the faintest grin, which I eagerly interpreted as some
kind of positive omen.

I lay on my bed and began to assess the glimmer of hope I felt I had been given. Five minutes ago I was 100 percent dead; now I was only 99 percent in the awful grave. I had gone from the worst moments of my life to the best in a few precious seconds. The remotest twinkle of light was infinitely better than total darkness. I covered my head with the bedclothes, and instantly the tears began to flood as they had done two days previously. That first time the tears were tears of despair; this time they told me I must strive with all my being to stay alive.

The matron entered. 'Sister, ye may have to put up with me for some while yet. Mr McGuinness seems to think the news is not quite as hopeless as he initially feared. What do you think yourself?'

'Oh,' she said, 'we are all praying for you. God is good. He will take care of you.'

'But, Sister, surely I have some chance now?'

'No one but God knows the answer to that question, my dear. It's up to you now. You keep up your spirits and we will keep up the prayers.'

As I regained my mental composure, my plight appeared less hopeless. The dreadful pressure in my head began to ease, and the minutes began to move along at a more normal pace. For the first time since the axe fell, I began to observe what was happening about me. Dr Riordan's wife walked briskly into the room and went to her husband without even glancing in my direction. It was immediately evident to me that she was behaving oddly. She leaned over and kissed her husband as he began to emerge from his anaesthetic, then seemed to peep furtively in my direction before turning back to her husband. She soon turned toward me again and, after a more prolonged scrutiny, asked, 'How are you today?'

'Great!' I said instantly.

'Great?' she echoed, as if surprised.

'Oh, yeah,' I confirmed. 'I got great news a little while ago - or at least I think I did.'

This lovely lady now stared at me and drew a deep breath. She then let go her husband's hand and walked to my bedside. She kissed me on the forehead, and with huge tears running down her powdered cheeks, said, 'I did not sleep one wink after hearing what that surgeon said to you. I was across the ward with Eugene and my daughter and clearly heard every word. We were all shocked. Eugene, who is eighty-five and was a surgeon himself in Newcastle, England, for forty years and a GP in Youghal since then, said that the way the surgeon broke the news to you must have shaken you terribly. Believe me, I am so happy to hear your good news.'

'Well, Ma'am,' I replied, 'I'm not too sure how good the news is, but at least I have some hope.'

When dinner was over, a nurse told me almost nonchalantly that I was free to go home whenever I wished. I did not need to be told a second time. My car was in the car-park, so I changed from my hospital attire, bid adieu to my genial room-mate, and proceeded to freedom.

The taste of the cool and wholesome fresh air welcomed me at the door of the hospital; the grey, overcast sky was a joy to behold. I told myself it was great to be free again, but I knew I was fooling no-one except myself. The past few days would have surely left an indelible indentation on me, whatever the eventual outcome.

I sat pensively in my car for a few moments. Involuntarily my eyes settled on an area where sapling trees had been recently planted. The freshly-turned clay stared conspicuously back at me. The mound seemed to grow into a much larger heap, and there beside it was a crowd, and Fr Andy praying over my coffin. Scalding tears came to my eyes. For a brief moment I began to panic - and wondered if it was the psychiatric hospital I should be going to rather than my own home.

After a short while my mind cleared, and I roused myself to start the car. As I engaged the key, the blare from the inserted cassette checked me from firing the engine. Bruce Springsteen's *Born in the USA* normally perked me up, but something was dreadfully amiss. For several seconds I could not explain my anxiety. Then the words of one of my favourite songs hit me with new and morbid significance: *I'm going down, down, down. I'm going down, down, down.* Panic! I thought someone above or below was calling me. Confused, I jumped out of the car faster than I was really able to. After a few moments, I realised I was letting my imagination run riot. I must act more rationally. Within a minute or two my head began to clear. I drove through Cork city to my home.

After a few days at home, I knew life could never be the same again. It was impossible for me to forget about my condition for even a single moment. Now it was clear that my former identities were of no importance, even to myself. No more was I McSweeney the individual. No more was I McSweeney the civil engineer. No more was I McSweeney the former inter-national athlete. Now I was McSweeney The Guy Who Has Cancer. Now I was the McSweeney who was fighting for his life. Now I was the McSweeney who had little or no chance of survival. Now I was the guy who was really hoping for a miracle.

People began to treat me differently. Friends and neighbours came from near and far to offer their sympathy and best wishes. The support I received was as astounding as it was welcome. Nevertheless, the pain in my lower back coupled with my mental tribulations overshadowed everything.

Everyday actions and events assumed a totally new significance. Daily prayer was something I had given little thought to since adolescence; now it became a tremendous succour - though I did wonder if the Good Lord would really lend an ear to such out-of-character supplications. Sunday mass became the most important event of the week. But again I felt slightly shamefaced about my newfound fervour. So instead of heading to my local church, I would travel to one at the far side of the city. Mentally, I felt like some kind of leper; I was getting a distinct feeling of isolation from almost every action I undertook.

The day of reckoning finally arrived: August 14th was the date I was to phone Mr McGuinness to get the results of the biopsy from Scotland. Now, in the comfort of my own home, my whole life was once again flashing in front of me. Making that call was one of the most difficult things I ever did. 542982 ... 'Hello, Bon Secours maternity hospital,' the voice said.

'Oh, I'm sorry - wrong number.' The momentary relief was enormous. But the correct number had to be found. 542807 ...

'Bon Secours.'

'Can I speak to Mr McGuinness please?' A voice told me to hold.

'Mr McGuinness's secretary speaking -'

'Yes, I'd like to speak to Mr McGuinness. I have an appointment. McSweeney is my name,' The heart was pounding in my chest.

'Hold the line for a moment, please,' the lady said.

That moment lasted an eternity - though it was probably only 20 seconds. Finally, I heard the doctor's voice: 'Mr McSweeney, I am very sorry, but you will have to undergo a further biopsy - the test results from Scotland were inconclusive.'

'Inconclusive, Doctor? What does that mean?'

'Well,' he said, choosing his words carefully, 'apparently they did not have sufficient tissue to make a definitive diagnosis. So now you must return to the Regional hospital this evening at 5 o'clock. We will perform a further biopsy in the morning.'

'Thanks, Doctor,' I said. 'But I wonder, since they say the result is inconclusive, does that seem to indicate good or bad news?'

'Neither,' he said bluntly.

I hung up the phone and laughed for the first time in weeks to think I had really said what I had said. 'Does this inconclusive result mean good or bad news?' must surely have been the most ingenuous and silly question ever put to a medic.

Nevertheless, things seemed to be looking up; I had at least had some kind of reprieve until the result of the next test in two weeks time. I phoned my dad and Fr Andy with the news. Dad seemed pleased, but Andy warned me to stop asking unnecessary questions, which 'rarely if ever bring good news'.

I relaxed for as long as possible and then packed my pyjamas and toothbrush in preparation for at least a week's confinement. As I drove my car, *Molly Bán*, out of the housing estate, my supercharged senses again began to play tricks. How, I wondered, could all those children be laughing and shouting and playing their carefree games; how could the grown-ups remain so sedulously immersed in their busy routines; how could the whole world be acting so normally, when I was in the throes of the greatest war of all time?

En route to the hospital I visited the smallest and quietest church I knew. Inside there were two people: a youngish woman and an elderly man. Again, I could not resist my tortuous speculating. The old man's presence was easily understandable. But what plight had brought her on a fine day like this into the House of God? I wondered if the young ever visited these spiritual oases by day except when, like me, they felt divine intervention was the last resort.

The sight of the Regional hospital itself had, like almost everything else, taken on a totally new perspective. Long past were the happy days, almost seven years previously, when I first arrived on the bare building site as a young civil engineer to supervise the construction of this brave new edifice. Now the monstrous red-brick structure seemed to magnetically repel me. I was terrified to enter, but entering was the only route to even the remotest chance of survival. As I drove toward the entrance my spirits plummeted and my heart began to pound. At the last possible moment I changed direction and motored past.

Briefly, I had scaled the prison walls. But a mile or so on, I woke up to the reality that my newfound freedom was a pathetic mirage. I stopped at the side of the road. My wristwatch said ten past five, so I was already late for my appointment. I turned the car, proceeded grimly to the hospital carpark, and stopped under the same tree I had perceived so dramatically from my bedroom window on the evening I received the dreadful news from Mr McGuinness. The tree was God's creation alright, but it no longer revealed the mystical aura I had discerned on that fateful evening. I kissed the steering wheel of *Molly Bán* adieu and prayed that I and not someone else would be driving her from the hospital.

The receptionist at the nurses' station escorted me to the same ward as before. This time my bed was by the front window. All five other beds were occupied, three by apparent accident victims, one by a teenager, and the other by someone who had his head covered by the bedclothes. I decided to postpone for as long as possible the donning of the claustrophobic hospital attire.

After a while a young nurse approached briskly - as they usually do - and pulled the curtains around my bed. 'You may as well get into your pyjamas now and make yourself at home. You'll be having your biopsy first thing in the morning.' She hurried away, returned with a fasting sign, and placed it on the end of my bed. I was now firmly in the grip of confinement and isolation.

After a long time my nearest room-mate emerged stealthily from under his covers and surreptitiously peered in my direction. He was as bald as a coot, desperately haggard, and had a frightening stare in his eyes. I judged him to be in his seventies - but later learned he was only 34. There was a chilling silence before he uttered a word. 'What is your problem?' he asked.

'Oh, I'm having a second biopsy on a tumour in my spine,'

'My God,' he said, 'you have the very same type of cancer as myself! Do you see that eighteen-year-old over there? He too has cancer of the spine. He walked to the bathroom today and had to be carried back to bed. He will never walk again and will be dead in a few months. I have it in the spine too, and I too will be dead in a couple of months.' And he was.

I was temporarily struck dumb. Cold goose-pimples stiffened on my arms and shoulders; the hair stood up on my head. The nightmare had recommenced in earnest.

After what seemed like a lengthy intermission in our conversation, I asked his name. 'John O'Brien,' he replied.

'John,' I instinctively said, 'no-one is going to die. We may have cancer, but this is 1986, and with all the innovations and breakthroughs in modern-day medical science we will survive for sure. Come on, we'll hang on in there together - and believe me, we will make it through.'

He slowly and deliberately sat up, fixed me with a frightening stare, and slurred, 'I know I am going to die soon. You haven't come to accepting it yet. When you get more strength mentally, like me, you will then accept that you are dying too.'

'John,' I said, 'I honestly do not believe you are correct in what you are saying. I do believe, though, that if you continue to think like that, then you are shooting yourself in the foot and greatly lessening your chances of survival.'

He continued to stare dementedly at me. 'All you are going to do is to prolong the suffering for an extra day or two - and I don't think it is worth it.'

'John,' I countered, 'I used to do a fair bit of running in the international arena, and I can definitely tell you that if you are not totally psyched up for the task ahead, then you have little or no chance. So, come on, John, let's tackle this together!'

He shook his head in apparent exasperation. 'You are telling me the same as everyone else. It sounds commendable, but you must face reality. I pray a lot that God will grant me a happy death. I was saying my rosary when you came into the ward, so if you don't mind, I'll pray under the clothes. I prefer it that way.'

I lay on my back gaping at the perforations in the tiles of the suspended ceiling and mentally regurgitating his every word. I felt desperately confused; I had been talking brave, but now 'grave' doubts were setting in. John's prognostic was founded firmly on medical statistics; my theories were based largely on the competitive psychology of amateur athletics. Undeniably, I was grasping at straws. John's opaque conclusions now became my latest source of torment.

Later that evening I asked one of the nurses to pull the curtain around my bed; I wanted to distance myself as much as possible from my life-relinquishing room-mate. I was expecting no visitors until the following evening at the earliest, but just then John Clifford - affectionately known as Waxie - poked his head through the curtains. 'Just called to see if you needed anything,' he said.

I put a conspiratorial index finger to my lips, and we chatted in normal tones while I used pen and paper to describe the plight of my nearest neighbour. Waxie had recently received an honours master's degree in psychology, and when I wrote that John O'Brien was from near Killarney, as was himself, he felt compelled to take up the challenge.

Waxie went to the bathroom, hoping to tactfully catch John's attention. Five trips were needed before John emerged from his ostrich-like prayer-chamber and contact was established. 'Oh, hello! Fanahan tells me you're a Kerryman like myself. I suppose you're a football addict like everyone else back home.'

'I used to be, but I have no interest any more. I haven't much time left. I suppose your friend told you I have cancer and that nothing can be done for me. When you're dying you have no interest in football or anything else.'

There was a chilling silence; neither poor Waxie nor any of his psychology courses had anticipated such a negative response. 'Ah, you'll be fine! You're a young and strong Kerryman, and it's not easy to get the better of a Kerryman.'

'You are all the same. When you have cancer and they can do nothing for you, then all you can do is to pray and hope to go to Heaven,' said the quite despairing patient.

'I'll pray with you now if you wish,' offered a sincere Waxie.

'Thank you, but I prefer to pray with my head under the bedclothes, because when I pray I cry a lot.'

'Okay, but when I go home I'll pray for you.'

'Thanks very much,' replied an apathetic John.

Waxie came back as white as the proverbial ghost. He put the sign of the Cross on himself, unable to say anything for fear that John would hear. 'Best of luck in the morning!' he wished me loudly, while still shaking his head in disbelief. 'I'll call to see you tomorrow evening after school.' He then disappeared into the corridor.

Soon the lights were dimmed, and I hoped to quickly fall asleep. But as I lay there in the corner of the room hemmed in by the two cancer patients, I felt as if I were sinking in a gangrenous cesspit. My scalp tightened up; the hair on my head began to feel filthy and matted; cold sweat congealed on my face. I seemed to be losing control of all my faculties. In the darkness I could see thousands of large-mouthed worms advancing on me from both beds. I began to panic; sleep was out of the question; I felt I had no escape.

In desperation, I jumped out of bed, grabbed my dressing gown, and ran into the corridor. The relief from the nightmare was instantaneous - but I knew the oppression still waited for me in that room. I stopped and tried to gather my wits. Standing in the middle of the long, silent corridor, I felt childish and stupid, but then genuine fear reasserted itself. I knew I could never return to that ward again.

I slowly headed toward the nurses' station and was spotted by the head sister, Maria Rea. Maria walked briskly to me and without my uttering a word said, 'I'm terribly sorry about what has happened. When I came on night-duty and learned that you were put next to John O'Brien I knew trouble was imminent. It was a stupid and insensitive decision by that young nurse. If the healthiest person in the world was put next to John, he would think his end was nigh. I have never in my life met a cancer patient who talked so openly and negatively about his illness. I am definitely not allowing you back into that room.'

'Thank God!' was all I could say.

She took me into the nurses' station and gave me a cup of tea and a sleeping pill. She then wheeled an old man in a bed from a nearby room, parked him in the corridor with three traction weights swinging from the end of his bed, and steered my bed to where his had been. The old man snored and grunted peacefully through the entire manoeuvre. I immediately fell asleep in my more agreeable surroundings - but all too quickly it was 6 am.

I was prepared as before for the biopsy. An orderly arrived with a wheelchair to take me to the operating theatre. I assured him I could walk the distance unaided, but he said regulations forbade that. The journey was an acute embarrassment: being wheeled helplessly along the same corridor I had once sprinted in my buildup to the European indoor championships. I was parked in a room next to the operating theatre, endured the usual agonising wait, and was then steered into the theatre and placed face down on the operating table. The familiar face of Surgeon Ryder approached and pleasantly asked, 'Good morning! How are you today?'

After a brief but relaxing chat, I asked if I could see the damaged vertebra on the TV monitor. 'I can't see why not,' he said. 'But I wonder if perhaps it would be best if you weren't aware of what's in there.'

'Oh, come on, Doctor, I'd like to see it!'

He moved the camera slowly from my neck down toward the damaged area. 'Do you see that vertebra and how it fills the screen?' he began to explain. 'Now, look at the next one - and the next.' He then focused the camera on the damaged area. What should have been an apple-sized vertebra showed up on the monitor as the slim core of a well-eaten apple.

The picture confirmed my worst fears. I thanked Dr Ryder and, strangely, felt new confidence in him. 'How do you feel now that you have seen the problem area?' he asked.

'Doctor,' I managed to say through my numbness, 'the sooner you put me to sleep the better.' He just patted me on the shoulder.

The anaesthetist took me by the right hand and said, 'As soon as I give you the injection, you begin counting to ten.'

The prick of the needle was gentle. I began to count: 'One, two, three, four, five, si... '

When I woke up at about three o'clock that evening, my first inclination was to check to see if both my hands and legs were intact. Then, remembering the blissfully pain-free aftermath to the previous biopsy, I decided to rise and go for a short walk. I drew on my favourite brown dressing-gown. My lower back was tight and stiff; I walked slowly along the corridor. Passing my former room, I looked in and saw poor John in bed with his head still covered. The very sight of his suffering took my breath away; I returned immediately to bed.

Soon my feelings of doubt and self-pity changed to joy as pretty Jacinta floated into the ward.

'Delighted to see you again, Jacinta. You're just great to take the time to call,' I said.

'No trouble whatsoever - I pass the door every day coming from school. Tell me, did you have your second biopsy?' Chatting with her cheered me enormously. She was a sweet, radiant girl. And though she had until lately been just a casual friend, she was now as supportive as if we had known each other for years. Time flew as we chatted animatedly about our several common interests; she, it turned out, was a former international swimmer who also played the piano. Soon supper arrived, and Jacinta left, promising to 'give me a shout' on her way home from school the following day.

The evening progressed, and the pain in my lower back and legs returned: a deep, throbbing sensation that made me crave the sleeping tablet that would induce blessed relief.

The first thoughts to flash through my mind every morning were always frightening: What new grim facts would be uncovered today? Would this be the day that my death warrant would be finally signed? I monitored every single expression of every nurse and doctor who entered the room, even if they were attending another patient. When they ignored me, I wondered if they had heard bad news and were too embarrassed to look my way. When they did greet me pleasantly, I wondered was I being psyched up for unpleasant news later on. Occasionally, my compulsive detective work made me doubt my own sanity. But there was little I could do to control my hyperactive imagination.

5   Angel from Heaven

The morning passed uneventfully; just the usual blood sample was taken. The evening, however, was to be as momentous as that of August 1st, when Surgeon McGuinness had shocked me with the bad news.

I was lying in bed staring pensively into space when two young women walked into the room. 'Hello! This is my friend Ann. We were passing along the corridor when we saw you.' I looked at the speaker and was speechless. If I had been given a magic wand and the power to conjure up just one girl in the world to visit me, I would unhesitatingly have selected this girl whom I scarcely knew. I had first met her, very briefly, seven years before, at a time when I was often invited to address athletics functions or 'officially open' supermarkets or pubs. On that occasion I was to be the guest speaker at an athletics banquet and was on the lookout for a female companion to take along. Come the weekend before the Tuesday night banquet, I still had not found a suitable partner - so my last chance was the Sunday night disco.

The shindig was nearing its end, and I was more-or-less resigned to going alone to the feast, when I decided to buy a drink at the bar-counter. There, standing next to me, was the most delightful creature I had ever set eyes on.

'My God, this disco-dancing is hard work!' I remarked with a smile.

She laughed. 'Well, I only hope you enjoyed yourself and that it was worth your while.'

'It's the same old story,' I joked, 'just like the Good Book: laboured all day and caught nothing.' I was beginning to enjoy our little conversation when I perceived a robust gentleman standing next to her and glowering at me in a way that reminded me of the evil eye the boxer Muhammad Ali used to throw at opponents. The prize looked divine, but there was no contest - I was only buying a bottle of 7-up and having a fanciful reverie. But perhaps I could glean vital information before beating a dignified retreat. Trying to ignore the glare of the brute, I said, 'You must be a stranger to these parts.'

'No, I'm from Clondulane, which is only a few miles from here. But I teach in Cork City and spend most of my time there.'

'Teach? Which subjects?'

'Maths and biology.'

'Maths were my favourite subject,' I said brightly.

'Really?' she replied as she was ushered away, apparently forever, by the brute .

I returned home that night with my faith in human nature and in God's creations reaffirmed. Meeting the brute's pulchritudinous partner had been the most pleasant 60 seconds of my life; it rendered immaterial my failure to find a date for the banquet. I wondered if I would ever meet her again, and what was her relationship with the hulk, whosoever he might be. At least, I reflected, she wore no ring of any description.

The following day I was sitting in my office when a flash of inspiration told me to attempt to contact her. But there were more than 20 secondary schools in the city. And I did not even know her name. I said the fastest prayer in history to St Christopher - the saint Mam always insisted could 'find anything' - and dialled the first number. Ring, ring ...

'Hello, could I speak with the lady maths teacher with the auburn hair from Ballypooreen?'

'I'm sorry,' was the reply, 'we don't have any maths teacher from Ballypooreen.'

'Gosh, I'm sorry too - I must have the wrong number.'

'We do have a lady maths teacher from that neck of the woods: a place called Clondulane.'

'That's the place,' I said, trying to contain my excitement.

'Would you like to speak to her?' the kind lady asked.

'Oh, yes please,' I said quickly.

'Hello?' said the new voice.

'Hope you enjoyed the disco last night,' I said.

'Yes. Who's speaking, please?' said the bemused voice.

Still not certain I had the right person, I said, 'How quickly some people forget! I was chatting to you after the dance, and you cannot even remember.'

There was a longish pause. Finally she said cautiously, 'Yes, you must be the tall fellow with the moustache.'

My heart missed a beat. 'I'm phoning you in the hope that you might do me a big favour, but, honestly, you are under no obligation whatsoever.'

'Try me,' she said in a not-altogether-unfriendly tone.

'Well, tomorrow night I am to give a little talk at an athletics function in Limerick, and I have just received two tickets in the post.' I was now lying through my teeth. 'I hoped maybe if you had nothing better to do you might come along. All I can promise you is a free feed, but there's always the outside chance you might enjoy yourself.'

She chuckled - and then said, 'Yes, why not.' She gave me her address. I omitted in the excitement of the moment to ask her name.

I was as proud as the proverbial peacock. Her pleasant and dignified manner on the telephone had reconfirmed my first impressions; and now I would be meeting her tomorrow night. I could not wait.

As the afternoon progressed, however, a strange tiredness came over me. My face felt drowsy and itchy. I found myself scratching and scrawling compulsively, all the time on the left side. As I left my office to go home, I visited the toilet and glanced in the mirror; a monster stared back at me. The left side of my face was grossly distorted. My mind flashed back to the final of the 400 metres in the national track and field championships a few months before. I had come out of retirement and won as a dare, without any training whatsoever, but was so exhausted after it that I could not climb on the victory rostrum for half-an-hour. Now, I told myself, I was paying for that folly with a heart attack or stroke. I rushed to the nearest doctor.

The recently-qualified lady GP at first thought I was playing some silly game. Then, when I was about to hurry away to find another medic, she called me back: 'You probably have Bell's palsy.'

'What in the world is Bell's palsy?' I stuttered.

'It's a disorder whereby a nerve under one of the ears gets a cold, and this in turn restricts or very much hinders the flow of blood to the other side of the face. This causes the muscles at that side to contract, resulting in this apoplectic appearance you have assumed,' she said, trying to conceal a smile.

'How long will I be like this?'

'The paralysis usually intensifies for about a week. Then it remains constant for a week or so. After a further week it will have disappeared. Of course the duration can vary. If it deteriorates for more than a week or so, you may have to have a special leather cage fitted to your head. Otherwise the muscles can become so stretched they never return to normal,' she said quite seriously.

'What are the chances I will be okay this time tomorrow?' I asked, with my big date back on the agenda, now that I apparently did not have a stroke or a heart attack.

'Quite remote,' she said, reaching for a large medical manual from which to cull the name of the drug to treat my rare affliction.

Having filled the prescription, I sought out a more senior medic. 'You must have been driving with the window of your car turned down or sleeping with the bedroom window opened too wide,' he said.

'What have I got, Doctor?'

'It's called Bell's palsy. It can happen at any age, but usually strikes an individual only once. It lasts for two to three weeks, or even longer.' He gave me a prescription identical to the first. A major calamity had been avoided - but another was looming.

The following morning my fate was abundantly clear; my face was unrecognisable and my speech unintelligibly slurred. I got a friend to phone the school and ask for the maths teacher from Clondulane; I feared that the secretary, on hearing my drunken diction, might refuse to put me through. Eventually, my prospective date was located, and I took over. 'Allo...its me againn...Fanahan. I'maffraid...I...have to canshell...t'night. Ihaav...Bbells Paaalsy inmy...fface. I...can scaarcely..taalk. I...hopeyou...cann...unnnerstand.'

There was a slight hesitation before she said politely, 'Oh, I understand perfectly. Thanks for asking me.' Then the phone went dead.

That was the end of the function and the end of my dreams. A month passed and so finally did the Bell's palsy. Several more months went by, and my elusive friend's path and mine failed to cross. The passage of time then seemed to drive a wedge between us. Since I had failed to find out her name, one of my friends christened her BP, as in Bell's palsy. During the following seven years I met her a few times, but it seemed the invisible wall of mistrust I had unintentionally created would always be there to keep us at a polite distance.

Now, lo and behold, BP had come to visit me in hospital! I quickly recovered from the delightful shock of seeing her and immediately wondered if I should tell her I had cancer or feign some minor ailment. I decided honesty was the best policy.

As I related my story, my two lovely guests seemed spellbound. BP showed wonderful concern; it was as if the embarrassing incident of seven years before had never happened. But just when we had dispensed with the inglorious past, in walked my friend Jacinta. 'Oh, your girlfriend is here,' quipped the two lassies in unison as they discreetly made for the door.

My spirits drooped. Fate had destroyed another chance to get to know the girl of my dreams. Jacinta was, of course, a delightful visitor, but just this once the lovely Jacinta was not wholeheartedly welcome. Like before, BP had entered and exited my life with tantalising rapidity. But this time, at least, we had established some rapport; should we meet again, we would do so on a pleasant footing. Reflecting on her brief visit, I even took morbid consolation from the fact that if I did not survive she would probably attend my funeral.

After the excitement of the evening had waned, the reality of my hospitalisation again became glaringly evident. I was at a loss to understand why my spine was so painful after this biopsy, since I had felt so good after the first one. Even though I was very much on a high after BP's visit, I still needed a sleeping-pill to quell the pain and induce sleep.

The agony was just as bad the following morning, and because I was to be discharged that day, I asked a young house doctor for some painkilling tablets. I also asked him to enquire if I could stay in hospital until the pain subsided. Soon after I issued my request, a nurse told me Mr McGuinness had left instructions for me to be discharged later that day and for me to phone him for the biopsy results two weeks hence.

Back at home, the pain did ease somewhat, and the lonely days passed all too quickly until it was time again to make the dreaded phonecall. Again, I became intensely religious; for an hour or more before I dialled Mr McGuinness's number I prayed constantly.

When Mr McGuinness answered he immediately said, 'We have the results back from Glasgow.' My heart pounded so much I could scarcely hear what he was saying. 'It's confirmed you have plasma cytoma.'

'My God, Doctor! What's the next move?'

'I would like you to enter the Regional hospital today at 1:45 for further tests.'

I put down the phone and tried to assess this latest news and consider my future if any. Yes, I definitely had cancer - but it was apparently not the worst type. It appeared the new tests were to find out if it had spread to other parts of my body. Now, I at least had some hope.

Feeling slightly more positive than on the previous occasion, I checked into the Regional. When the usual blood-samples were taken, Mr McGuinness arrived and in his customary businesslike manner told me a complete set of tests would have to be run before a conclusive diagnosis could be made. The first of these was to be an 'ultra-modern' CAT scan, which could only be done in the New Mater private hospital, in Dublin, 160 miles away. Transport would be arranged.

That evening, student nurse Elma Kenny whispered to me that some other patient was to be flown by helicopter to Dublin and that I would surely get a ride. The evening passed with me keeping a weather ear out for the distinctive sound of the big whirlybird. As sleeping time approached, I walked to the nurses' station to get a sleeping pill. A very surprised senior nurse Eileen Walsh said, 'You are supposed to be in the Mater - in fact you should be on your way back by now. I may get in trouble if this is found out.'

'If someone can sneak me onto the early morning train, I can have my friend Fr Andy Sheahan collect me at the train station and can be back here tomorrow evening,' I volunteered.

'Will you be able to travel on your own?'

'I'm sure I'll be fine,' I replied confidently.

'Phone Fr Sheahan now,' she said.

Andy answered the phone in his usual way: 'The Vatican speaking.'

'Andy, I'm to go up to Dublin in the morning for tests. Any chance you could collect me?'

'Of course, no problem at all. What time are you arriving?'

'Half-past nine.'

'Oh, I'm to say nine o'clock Mass. Not to worry - I'm sure Fr McDowell will say it for me.'

'Thank God!' said Eileen. 'I'll drive you to the station in the morning.'

Eileen was a wonderfully caring and dedicated nurse; it always seemed to me that the stipend she got for her labours meant much less to her than the satisfaction she derived from caring for others. I also suspected that she knew more about my condition than she pretended, yet I could glean very little information from her either directly or indirectly. 'What you will be going through from now on won't be easy mentally or physically. Your own attitude will play an ever-increasing role. So be strong and tough, and a little prayer would do no harm either,' was the gist of all she would say to me.

The long journey to Dublin was an early morning nightmare. The modern carriages had the seating stacked so tightly together that I was forced to sit upright all the time. From the start, the throbbing pain from my lower spine darted down my legs and made it impossible to sit. I got some relief by tucking my left ankle under my buttocks, but could endure that position for only about ten minutes. Clearly, there was no way I could survive the entire journey in a seated position.

I decided to visit the lavatory. At first, I was scarcely able to stand; then my numbed legs began to cramp as I shuffled toward the toilet at snail's pace. Once in the tiny cubicle, I placed my elbows on the stainless-steel wash-basin and tried to find a position that would exert some traction on my spine. Very soon my elbows began to hurt, so I straddled the toilet bowl in another search for pain-relief. Unfortunately, whatever relief I gained was well nullified by the unhygienic and claustrophobic position. Knocks on the door were answered by shouts of, 'Please go to some other lavatory - I'm getting sick!'

Having alternated these two positions several times, and begun to grow uncomfortably warm, I opened the small porthole window and stared at the pretty, green patchwork of fields flashing by. As we slowed on the approach to Mallow, a town well known to me, the large cemetery suddenly swung into view. I had known many of those interred there. An uncanny chill gripped me; then, paradoxically, I started to perspire. Scary thoughts invaded my mind. As the hundreds of Celtic crosses swam before my eyes, all those dead people seemed to be terrifyingly beckoning me into their midst.

I panicked, rushed out the door, and knocked straight into a ticket-collector, who was probably coming to investigate the strange goings-on in the toilet. 'Are you feeling okay?' he asked with a surprised look on his face.

'I'm as sick as a dog,' I gasped. 'My back and legs are killing me. If I don't lie down I'll conk out.'

'Oh, my God! There's no place on this train where you could lie down except the mail carriage, and for security reasons no-one is allowed in there.'

'Look, Sir,' I pleaded, 'I have cancer in my spine, and I'm on my way to hospital for special tests. Honestly, if I don't lie down I'll fall down.'

'Oh, my God!' he repeated. 'My own sister - God rest her soul! - died from the same disease last year. Oh, sorry, I shouldn't have said that. Come with me.' Within a few minutes I was stretched on the most comfortable bed I had ever lain on.

'I'll lose my job, you know, if you are ever found in here,' he said as he left and locked the carriage door behind him.

'You'll go straight to Heaven some day for your corporal work of mercy,' I promised him, as if I had a direct line to God Himself. He shook his head and smiled.

Nobody who has not slept in a mail-carriage knows how comfortable thousands of letters, bills, and postcards can feel. Once I worked my body into position, I felt blissfully at ease. Strangely, the vibrations from the tracks enhanced the soothing effect. Time now moved quickly; soon my newfound benefactor unlocked the door and helped me to my feet as we clanked into Heuston station.

Fr Andy was waiting. 'Where's your bag?' he shouted.

'I'm travelling light - I have to be back in the Regional tonight.'

Andy made me as comfortable as possible in the reclining front seat of his car and, as we drove to the Mater, asked for the latest news.

'I just cannot believe what is happening,' I said. 'Just one month ago I thought I would live forever. Now it looks like I'm on my way out. No-one will give me a direct answer. The more I'm left in the dark, the more hopeless I feel the situation is. I honestly don't know.'

He did his best to cheer me up: 'Come on, let's take each day at a time, and let the last hour be the hardest.'

'I know you mean well, Andy, but when it's your own body that's at stake it's a totally different ball game.'

'I tell you, live each day as if nothing is wrong - and don't ask any of those doctors for their opinions. These fellows like to play God. When the patient survives the doctor was responsible and gets the credit. But when the patient dies it was God's will. Come on, let's begin to enjoy every second not to mind every minute.'

'I'll try, Andy, but believe me, it's easier said than done.'

6 Endless tests

We arrived at this ultra-modern hospital and were escorted to the inevitable queue. Andy sat with me and joked incessantly. Eventually, I was escorted into a space-age room and dressed in the usual paper gown. I was placed on my back on top of a narrow bed-like conveyor-belt, which transported me into the circular aperture of a futuristic cockpit-like contraption. I lay there motionless while I was scanned by this giant X-ray machine. Then the conveyor-belt returned me to the starting position. 'You are now free to return home,' the operator said pleasantly.

'How was the pussy scan?' asked Fr Sheahan.

'It's called a CAT scan, not a pussy scan. For God's sake, Andy, don't tell any of the lads I had a pussy scan!'

'Why not?' he asked in genuine innocence.

'I'll explain some other time,' I said, barely stifling a laugh.

We drove aimlessly around the crowded city, chatting about everything except the problem at hand. 'How about a pint of beer?' I suggested.

'I can't - I'm off the cursed thing until Christmas night.'

'I'm granting you a temporary dispensation, Father,' I said. 'After all, you gave it up on account of me.'

'That's a good idea, especially since it will be our last drink together for a while.'

The pints tasted wonderful, and the fact that the sign on the wall of the Brazen Head said we were in the oldest pub in the country made our session seem even more significant. When I reached the half-gallon mark, the pain had almost totally deserted me. 'Andy, I think it's best I head for the station. I must be back in hospital tonight.'

'Not at all,' said Andy. 'Let's go out and have one last good meal together. We'll call it the Last Supper.'

'The Last Supper,' I said, shocked. 'Not the Last Supper - but okay, let's go and have a good feed anyway.'

'Come on,' he persisted. 'You must be strong. You must face up to reality. Now is the time to begin. We're calling it the Last Supper. If you go along pretending nothing is wrong, it's going to be much tougher on you in the end.'

'Andy, I'm so scared of dying that I'm doing my damnedest to be positive - otherwise I'll have no chance at all. If I begin to prepare for the inevitable, then the inevitable will surely come.'

'What you say doesn't make sense to me,' he said. 'But come on, let's have that meal anyway. The tab's on me.'

We went to the Kingsland restaurant and ordered the best steaks and the most expensive bottle of wine. When we had paid the bill, we decided to return to the Brazen Head. Innumerable pints later - and with the clock past midnight - we were ushered out with the rest of the drunks.

The knock on the bedroom door woke me. Andy charged in shouting, 'Up, up! I have the breakfast ready. I'm off to mass; I'll be back in half-an-hour.' He then gasped and roared: 'Good Lord, you've been sick all over the bed! Your hair is a mess - you better hit the shower quick.' He was laughing as he ran out the door.

Never before had I felt so ashamed, and never again, I promised myself, would I so debase myself with alcohol. The cleansing shower and the nourishing breakfast made me at least feel human again. Andy returned from mass still grinning broadly: 'How's the head this morning?'

'Bad but improving,' I groaned.

'I never thought I'd see you drunk, but you were sure drunk last night. I really enjoyed it. Come on - you can still catch the ten o'clock train. By the way, don't tell the doctor that a holy priest kept you out drinking all night.'

The return home was almost as traumatic as the start of the initial journey. Fortunately, the morning train was half-empty, so I lay on my stomach on a table between the seats, stretching my spine and so easing the pain. The relief was partly offset, however, by the embarrassment whenever a fellow-passenger walked through the carriage.

I had intended, on arrival in Cork, to take a taxi straight to the hospital. But the smell of freedom and the fear of returning to traumatic news led me to skulk through the back-streets of the city. Semi-comatose and wandering aimlessly, I was eventually spotted by a friend, who insisted on driving me to the hospital.

It was around 5 o'clock when I arrived back in the ward. Nurse Breda Murphy stared at me as if she had seen a ghost. 'Glad to see you back, Fanahan. What happened? We thought you had gone to your brother in the States when you didn't return last night.'

'Why did you think that?'

'Well,' she said, 'sometimes when patients hear bad news, they react irrationally; they may go to another hospital for a second opinion or even leave the country altogether. When someone said your brother in America was a doctor, we assumed you had gone to him. Anyway, now that you're back, you'll probably have the bone-marrow taken that was scheduled this morning.'

'Bone-marrow?' I stuttered. 'That sounds like more pain.'

'Come on, give me a break - you're a big boy now,' she said as she bustled from the room.

An hour later, a doctor approached equipped with needles, syringes, and several small glass plates, and trailing half-a-dozen students. He pulled the curtains around my bed and said, 'Relax. I'm going to give you a local anaesthetic in the hip and take some bone-marrow. You'll feel uncomfortable, but don't worry - the sooner we begin the sooner we'll be finished.'

'I'm ready when you are,' I replied.

He hardly spoke to me thereafter, but continued to converse with his minions. He rolled me on my side and measured some precise distance from the apex of my hip-bone with his fingers. 'I will insert the needle here to deaden this area,' he told his docile proteges. Feeling like a cadaver or at best a guinea-pig, I tried to conjure up happier thoughts of my past life as a diversion from the unpleasantness at hand.

I could feel some kind of corkscrew being hand-twisted through my hip-bone. 'Turn slowly and carefully,' he said, like a TV gourmet explaining how to prepare a special dish. 'Watch right here and you will see the liquid appearing. Twist a little more and we should be through. No, nothing yet - twist some more. Keep watching - we are almost there now.'

The awful sensation and sound of the hip-bone being augered through was like nothing I had ever endured. The audible cracking and chipping and gouging turned my stomach. Eventually, 'oil' was struck, and placed between the various glass plates. Very soon my tormentor and his silent henchpersons had departed.

Student nurse Elma Kenny entered and whispered, 'How was it?'

'Real easy,' I fibbed nonchalantly.

'Really?' she replied in some surprise.

'Hell no! But it's a step in some direction at least.'

'You have another test this very minute,' she said gravely. 'This time much more serious than any bone-marrow op.'

'Oh God, no! Not so soon, surely.'

'This is a different kind of test,' she said, a smile lighting up her pretty face. 'There are two girlfriends to see you. One I saw before, but the other says she has travelled two-hundred miles, and believe me, she means business.'

'Elma,' I said, 'you'll be a friend for life if you can get me out of this one.'

I did not have to ask her twice. She walked straight into the corridor and was back in a few minutes laughing. 'Marilyn will be back at eight tonight. Jacinta will call at four o'clock tomorrow.' Before I could thank her, she breezed out of the ward.

Marilyn, once a casual girlfriend, arrived later with a delicious apple-tart. It was great to see her again and to hear all her news, but as long as she was in the ward one of my eyes was trained on the door in case my heart's desire, the delectable BP, might perchance call again. As Marylin left, she said, 'I'll call to see you again tomorrow after dinner.'

She arrived punctually at two o'clock the next day with another excellent apple-cake, most of which I would later eat in the toilet because everyone else was on a special diet, and nurse forbade me to share it. Delighted that her cake was so welcome, Marylin left with the promise, 'I'll bring another one tonight.' That was when it occurred to me that this particular friendship could eventually spell trouble.

That night, a nurse raced into the ward saying my brother Terry was on the phone from the USA. 'How are you doing, Fan?' he asked. Dad rang to tell me you have a tumour in your spine.'

'Yes - the diagnosis is plasma cytoma. At the moment they're doing further tests.'

'What kind of tests?'

'I had a CAT scan in Dublin, after which I drank the most of two gallons of beer with Fr Andy.'

Terry roared with laughter. 'Andy is great; he makes light of every situation. But what other tests have been conducted?'

'As soon as I came back here they took bone-marrow. I should have the results of that test tonight. I believe I'll have several more tests soon.'

'What's happening to you is rough. You'll have to be very strong. Best of luck with the tests. I'll give you a buzz again soon.'

After breakfast the following morning, a wheelchair arrived to transport me to my next scrutiny. 'I'm to take you for a skeletal survey,' said a tall, moustachioed attendant.

'There's no need for the wheelchair - I know exactly where to go. I'll be able to walk unassisted.'

'Look, my man,' he said firmly, 'I'm not trying to make a cripple out of anyone. All I'm trying to do is protect my own job. I have a wife and four children, and if I am found farting around the hospital with no-one in my chair, then I could easily get the sack. Surely you've heard about the health cutbacks.'

I could not help laughing: 'You have made your point beautifully. There's nothing I dislike more than a farting pilot. Hold tight while I get on.'

We laughed and joked our way at high speed through the long corridors to the X-ray department. His hilarious manoeuvres with the wheelchair recalled happy scenes from the fairgrounds of childhood. 'I'll be back for you later on,' he said playfully as he deposited me at my destination.

When I had been photographed from every angle, I asked the radiologist to phone for 'Speedy Gonzales'. 'The walk won't do you any harm. Surely you don't need a wheelchair, do you?' she said.

'I can get back under my own steam all right, but it seems five lives are depending on me going back on Speedy's carriage.'

'What in the name of God are you talking about?'

'Oh, it's a long story. But I think it's best you call Speedy.'

My entertaining chauffeur whisked me back to base, where I was startled to see the curtains pulled around my bed; normally they would be drawn only when an examination was imminent. Nurse Kenny was perched at the far side of the bed, deeply immersed in conversation, it seemed, with a patient - which struck me as odd at such a busy time of the day. The rest of my room-mates seemed preoccupied with imaginary happenings on the ceiling, while Speedy held onto his chair at the door with an untypically intelligent look on his face. I sensed a prank - and decided to play along.

'What in the hell is going on over here?' I said, as I shuffled toward the suspicious-looking drapes. Before I had time to fully investigate, everyone burst into laughter. When I saw the set-up, I laughed longer than anyone. A rope about six feet long hung from a pulley suspended over the end of my bed. A large weight was attached to the rope near the floor. A condom-like rubber tube called a unidorm - designed to prevent old men from wetting the bed - was fixed to the other side in the centre of the bed.

'Is someone trying to tell me something?' I asked rhetorically. That little practical joke made me feel 'at home' in hospital for the first time.

All my visitors that evening were entertained by the unidorm; and they all added a new word to their vocabulary. The whole atmosphere in the ward had changed unbelievably for the better, clearly proving to every one of us the old adage that laughter really is the best medicine.

Early the following morning, 'Speedy' arrived to take me to another section of the X-ray department. This time I was to have a radioactive dye injected in preparation for a bone-scan later that day. A foreign-looking gentleman approached and said, 'Hello, my name is Dr Prikash. I shall give you a small jab in the arm in a very soon moment. It shall hurt only a little. You shall please return in four hours and we shall conduct a total bone-scan. In the meantime, please refrain from contact with pregnant women and small babies, as radioactivity emitting from your body may be injurious to them. Do you understand me, please?' For a second I suspected another practical joke, but very soon realised he was deadly serious.

A nurse sterilised my arm as I caught an unwelcome glimpse of a large syringe full of radioactive dye. The colouring was administered painlessly.

Later that evening, I returned for the scan, lying there patiently for almost an hour as the giant machine moved slowly in front of me from head to toe, and then in the opposite direction behind. As I lay there, my mind began to conjure up visions of my plight should the tests reveal bad news, and I found myself again sinking into a depressive quagmire.

The following week was taken up with innumerable blood-tests, examinations, and scans. The more scrutiny I was subjected to, the more parlous and precarious seemed my situation. I had no option but to wait and hope and pray, but the waiting was becoming more intolerable each day. Hope I tried to gauge in percentage terms, but the most optimistic figure I could come up with was only marginally above zero.

Prayer, and my ambiguous attitude to it, now became the source of much scruple. I was pleading with my Maker to save me - but was I being a hypocrite? Perhaps my beseeching the Good Lord in a manner quite uncharacteristic of me was tantamount to mockery. 'Dear Lord, if You will give me one more chance, I'll -' Who was I trying to fool? During my life I had made several similar requests - and always reneged on the promise. Petitioning for the easy way out sometimes seemed both cowardly and negative.

Only one thing was guaranteed to lift my spiritual confusion: a phone-call from Fr Andy. He had the power to strip away my doubts, so that for several hours, or even longer, prayer would become a passion and a powerful tonic. Then my scrupulous and guilty conscience would intervene, and I would feel ashamed to continue.

The days passed and all tests were complete, but the results were slow in coming. The diversion of the tests themselves was now absent, and my mind hurt so much that I frequently had to hold my temples between my two hands to ease the tension. Trying to come to terms with a death sentence for something I did not do was proving incredibly difficult. I thought of the guilty criminal awaiting the pronouncement of his death sentence. Even for the perpetrator of hideous crimes, the ultimate penalty must surely be a hard one to accept. But my fate was infinitely more cruel; I was being sentenced to a horrible death for having committed no crime whatever. And I had no legal recourse; all I could do was sit and wait. Indeed, that simple four-letter word - 'wait' - now became my most feared enemy.

Jacinta continued to cheer me with her almost-daily visits; Marylin's apple-tarts were delicious; but BP was conspicuous by her absence. Friends from the past and present dropped in to wish me luck. Old flames called, some with their husbands, others with their children. Some situations were embarrassing, but everyone meant well. What cast a cloud of unreality over it all was that I felt deep down I was seeing them all for the last time.

I was shuffling along the corridor one evening when I encountered a doctor I recognised as the one who extracted my bone-marrow. 'Hope the bone-marrow was okay, Doc,' I said nonchalantly, almost without thinking.

'Fine, I believe,' was his reply. I could not believe what I had heard. This was the briefest conversation I ever had in my life - and possibly the sweetest. I retreated to my boudoir to reflect on what seemed to be great news. Soon, though, I began to question the foundation of my sudden joy. Did I really speak to the correct doctor? Was he scared to tell me the real truth? Was this another figment of my imagination?

I became confused, and angry at myself for my bizarre and eccentric behaviour. Then I began to retell the supposedly good news to my visitors, and to believe it again myself. Later, Terry phoned from the States: 'How are you doing, Fan?'

'Not too bad, I think, Terry. I believe the results of the bone-marrow tests are good.'

There was a deep sigh and a long pause at the other end. 'Thank God!' he exclaimed. 'If your bone-marrow had been affected, you would have been dead before the drugs could have killed off the infection. Boy, I'm glad you're over that hurdle!'

'Is it that serious, Terry?'

'Oh, yeah,' he said. 'Now put that one behind you and hang on in there and fight like the devil.'

When Terry rang off, I lay on my bed semi-paralysed, telling myself that the news on the bone-marrow had better be correct. An alarming numbness engulfed me, relieved only by the horrendous migraine that was trying to force my brain out through my temples. Andy was all too right, I concluded: never ask the medics anything, since they rarely if ever give good news. By disdaining that advice, I had unwittingly created a dark, terrifying scenario for myself which could only be brightened by a definitive diagnosis.

Later that night nurse Eileen Walsh entered the room. I called her over, told her what I had discovered about bone-marrow, and pleaded with her to tell me if she knew anything about my results.

'Fanahan, it's time enough to worry if and when you receive bad news. But fretting about something that may not be true is stupid. All I know is that at noon tomorrow a meeting will be held in the conference room and all your tests will be evaluated. Until then, try to relax and get a good night's sleep.'

'Pauline, tomorrow my death sentence may be confirmed, and now you tell me not to worry. I can tell you that's much easier said than done. All I want now is for you to give me a double or even a treble dose of sleeping pills.'

'No problem,' she said. 'Did I ever let you down before?'

'Don't mention that word 'down' - it scares the life out of me.'

The tablets worked like a dream, and I awoke the following morning acutely conscious that this was going to be the most significant day of my life. During the morning, Fr Andy phoned.

_'Say a prayer for me at around twelve today,' I told him.

'Indeed I will. I'm still off the booze and will be until Christmas Day. If there is any power in suffering, then you have nothing to worry about.'

Twelve noon struck. I sat in my bed in a semi-trance, my mind totally focused on the imagined events in that familiar conference room. During the construction of the hospital, I had supervised every steel bar, every cubic metre of concrete, every electrical and mechanical fitting, and every other component of that large room. Indeed, I had made many decisions in that room about the hospital's construction. Now my own future was being thrashed out in the very same room.

Dinner time arrived, but not my appetite. I managed to swallow some jelly and ice-cream and a glass of milk, but nothing else would go into my mouth. Again, I kept brooding about the prisoner on death-row, and reminding myself that I was much worse off. 'He, at least, has committed a crime which society deems worthy of the ultimate punishment. I, to my knowledge, have done nothing wrong. And now I cannot even speak in my own defence.' As to why I tormented myself with these fruitless mental gymnastics, I could never find a satisfactory answer.

The minutes crawled by; the smell of death was in the air; the nurses, knowing my predicament, tended the other patients silently. They wanted to be positive, but sometimes words are best not spoken. Thousands, perhaps millions, of permutational words whizzed through my mind, all theoretical diagnoses, all escape routes - all entirely meaningless. There was nothing to do but await my 'executioner'.

My super-sensitive ears monitored every sound from the long, tiled corridor outside. Finally, from the far distance, the scarcely-audible but unmistakable military cadence of Mr McGuinness hit me as loud as the close-up din from Concorde. Time stood still.

He marched in, followed by his large entourage. A nurse diligently pulled the drapes encircling my bed. Feeling shockingly vulnerable and helpless, I looked directly into my reluctant executioner's eyes.

'Well, Fanahan,' - he seemed nervous - 'as you are aware, you have a tumour in your fifth lumbar vertebra. Fortunately - and amazingly, since there has been so much degeneration - the plasma cytoma has not spread. First, you will have to speak to Dr Curley in radiotherapy tomorrow morning. Then we will decide whether you have radiotherapy and chemotherapy here or in St Luke's in Dublin.'

'Doctor,' I blurted, 'the fact it hasn't spread surely sounds like good news?'

'Yes indeed. But I should add that the tumour is positioned at the front of the vertebra and so is particularly inaccessible. First the tumour will have to be removed - and then what remains of the vertebra.'

'What then, Doctor?'

'Oh, that's a long way off. We will just have to wait and see.'

'Does this mean I'll be paralysed?'

'Hopefully not. But again, as I have said, we will take each step as it comes. You will see Dr Curley tomorrow. Best of luck!'

'Thanks, Doctor!' I shouted as he led his silent retinue from the room.

As soon as the surgeon stepped out of the room, I told myself that at least I was not going to be dead in a few weeks. Since the cancer had apparently not invaded the rest of my body, I must have some chance of survival. Even the slightest glimmer of hope was infinitely more comforting than none at all.

I thanked God many times that day for this reprieve, temporary though it might prove. For the first time since my nightmare commenced, every word I directed heavenward came straight from the heart. I felt immensely grateful that I would be alive for some time, perhaps even a few months.

I spent the rest of that evening on cloud nine - until Nurse Eileen came on duty. Her, above all the staff, I expected to immediately rejoice with me. But when she entered the ward only briefly, and left without saying a word, I sensed something was desperately amiss. Almost immediately, I was plunged back into morbid speculation; I covered my head with the bed-clothes as an embarrassing mist of tears blinded me. Once again, I had taken refuge in a mirage. Oh, cruel world!

After a short while, a gentle hand descended on the bedclothes. Then a kindly whisper: 'Hi, it's me - Eileen.'

I waited for a few seconds before gradually letting in the light. A warm smile greeted me. She kissed me on the forehead. 'I just heard your great news. I'm so happy for you.'

'Is it really true, Eileen?' I asked childishly.

'Oh, yes. Since it hasn't spread, you have a fighting chance. I bet you won't need your sleeping tablets tonight,' she laughed happily.

This was surely the happiest evening I had spent in hospital; I was euphoric. But I did not forget the harsh reality of my situation. The confirmation that I was not 'riddled' was, under the circumstances, *summa cum laude*, but I still had a huge cancerous tumour which had eaten away four-fifths of my L5 vertebra. The important thing was, though, that I had won the first battle; it was all I could possibly have hoped for on that glorious day. Later that night, Eileen gave me my usual sleeping tablets, since now I found it difficult to sleep for a totally different reason.

Soon after breakfast the following morning, 'Speedy' arrived to transport me to Dr Curley's office in the radiotherapy department. Dr Curley was, according to the nurses, a charming and approachable man. My heart pounded with excitement as I awaited my new saviour: the man who through his skills would rid me of this malady.

He entered, shook hands, and smiled: 'Fanahan, I followed your athletics career down through the years, and I -'

'Doctor,' I interrupted, 'what can be done to burn the tumour from my spine?'

He shook his head and continued as if he had not heard my question. 'I remember you missing out in Munich by - was it one-hundredth of a second?'

'Doc,' I again cut in, 'what's the next step in my treatment. Am I to get radiotherapy, chemotherapy, or surgery? Please tell me.'

He seemed taken aback by my unwillingness to talk about running, but said, 'Well, initially you will undergo a course of radiotherapy either here or in St Luke's.'

'Doctor, thanks a lot,' I said almost sarcastically. 'I'm not feeling very well right now - I think it's best I return to bed for a rest. Thanks, Doc. Thanks very much.'

Without bothering to summon my friend Speedy, I walked the distance of about 100 yards back to my ward feeling bitterly dejected. Why, I asked myself, had I behaved like such a beast toward this good and friendly man? After some soul-searching, I decided the answer lay in a comparison of Dr Curley and Mr McGuinness: McGuinness's confidence and near-bluntness tended to inspire implicit trust in his expertise; Dr Curley's easygoing friendliness, on the other hand, left me doubting his professionalism. I would soon learn that I had cruelly misjudged Dr Curley.

Later that day I happened to meet Mr McGuinness on the corridor. 'Doctor,' I said, with tongue partly in cheek, 'I met Dr Curley this morning. He mentioned the possibility of my going to St Luke's. Since it's the premier cancer hospital in the country, I'd prefer, given the choice, to go there. I have several good friends in Dublin. In fact, one of my very best friends, Fr Andy Sheahan, is up there and would be a great help to me spiritually and otherwise.'

He seemed surprised that I would be willing to travel 160 miles rather than attend Dr Curley nearer home. But after brief deliberation he said, 'Fine. I will have a chat with the powers that be, and try to set up an appointment in St Luke's. I'll be in touch with you later today. And since all the tests are complete, you can contact your family and have someone collect you this evening,'

'Thanks a lot, Doctor, but it won't be necessary to contact anyone - I have my own car waiting in the car-park.'

'My God,' he said, 'don't attempt to drive with all that medication you have taken! It would be extremely dangerous.'

'Okay, Doctor,' I said, and added as he was about to leave, 'By the way, many thanks for everything.'

'I'm delighted the prognosis is more hopeful now - and sorry it appeared so bleak at the beginning,' he said with obvious sincerity.

'Don't worry for a moment about that. Your initial diagnosis did more to secure a place for me in Heaven than all the priests and ministers could ever do. My new approach to the Man Above even startles myself; He's so much more real now than ever before.'

He laughed, and as we shook hands warmly, said, 'Be nice to Him - you have a long, rough battle ahead of you.'

As evening approached, some friends arrived and were preparing to take me home. Strangely, I began to feel I might be wiser to stay in hospital. My legs were both numb and painful from the spear-like sensation in my lower back. Walking above snail's pace was impossible. The DF118 painkilling tablets I was gulping down four times a day appeared to be having little or no effect. A young Pakistani doctor now topped me up with a prescription for further painkillers.

By now I had donned my civilian attire and bidden adieu to my five room-mates. As I was being escorted down the corridor, Nurse Eileen came rushing after me. 'I'd prefer if you took these,' she said, handing me a small box of painkillers. 'If you take that other prescription, you'll get hooked on codeine. Take these with you and tear that prescription up.' I did as she said, then headed homeward from the hospital, driving my own car.

7 The Gates of Hell

The trip home across the city was intensely pleasurable. Briefly courting normality amid the distractions of the ever-busy metropolis almost allowed me to forget my dilemma. It was delightful, too, to return to the comforts of my own home. But I was now in a non-medical environment, in dreadful discomfort, with a collapsed vertebra and a cancerous tumour. It seemed certain that without imminent medical treatment I was bound to deteriorate rapidly. I was therefore almost looking forward to my sojourn in St Luke's. The sooner treatment began there, the better would be my chances.

Mr McGuinness's secretary duly phoned to confirm that I had an appointment in St Luke's hospital, Dublin, with a Dr Breslin. He would carry out a complete diagnosis and then decide on a course of treatment. It all sounded a bit vague for my liking; the nerves began to tighten. The only thing that seemed clear was that I was unlikely to be kept in on the first visit.

Against Mr McGuinness's advice, I set out on the 160-mile odyssey in my own car, feeling extremely frightened and lonely. I had forewarned none of my friends in Dublin, not even Fr Andy. For some perverse reason, I wanted my first trip to the largest, most famous cancer hospital in the country to be as low-key as possible.

The pain in my spine forced me to stop three times for spells of rest punctuated by bouts of empty retching at the roadside. Finally, I was negotiating Dublin's busy suburbs on the way to Rathgar. I drove through imposing gates to the car-park and gazed at this surprisingly-small old hospital. I then impulsively restarted the engine and drove to the rear of the hospital, so as to familiarise myself with the place where my future was about to be assessed.

Eventually, I plucked up the courage to venture in. As I entered the foyer, I immediately detected an odour very different from that of regular hospitals. Soon I was directed to a huge waiting-room, where four or five long queues awaited various physicians. Before I joined Dr Breslin's queue, I walked slowly to the bathroom and began to observe those in the line before me. Their ages varied greatly, but most were middle-aged to old. A few were in their teens. Three were as young as four or five. None of these children had a rib of hair on his head. Nor had several of the adults. But it was the expression on the faces that was really frightening. And most alarming of all was the realisation that all of us had one thing in common - cancer.

I joined the very slow-moving queue, took out a tiny finger-ring rosary beads, and began to pray. Continuous and repetitive prayer was something fairly new to me - but I prayed like the devoutest nun in Christendom. I prayed as if in a queue outside the Gates of Hell. Fellow patients occasionally looked in my direction, but they seemed to be looking through me rather than at me. This, I thought, was surely the last place on earth anyone would wish to be. Most of the patients in line with me had either parents or friends along for support. Four people surrounded the person immediately in front of me. As we neared the front of the line, my spirits soared at the sight of the long, well-groomed locks of this slim young lady. Then her friends rose to leave, and she glanced toward me. To my horror, the young woman with the lustrous hair turned out to be an old woman with a wig. The hairpiece had slipped halfway down her forehead, and as she tried feebly to adjust it, I did not know whether to laugh or scream. The brutal reality of St Luke's could not have been more graphically illustrated.

I was eventually taken into an examination room to await, with great trepidation, the arrival of Dr Breslin. Suddenly this grey-haired man sped in on a wheelchair. 'Hello, I'm Dr Breslin. Welcome!' he said with a smile.

This was the first I knew of him being incapacitated. Cruelly, my immediate thought was, 'If he cannot cure himself, then what chance have I?' Straightaway, however, he won my confidence; everything about him bespoke intelligence, competence, and dignity. I was delighted I had decided to come to St Luke's.

'I have studied all your reports from Mr McGuinness and will have some scans carried out here now, so please go with my assistant, Dr Hollywood, and I will see you later.'

Five minutes earlier I had sat in terror alongside the old woman with the wig at, or even one step inside, the Gates of Hell. Now Dr Breslin had rekindled my spirit - almost by the tone of his voice alone - and I was suddenly ready to take on the world.

Several scans were taken in space-age, 21st-century surroundings. Young Dr Hollywood was an athletics fan and seemed to be familiar with every sprint I had ever run. His enthusiasm and wit were a welcome diversion from the main event. I was feeling more confident and relaxed by the minute.

Later, Dr Breslin informed me that I was to undergo at least three weeks of radiotherapy, beginning three weeks hence. I was inclined to ask further questions, but with Fr Andy's advice ringing loudly in my ears, I suppressed the urge and departed the hospital with confidence and hope renewed. Presumably, when they had burned out the tumour, they would effect some surgical repairs. Then, if everything was stable, I would be free. The only nagging mystery was why I had to wait three weeks in agony.

I was temporarily free now, and not about to waste precious time; I immediately got in touch with Fr Andy. We devoured a large meal, and I quaffed several pints of porter as an anaesthetic for the long journey home. Astonishingly, Andy continued to refuse all alcohol; he was now unshakably set in his resolve to remain on the dry until Christmas Day.

8 A night to remember

I reached Cork and home completely exhausted, after having to stop several times to disgorge the food and drink consumed with Andy. But a thrilling
surprise awaited me inside my halldoor: a postcard with three red apples on
the front and a message on the back: 'Sorry to hear you are still under the
weather. If you ever feel low and would like to talk to someone, please
phone me at 025-31928.' A name was written on each apple: Anne, Eileen,
and Jean. By a process of elimination I was now able to deduce that BP's
actual name had to be Jean. I was madly eager to talk to her and meet her,
but decided to wait a few days. Past experience had taught me that, in affairs
of the heart, unbridled enthusiasm is not always appropriate.

Each day was taken up with people calling and phoning. My great friends
the Allisons phoned from Lake Charles, Louisiana, saying that all their fellow Methodists in Sunday school were praying for me. So too did the
Robinsons from Baton Rouge; seemingly all the Jehovah's Witnesses were
similarly wearing their knees out. My former coach Sean Kyle from
Ballymena told me that 'every black Protestant' in the North had me in his
prayers. So too had my good friends Billy and Myrtle Forde nearer home.
As for Fr Andy, he had suffered beyond reason - eschewing alcohol for several long months - on my behalf. There was great comfort in the fact that
almost every spiritual angle had been covered. But it often amused me that
I was heading for a destination to which there were so many unequivocal
and uncompromising roads.

A week passed before I plucked up the courage to phone BP - or was it Jean?
Our conversation went like a dream; she laughed and joked and almost convinced me that my condition was much less serious than I imagined. She
also told me that since she had a sister resident in Dublin, she hoped to visit

me sometime in St Luke's. She sounded so warm and caring that I decided to press my luck: 'I won't be going back to Dublin for almost two weeks. Maybe you could join me some evening for a drink.'

'That would be lovely,' was the sweet-sounding reply.

'Seeing as this will probably be my last night out in a long while, we might even go out early and have dinner as well?' I suggested nervously.

'Sounds even better.'

By now my brain was in top gear. What night was she least likely to have a date with someone else? I suggested the following Monday. Amazingly, she agreed.

I spent the following few days in a state of delicious anticipation, looking forward to a date with the most beautiful woman I had ever met. And yet, I still could not entirely exclude my medical problems for more than a few seconds at a time.

Monday arrived, and as I intended to drink, I decided to forgo my usual quota of painkillers, for fear the combination of drugs, alcohol, and driving might prove disastrous. So when I arrived at Jean's lodgings, I could scarcely bear the pain in my lower spine. While Jean readied herself, I chatted with Ann and Eileen - but all the time I was subtly studying the delightful Jean. After almost eight years, the big moment had come. As we drove away, she enquired as to which 'surprise' hotel we were going.

'Take your pick,' I said obligingly. 'I'll leave it up to you.'

She laughed a surprised laugh. 'Oh? I could have sworn you told me you had a special surprise all lined up for me.' In fact I had spoken rashly, trying to impress her. I decided that wherever we ended up would have to be fairly special, some romantic spot in the country.

The Rinn Ronain hotel was in an idyllic, rustic setting, perched on the banks of the River Lee. As we passed through the foyer, Jean noticed a goldfish tank and paused to admire its exotic denizens. There, in the soft, reflected light, I received my first real close-up view of the girl I had imagined over the years was the loveliest I had ever seen. She was even more beautiful than I had believed.

The dimly-lit meal was delicious, and the conversation of my cherished companion was on a par with her beauty. Never had I been so enthralled and enamoured. Long before dessert was served, I felt as if I had been best friends with her all my life - and I promised myself that if I survived this cancer, I would ask her to be my wife.

When dinner was over, we decided to retire to the bar. As I tried to rise from the chair, I was horrified to find that my spine had locked. I tried to disguise my difficulty, but Jean jumped from her chair, grabbed me around the shoulders, and loudly whispered, 'Steady, please be careful. Come on, let me help you to your feet.' She carefully held me by the right shoulder and firmly but gently raised me to my feet. As she patiently ushered me toward the bar, I imagined ruefully how she must feel - out for one night with an acquaintance who was semi-paralysed and probably going to die very soon from cancer - and asked myself how it was possible to be so happy and so sad at the same time.

At the bar, she recounted several hilarious incidents of her youth back on the family farm. The more she talked, the more I realised we had in common. By now, the Guinness was working its soothing magic, but alas, the old adage that time flies when you are having fun was proving all too accurate. At least, I told myself, whatever my future held, this lovely girl would be somehow a part of it, helping me battle with those two ugly and alliterating intruders into my life - cancer and coffin.

On the way home, I wondered if this would be the last really pleasurable night of my life. Outside her apartment, she leant toward me and said, 'Thanks for the lovely meal and evening - I really enjoyed myself. I'm looking forward to another when you return from hospital. Of course, I'll call to see you up there.' With that she alighted from the car and shouted, 'Good luck!' before disappearing indoors.

Taking Jean out had infinitely gladdened my heart. But soon it was time to set out on my return trip to St Luke's. By now I was feeling well rested and decided again, despite doctors' orders, to drive. I left my house early on a quiet Monday morning and dropped in en route to my parents' home. My father told me discreetly that Mam thought I had simply strained my spine; she had been told nothing of cancer. Nevertheless, as I was leaving she began to sob uncontrollably. That brought back memories of the previous time I had seen her cry: she was standing in exactly the same spot and I was about to be the first offspring to leave the nest - setting out for Louisiana to attend McNeese State University. Now Dad shook my hand and wished me the best of luck. Driving away, I glanced back and wondered would this be the last time I would see the house where I was born and reared. These were tough moments to endure.

A few miles further on, I decided to make one other stop. The Palmers had been lifelong friends: in my youth, Tom had taught me everything there was to know about hunting and fishing; his wife, Mary Liz, was of course the patient I had shared my grief with on the night McGuinness dropped the nuclear bomb.

Tom greeted me at the door: 'I'm delighted you called. It's just like the old times when you would give us a shout on your way to those international races. You can do it this time too, kid. I know it.' His voice was full of determination as he went on, 'By the way, I still have the hat you wore during the opening ceremony in Munich - it was the best present I ever got. But the present I want from you now is to return here with the most important gold medal of all - good health. I know you can do it, Fanahan. You never let me down before.'

As he spoke, Mary Liz limped slowly from the bedroom. She did not say one word, but began crying inconsolably, just like my mother, and embracing me fervently. The behaviour of this lovely lady took me totally by surprise, and I felt it would be better for everyone if I continued on my journey forthwith. I kissed Mary Liz on the forehead and shuffled out the door.

The three-hour journey took almost five hours. I stopped at least ten times to admire the fields and the trees and mountains. For the first time in my life, I marvelled, almost in a trance, at God's beautiful handiwork. Then, emerging from my trance, I would again wonder - as I had done when leaving my home - whether I would ever pass this way again. Then my eyes would fill with tears and I would tell myself I was unnecessarily making my journey more difficult. A few miles farther on I would again pull off the road, go through the empty retching, rest for several minutes, scramble out of the car, and become absorbed in some cloud or leaf or trickle of water. Then, having regained my composure, I would recommence my arduous journey.

9 Into the frying pan

Soon - too soon - I was again sitting in Dr Breslin's queue. This time the place looked much brighter and more ornate than before, but the faces waiting in line were as vacant and shellshocked as ever.

Meeting Dr Breslin was like bumping into an old friend. He explained that the tumour was positioned at the front of the L5 vertebra, and that the first course of action would have to be radiotherapy. Further assessments would be made at specified intervals. I asked him for more detail, but he declined. 'This is a most unusual case,' he muttered while absentmindedly shaking his head. I did not know how to interpret that action. But, remembering Fr Andy's advice, I decided to ask no further questions.

My friend Dr Hollywood escorted me to a hi-tech room. I was strapped securely to a sophisticated conveyor-belt-cum-stretcher, which transported me several feet into a jungle of telescopic cameras and probes. Dr Hollywood and his colleagues began scrutinising my insides through several monitors situated in an adjoining room. Calculations were made as I was repeatedly loosened and restrapped to my slim bed. Then, with painstaking accuracy, several indelible red marks were inked on my stomach and side. I was then rotated 180 degrees and had another set of red crosses and dots printed on my lower back.

The atmosphere during this entire half-hour procedure was tense and businesslike. I got the impression that the serious expressions on the faces of the doctors and technicians probably reflected the gravity of my spinal deterioration. Finally, I was told radiotherapy would begin at eleven the following morning. It was with a great sense of relief that I sat into my car and set out for Fr Andy's house.

Andy greeted me Indian-style as usual: 'Ah-hum-a-ha-chi! How did things go in St Luke's?'

'Quite good I think. Evidently they've pinpointed the tumour. Blasting will begin in the morning.' As I spoke, I loosened my shirt buttons and showed him my several red marks.

He laughed heartily. 'You remind me of the raddle my oul' fellow used to put on the belly of the ram. It was his foolproof method of finding out which of the ewes was in the family way. Lord forgive me for laughing, but you look very funny!'

Andy had the guest bedroom ready for me; I could stay for a few days or several weeks, depending on the outcome of the radiotherapy. When he came back after celebrating seven o'clock mass, he overloaded the frying pan with enough rashers, sausages, and pudding to feed five very hungry men. As he laboured at the cooker, the phone rang next to the reclining chair on which I was stretched; I raised the receiver.

'Father, I'm going to kill myself,' said the demented male voice at the other end of the line.

'Hold on one moment, please - I'll get a priest for you.' I travelled faster from lounge to kitchen than I had moved in the previous six months.

'Andy, quick! I'll take over the frying pan. Get on the phone - some fellow says he's going to kill himself.'

'Tell him call back in half-an-hour,' he replied without batting an eyelid.

'No way, Andy! This guy sounds serious. Give me the frying pan.'

Andy paused for a moment, then said, 'Here, I'll put the skids under him.' The phone conversation that followed went thus:

'Hello, Fr Sheahan here.'

'I want to speak to the priest because I'm going to kill myself.'

'I'm not on duty today. But hold on - I'll give you the parish priest's number. Today is his day on duty.'

'To hell with the parish priest! I'm going to fuckin' kill myself!'

'Where do you live, my good man?' asked Andy.

There was a long pause while the caller tried to come to terms with the shockingly unorthodox response of his hoped-for counsellor.

'Galtymore road.'

'Well, if you can come down in half-an-hour's time we can have a quick chat. Okay? God bless!'

As we we sat down to an enormous meal, I managed to splutter, 'Andy, you better get your act together. This guy's life may depend on how you handle the situation.'

'Don't worry about that for one moment - I'm dealing with that type of situation every day of the week.'

Andy was dressed casually, as usual, but decided it might be appropriate to greet his caller in style. He went to the closet in the hall and returned with a long, black cloak with splendid red buttons running down the front for almost five feet. 'Got this years ago from an old bishop in Scotland who was on his last legs. How does it look?'

'Your man is guaranteed a laugh anyway. I never saw anything so musty in my life'

A brush was found, and the job of decontamination was done in the garden lest we pollute the house. Soon, Andy was looking like a very chic young bishop. When the doorbell rang, he winked and said, 'I bet you I'll sort this fellow out in jig time.' He ushered his parishioner into the study and left the door slightly ajar; I could hear every word.

'My good man, sit down there for a minute and tell me your tale of woe. I'm sorry to hear you're having a rough time.'

'Well, Father, 'tis the wife. Things are very bad between us. To tell you the truth, she won't sleep with me. I'm in the room on my own for more than a month now. Life is not worth living. I tell you, Father, I can't fucking take it anymore.' He sounded dangerously overwrought.

'I'm very sorry to hear that, but on the phone you mentioned suicide. Tell me why you were thinking of taking your life?' asked Andy boldly.

'Well, Father,' he shouted almost hysterically, 'the likes of you don't understand. Ye don't understand what it's like to be shunned by your own wife.'

'Hold on a moment,' said the priest slowly and deliberately. 'Are you seriously telling me that you are thinking about killing yourself because you have not had a bit of sex in a month?'

'Be Jaysus, Father, I think you're finally getting the message,' was the exasperated reply.

'My good man, you have me all confused. I would say you are about the same age as myself - forty-five or forty-six?'

'Forty-five is right.'

'I was thinking you were around the mid-forties all right,' said the very sincere-sounding Andy. 'I just can't understand you at all. You say you are going to kill yourself because you haven't had sexual intercourse with your good lady in a month. Why I'm so baffled is because I never had a ride in my life - and the last thing I am going to do is kill myself.'

There followed a long, wordless pause. I was chewing my lower lip to suppress the laughter. The poor soul grunted and groaned. He sounded like he was trying to swallow huge breaths, as if to prevent himself from laughing. He asked for no more advice, but apparently jumped from his chair. As he sped out the front door, shaking his head and smiling ruefully, he shouted back, 'Thanks, Father!'

Andy returned to the lounge. 'What did I tell you? That didn't take long. I was quite correct - there was nothing the matter with him. He just thought he had a problem.' I could not help thinking that if that parishioner had gone to a more orthodox cleric, he might now be heading for the river.

I was already enjoying my stay in this presbytery, the atmosphere of which was so refreshingly untypical. Andy was always joking, singing, or laughing.

As I thought ahead to my first radiotherapy session the following morning, the tension started to build. 'I could murder a pint,' I said tentatively.

'So could I,' he replied quickly. 'Och aye - but promises have been made and cannot be broken.' And that was that.

The following morning after ten o'clock mass, I headed for St Luke's. There was no queue for radiotherapy, just one pretty girl in her mid-twenties with long, straight blonde hair. I would never have guessed she was a patient but for the 'raddle' marks tattooed on the side of her head. After a few moments, a smiling lady in her fifties approached. 'Are you Mr Fanahan McSweeney?

'No, just plain Fanahan McSweeney,' I replied.

'Oh, good. You can come along with me.' She then introduced me to John, Peter, and Mary, all of whom I was to become well acquainted with in the following weeks. The atmosphere was cheerful but businesslike. There were three or four TV monitors in an oval-shaped observation area outside the huge door to the radiotherapy room. I caught a glimpse on one screen of the blonde being laser-beamed - just before the monitor was swivelled discreetly out of my line of sight.

After about ten minutes the blonde lady emerged, and I was taken through the massive, slow-opening, and thickly-leaded door. A corridor changed direction three times before leading into a room measuring about 30 feet square. To one side was a huge white machine, on which was a dial three feet in diameter with graduations from zero to 360 degrees. A gigantic arm protruded from the top of this machine and extended about six feet over a slim-line bed, and at the centre of this arm was connected a conical device pointing toward the bed. Seemingly it was from this large cone that the radiotherapy beams would be emitted.

I was carefully raised onto this slim metal bed and put lying on my back. The large arm moved, and finally positioned the cone over me according to precise instructions. I was told to lie absolutely still. Three of the four operators left the room, while one ensured that I did not move. After a minute or so, all three returned and made minor adjustments. This operation was repeated four times. They then left individually. Finally, I heard the thud of the heavy door closing. I felt helpless and scared. My future was now in the hands of these people and this machine.

For a few pregnant moments there was absolute silence. Then my heart jumped to the shrill of a piercing noise. Snake-like hissing continued for about two minutes. Suddenly the hissing stopped, and the doctors and nurses hurried in. 'You will now be placed on your tummy and the whole procedure repeated,' someone said.

As I was being rotated someone asked, 'How did you find the first session?'

I did not immediately know how to describe my feelings. 'It was as if I had one of my fingers severed by an axe: I know something traumatic has happened, but as yet I can feel no pain,' I said, struggling to find a suitable analogy.

'That's the first time I ever heard it described like that, especially from someone with all ten fingers,' was the reply.

In the prone position, the procedure was exactly as before. My head was turned slightly to one side; my big toes were placed together, and my heels were placed apart; my arms were extended, and the palms of my hands were placed beside me on the bed. Everyone exited like before. Soon the hissing began. I closed my eyes and prayed. Two to three minutes later the noise stopped. The four operators returned, removed my shackles, and helped me carefully back onto my feet. I walked out of the hospital delighted to be feeling tolerably human after my first encounter with the dreaded laser beams. My second encounter would be on the morrow.

Back at the presbytery, Andy was just leaving to drive to the nearby Phoenix Park, where he would jog six or seven miles. When he enquired how I had fared in radiotherapy, I told him about the unearthly hissing noise. 'They were probably letting some of the hot air out of you,' was his unsympathetic comment.

I decided to spend the early evening in bed and to go with him later to hear him sing with the Holy Show.

When Andy returned from the Park, we consumed an enormous fry, then travelled a short distance to the tiny house of an old man named Joe and his infirm sister, Mary. Andy had promised to say mass there. The rickety kitchen table became the makeshift altar: the priest donned his colourful robes and carefully took the chalice from its container. In the tiny room, I was much closer than I had ever been to any priest saying mass. And so I was able to observe a remarkable transformation in my friend: as soon as he intoned the first word of the sacrament, his usual jovial lilt gave way to a tone of profound devotion and solemnity. It was as if this was the most important mass he had ever said. The homily was humorous, yet sensitive and full of wisdom. Joe and Mary appeared to be the happiest people in the world. Old Joe would die within the week. When I heard the news, it struck me that - since Andy had honoured him by saying mass in his little house - poor old Joe must have been almost looking forward to meeting his Maker.

Having said our farewells to Joe and Mary, we set out for the Green Isle hotel, but had barely started the journey when, without warning, my stomach began to explode. 'Stop the car quickly!' I roared, placing my hand over my mouth but totally failed to prevent the inevitable. I jumped from the car and buried my head in the shrubbery of the nearest garden. My whole body began to shiver; water poured from my eyes.

Andy walked from the car, laughing loudly. 'It's that damn fry,' he said.

Dizzy and disoriented, I was temporarily speechless. Eventually, I managed to gasp, 'It's not the fry but the radiotherapy. It feels as if I've drunk a gallon of poison.'

Andy patted me on the back. 'Come on, throw up some more. It's just like after a feed of booze - the more you get up, the better you'll feel.'

Before long, I was well enough to continue the journey. But ten minutes later I had a repeat performance. This time, fortunately, the trauma was less severe. I sat on a wall in the cool night air and rested. 'We better hurry,' said Andy. 'There will be three to four thousand people here tonight.'

Andy rushed into the hotel and pulled on his kilt, sporran, knitted white socks, 'scian', and buckled shoes. He wrote the names and relevant keys of four or five Scottish, Irish, and Italian songs on a piece of paper and handed it to the backing group. He then gave a couple of yodels as if to clear his throat, and waited for his cue.

'Ladies and Gentlemen, the priest with the lilt and the kilt. From Ireland via Scotland, Fr Andy Sheahan!' Soon, the powerful and melodious voice had the audience in thrall.

More than anything else, Andy loved singing and entertaining. He unashamedly lapped up the applause and adulation. And his enthusiasm was infectious. Halfway through his repertoire he would always sing a slow, semi-religious song, during which you could hear the proverbial pin drop. But the most gratifying aspect of the entire night for me was that Andy had invested at least as much attention and effort into saying mass for poor old Joe and Mary as he did into entertaining several thousand people in the glare of the spotlight.

The following morning I drove the lonely half-hour journey back to the hospital. In a sense, I looked forward to the radiotherapy. My mental state was fast becoming intolerable, and any amount of pain or turmoil would be welcome if it contributed to a favourable long-term prognosis. The treatment might be and was burning away part of my body, but I had to believe it was the only means to saving my life.

When the treatment was over for that day, I told Dr Hollywood about my enteric convulsions of the previous night. 'That's nothing to worry about,' he said. 'In fact, it only shows that your body is reacting in a healthy way against the alien radiation.' When I informed him of the increasing agony in my legs and lower back, he gave me a prescription for a special corset.

My next treatment would not be until the following Monday morning. Normally, I would have looked forward to the long weekend; now I only wanted to get off my feet and rest.

Andy was heading out for a night's salmon-fishing with friends. Before leaving, he brought a television set from the lounge and put it on top of the wardrobe in my bedroom. He also placed a bowl of fruit and milk within my reach.

With my tightly-adjusted corset imparting some traction to my spine, I rested in comparative comfort for a few hours. Then, near midnight, I had to go to the bathroom. As I tried to sit up in bed, my troubles began: my spine locked; I was totally unable to move. After a few minutes, I rolled to one side and allowed my legs to slip toward the floor. Then, with a rotary movement, I sat up at the side of the bed. My absolutely leaden legs seemed to be bursting with pressure from within. I tightened the straps on the corset and gained some relief. I stood up slowly, but had to lean against the bedroom wall to keep my balance. It took an interminable and gutbursting struggle for me to reach the bathroom, perform my toilet, and get back to the safety of the bed.

Andy returned in the small hours with a bag of salmon. 'The best night ever,' he said excitedly.

'How many did ye catch?'

He placed his finger to his lips, as if to silence me, and said in a confidential whisper, 'I think it may be better not to answer that question.' I did not pursue the matter; it was clear he did not want to further rub in the fact that I had missed a rare night's entertainment.

The weekend was long and painful, and spent almost entirely on the horizontal. On Sunday morning, Andy ordered me to lie on, because attending mass might be too stressful. He relented only when I insisted that, now more than ever, I felt drawn to the sacrament. With the support of a walking-stick unearthed by Andy from his garage, I stood at the rear of the chapel in case

I needed to exit in a hurry.

Again, Fr Andy was a revelation; I began to understand why many of his flock reportedly went out of their way to attend his masses. The theme of the sermon was 'confession'. From beginning to end, it spoke directly to me in the context of my need to make peace with God. He listed, then gently debunked, the diverse reasons why people turn away from God and from confession. An example was the would-be penitent put off by a grumpy confessor.

'Don't tell me you stayed away from the confession box just because one priest was less than friendly to you years ago. Believe me, it's important to look at the situation from the priest's side; we are as much human as you are - there are two sides to every story. Just think - maybe you were telling your sins to an oul' fellow whose nerves were at him. How long had he been shut in there listening to people's problems? How would you feel if you were locked into your wardrobe for two hours? I bet you wouldn't be feeling the best either.'

I got out of bed unaided on Monday morning, spurred by the fear of being confined to bed in St Luke's should I miss an appointment. Andy arrived with my breakfast and was astonished to find me freely moving about the room. With the intention of driving me to the hospital, he had already arranged for the parish priest to say ten o'clock mass. But I insisted that my temporary paralysis had vanished and that I was well able to go it alone. It was a foolish miscalculation.

The journey to the hospital was a nightmare. Every time I passed over a hump or a hollow on the road, it was as if a dagger were being pushed further into my spine. Getting my legs out of the car was pure torture. When I raised myself from the seat, my head spun, and I was afraid to move. I raised my two elbows onto the roof of the car to rest a little, and gradually regained confidence. Eventually, after a short walk through the beautiful garden, I ventured inside.

I walked bravely into the radiotherapy department and took my treatment - like any other day. I also told Dr Hollywood about the increasing pain, without, of course, letting him know that I could barely walk. He took me for a scan, which revealed that my damaged vertebra was becoming sponge-like. He prescribed stronger painkillers and urged me to notify him of any worsening of symptoms.

With new peace of mind, but feeling highly emotional, I headed back toward Blanchardstown and Fr Andy's new presbytery (he had just moved parishes). My terror of being kept in had obviously run even deeper than the conscious, because as I drove from the hospital environs, an oppressive numbness descended on me, and hot tears burned my eyes, which made it increasingly difficult to negotiate the crowded city streets.

The relief of having avoided hospital imprisonment was immense, but it was obvious my freedom would be short-lived. I felt as if my spine was on the point of collapse; perspiration accumulated on my brow; I began to shiver and shake. My breath came in rapid gasps, and my heart pounded. My leaden and tingling legs itched so much I could hardly operate the pedals and was in imminent danger of wrecking the car. Even though I needed to call to a chemist for my tablets, I was in such distress that I decided to make straight for Fr Andy's.

Unfortunately, I was now so disoriented that I could not find the presbytery, though I knew the route well. I drove into a filling station and asked the attendant if he knew how I could get to Fr Andy Sheahan's house in Blanchardstown. The kindly man apparently gave me something to eat and drink and insisted I rest for a while. I dozed off.

Andy and his friend Larry roused me with a shout. I was more than 20 miles from my destination. They carefully transferred me to the passenger seat of my car and drove back to the presbytery. Alighting from the car was a delicate and embarrassing procedure; both men had to lift me like a baby and, while I clung to their necks, carry me into bed.

After a sleepless night, I ate breakfast in bed. But when I tried to rise, I could not move. Andy had to dress me from head to toe and carry and drag me to his car.

The trip to the hospital was another catastrophe. As we drove through the Phoenix Park I began to get sick. Andy stopped and helped me from the car. I staggered to a large metal railing and clung to it like a drunk. Only the cold air against my forehead saved me from fainting. After several minutes, Andy placed me on my back on the rear seat of the car and drove with the utmost care to Rathgar.

Getting out of the car was another painful struggle. When Andy had me vertical, I asked him to take me on one final, short walk so I could regain composure before entering the hospital. 'I suppose this will be my last time on my feet for some while - a few weeks, a few months, ever?' I said forlornly.

'Come on, try to cheer up. You never know what buttons Dr Breslin might press,' joked Andy. 'You might come out of here faster than myself in half-an-hour's time.'

We sat and chatted in my usual spot in the waiting room. When the name McSweeney was called, I instinctively tried to jump to my feet, making a special effort to disguise my immobility. As I began to rise, something audibly clicked in my spine; I became instantly paralysed. Medics ran to help. Andy grabbed me by the upper arm and began directing proceedings. Almost immediately, a high stretcher was wheeled in, and I was carefully place thereon.

I was wheeled into the radiotherapy room and slid sideways onto the metal bed. Soon the 'sizzling' started. Before I closed my eyes to pray, as was now my habit, I checked that the indicator was pointing to precisely the same graduation mark as before. Eventually, I was rolled over onto my stomach, and the hissing resumed. Finally, I was trundled back into the waiting room.

Andy gave my carers a laugh when he said to me, 'This is the first time I ever saw you in the one spot for more than a second.' He then turned serious. 'I'm told you'll be staying here for the rest of your treatment.'

'I was expecting that. There really isn't a chance in the world that I could even attempt to stand up.'

Andy insisted on wheeling me to the ward. 'Got to make sure you are well taken care of,' he said as he negotiated corridors with an orderly. We wound up in a large, open-plan dormitory with about 40 patients. I was steered into a section with two beds facing two others and raised hammock-style onto my new bed. Andy's parting words were, 'Keep up the spirits - I'll see you tomorrow.'

It was grimly sobering to realise I was almost totally incapacitated in a bed in the largest cancer hospital in the country. My closest room-mates were two old men and a fellow about my own age. The atmosphere was quiet and peaceful, but the feeling of morbidity was heavy in the air. My nearest neighbour told me his name was Pat. He had fallen from scaffolding a couple of years before, and a tumour the size of an egg had grown against his brain. He said he was hoping radiotherapy would burn the tumour out, but that he had to cover his head for three or four hours every day after treatment, so violent was the pain. I reminded myself that I should be thankful for small mercies.

'Pat,' I said, 'to look at you, one would assume you hadn't a care in the world.'

With that, he grabbed the wavy hair on his head, raised the entire mop, and exposed the proverbial billiard ball. 'After two days of radiotherapy, the hair began falling out in chunks onto my food. I decided to shave it all off, seeing as it was going to fall out anyway. When I realised what I had done, I panicked and rushed into town and bought this hairpiece. Now I don't look like myself either way.'

'You look fine to me. How do you like it here anyway?'

'Well, the nurses are gorgeous, and the food is great. But, to tell you the truth, I'd rather be anywhere else in the whole world. By the way, my girlfriend is calling this weekend, and I don't know if I should wear the wig or not when she comes.'

Pat enquired if I had a girlfriend. I told him a little about Jean, but thought it wise not to over-elaborate, since there was no guarantee I would see her again. Soon, however, I was to receive a wonderful boost; as we talked, a beautiful blonde entered the ward and approached me.

'Fanahan?'

'Yes,' I affirmed.

'My name is Ellen Dorgan - Jean's sister. She asked me to phone St Luke's, and when they told me you were here, I thought you might like a visit from someone from back home. I live just around the corner.'

Ellen was almost too good to be be true. From the moment she walked in, everyone was staring at her. For her part, she felt obliged to 'visit' everyone, walking from bed to bed and chatting. By the time she left, the atmosphere in the ward had changed utterly. 'I'll give you a shout again in a day or so,' she said before leaving.

Pat was overwhelmed. 'Dear Lord, I never saw anything in my whole life as beautiful and lovely as Ellen! She looks better than any Miss World.

Does her sister look anything like her?'

'Even better,' I replied smugly, thrilled that her surprise visit had done so much for the morale of my beleagured companions.

Soon I felt the urgent need to visit the toilet, but was scared to even begin to attempt to leave my bed. Pat summoned a nurse, who quickly produced a cardboard container which she called a 'pigeon'. Some patients still had visitors - so discretion was paramount. I slipped the container into place and, with my hands innocently positioned out over the bedclothes, tried to fill it. After half-an-hour, and with pressure mounting inexorably, I had Pat pull the curtain around my bed. Soon the mission was accomplished, and Pat got rid of the 'pigeon'. I now began to realise that in my confined but semi-public state a new set of rules would quickly have to be learned and obeyed.

As sleeping time approached, a nurse wheeled a mobile medicine cabinet by my bed and asked if I would like some sleeping tablets; I gratefully accepted. There followed the fullest and most welcome night's sleep I had enjoyed in ages.

I awoke at seven o'clock, glad to note that the savagely early call common to other hospitals seemed not to operate here. A nurse brought me a pan of hot water, pulled the curtains around my bed, and said, 'Time to wash and shave. I'll help if you want me to.' Life was sure taking on a totally new format. The last time I had been washed in bed I was a very young lad indeed.

After a splendid breakfast, everyone began to look forward to eight-thirty mass. It struck me forcibly that I was now in an institution where God and mass and radiotherapy and chemotherapy had absolute priority.

All 40 or so of my room-mates went to mass, so for more than half-an-hour the ward was deserted except for myself and a middle-aged man in the far corner - both of us being confined to bed. He, it seemed, was deliberately keeping a low profile; the curtain remained all the time around his bed. But when the place had emptied, he peeped several times in my direction. I could see him clearly, but pretended, lest I embarrass him, to be short-sighted. This unfortunate man was missing his entire lower jaw and also, it seemed, his upper lip. From the side, his silhouette was ostrich-like. I was shocked to see a living person who more resembled a cartoon character than a human being.

I closed my eyes and wondered if this tragic fellow's problem was directly caused by smoking. Being a non-smoker, I mused that if nicotine was the prime cause of his horrific deformity, then the whole world should be informed of his plight; even his photograph should be put on every packet of cigarettes. I then wondered which if either of us would be still above ground in six months. I told myself that, despite his condition, I would gladly exchange places with him if it meant my survival. I then inhaled a large draught of hospital-smelling air and, not for the first time, asked myself if I was really stuck in this hell-hole.

At eleven o'clock I was wheeled in my bed all the way to the radiotherapy department, a welcome diversion from boring immobility in the ward. Obviously, the sooner radiotherapy was concluded the better. Even the treatment itself was becoming less scary, since among other things, I was becoming fast friends with the operators.

The transfer from my bed onto the radiotherapy machine was traumatic, but it was a great consolation to be among professionals. After treatment I was taken straight back to the ward, where a delicious meal was being served; I eagerly partook of several helpings of meat and vegetables.

I had now spent one complete day in my new environment. It was as frightening as I had expected, but the food was great, the staff were exceptional, and I was lucky to have someone my own age in an adjoining bed.

In the middle of dinner, Andy breezed in. 'Just popped in to see how you are. I'm off to the mountains - hoping to get a shot at a deer or two. I'll give you a shout sometime tomorrow,' he whispered, as if we were both involved in a fantastic conspiracy.

Andy's visits cheered me greatly; his childlike devilment was an unfailing source of entertainment. He always had a joke or a tall story, upon the telling of which his hearty laughter would echo round the hospital. When he would leave after one of his all-too-brief incursions, I would lie on my back motionless and just stare at the ceiling. Ever since first hearing my bad news, I had lost all interest in reading. Even the sports pages had lost their appeal. Political developments, too, were meaningless. I now had just one overriding preoccupation: my own survival.

10 Enema territory

Pat used to purposely relax and rest for some time before he would walk unaided to the radiotherapy room. 'Pat,' I said, 'please give me a pigeon - and when you return you must help me get to the bathroom. The nourishment here is almost too good.'

'When I get back I'll be as sick as a dog for a while, but I'll gladly help you.'

I waited in ever-increasing pain for his return. Amazingly, when the pain of the turmoil in my stomach exceeded that in my lower back, the back pain seemed to disappear altogether. I tried to sit up in bed, but could not raise my head more than a few inches above the pillow. I began to realise that my prudery about the pigeon was bringing needless agony on myself.

At the height of my discomfort, a good friend from home arrived. Willie Murphy was a running colleague with a great sense of humour who always spoke his mind.

'Jaysus, Fanahan, how are you doin'? You've lost a ton of weight. This is some whore of a spot you've landed yourself in. Look at them - they all look like zombies. I suppose they're all drugged up to the eyeballs -'

'Ease up, Willie,' I interrupted. 'It's not such a bad place. You should see the nurses - they're all smashers.'

'Thank God!' he gasped, in obvious relief. 'With comments like that you can't be too far gone. You haven't changed one little bit.'

As we chatted, Pat returned in apparent agony and immediately jumped into bed and covered his head. The clean-shaven head startled Willie. 'What's the problem with that poor lad?' he whispered.

Willie was a true friend, as his travelling 160 miles to see me proved. But I decided his cruel comments about my fellow-sufferers merited a little retaliation - just for fun.

'Cancer of the brain,' I whispered crudely. 'He has a tumour in his skull as big as an egg. It doesn't look good at all.' I shook my head somberly, noting at the same time that Willie was becoming acutely uncomfortable. Almost immediately, he took a deep breath, stood up, and as he headed for the door, called back, 'I'll drop in again next week. Best of luck!'

The fun in scaring the living daylights out of my straight-talking pal had temporarily taken my mind off my constipation. But when he had gone, my discomfort rapidly intensified. Pat emerged from underneath the covers at suppertime and said, 'Thank God, I feel much better now. I felt so sick after the radiation I would prefer to be dead than to go through it again. And still I know I'll have to go through it all again tomorrow.'

My constipation had by now reached crisis point. Shortly after supper, Pat agreed to help me to the bathroom. He grabbed me by the shoulders, and I made an earnest attempt to rise, but I was glued to the bed.

'I'll call an orderly. I'd never manage you on my own,' said a concerned Pat.

'No,' I replied quickly. 'An orderly would have to get permission from the big matron, and I know she'd insist on the dreaded bed-pan. That's the last thing I want.' I resolved to relax for a few minutes before making a really concerted effort. This time I had to succeed.

Having never been constipated in my life, I was astonished to find the pain could be so intense. I psyched myself up to bursting point - but still could not move an inch.

'Turn on your side, let your legs fall over the side, and I'll lift you,' said my solicitous room-mate. He grabbed me and, before I realised what was happening, had raised me to my feet. Instantly, a dagger-like pain shot through me, and a cold sweat erupted on my forehead. Suddenly, my 'good' right leg, which had never before troubled me, was useless: I could neither put any weight on it nor even straighten it. Pat shouted for someone to fetch a walking aid. This supported me, but I could make no forward progress.

'How about that mobile medicine cabinet over there?' said Pat.

I grabbed the horizontal bar on top, while Pat began to drag the cabinet the 30 or so paces to the bathroom. I did my utmost to shuffle along behind, but I was scarcely halfway across the floor when I knew it was useless. 'Get help quickly! I can't go any further. I'm going to fall.'

My next recollection was being back in bed and unable to straighten my right leg, the pain of which was now vying for supremacy with my constipation agony. It occurred to me - and I was horrified - that it might be a long time before I would walk again. My whole world had shattered into smithereens in a ten-yard shuffle.

One of the nurses, Caroline, brought me a stainless steel bedpan and said, 'I'll pull the curtains around your bed. You can use the pan when you wish.' I badly needed to use it there and then, but a new complication arose when I could not reach the desired position. My ten-yard odyssey had further stiffened my spine, which now resisted all bending.

I summoned Caroline again. She did her utmost to put the pan in place, but gave up when it was clear my weakened spine could not support my weight on the pan. She decided the only way to avoid further trauma to my spine was to slip a large waterproof sheet under me. She rolled me on my side, then to and fro gently a couple of times, till eventually the sheet covered more than half the bed.

'I'll leave you alone. You can shout when you want me,' she said.

'How about my underpants? I can't reach that far.' By now I had abandoned all inhibitions.

'I never had a request like that before. I'm not sure what to say,' said the pretty, smiling blonde.

'Quick, quick!' I shouted, pretending something was imminent - which, alas, it was not. The pants were removed in high haste, and I was left to brood in the privacy of my screened-off bed and my oversized napkin.

In this ideal environment, I rapidly gained confidence. I was now behaving, I told myself, in a way that would delight any maternity nurse. My effort was easily on a par with that of a woman in labour, and even matched the exertion of any 400-metre race I had ever competed in. My resolve was wholehearted and my heart was racing - but all I had to show for my labours were beads of sweat.

Caroline returned and was surprised to see me still in labour. 'There's only one thing for you now - the Pink Lady.' She was back again in a few minutes, shaking a reddish bottle. 'One spoon of this and you'll be in orbit in no time at all,' she said, with a great big smile. The Pink Lady had an acrid taste, but that did not deter me in the slightest. This was guaranteed to stir up everything inside me; the resultant evacuation would be easy.

It was a long night. I lay there looking at the dark ceiling and waiting for something to happen. How, I wondered, could a natural, everyday function, which I had always taken so much for granted, now be the root of so much turmoil. Much earlier than anyone else in the hospital, I heard the birds herald the dawn. Finally, breakfast arrived, and even though I had totally lost my appetite, I decided to cram in as much as possible - the idea being to build up the pressure to irresistible levels. Surely, I reasoned, the first law of physics would come to my relief: P1 x V1 = P2 x V2?

The screen around my bed remained tightly drawn. All my thoughts and energies were channelled into the job at hand - but the triplets refused to emerge. Just before eleven o'clock, an orderly arrived to transport me to the radiotherapy department. By now, I was not in the least concerned that the Pink Lady might produce the goods in transit, so dramatically had my inhibitions been lowered in the space of a week.

The hissing from the radiotherapy machine frightened me as always - but not sufficiently to induce a 'result'. The vibrations from the bed travelling back along the corridors also gave a glimmer of hope, but I arrived back to the ward without issue.

After a short rest, the crisis deepened. I summoned the head nurse, Betty. 'I'll have one of the nurses give you an enema,' she said.

'I hope that's not another name for the Pink Lady,' I groaned.

Betty smiled. 'Actually, it's a soapy purgative which will be injected in through your colon by means of a syringe.'

I took a few seconds to digest what she had said, then in some amazement replied, 'You're joking, of course.'

The smile grew broader on Betty's lovely face. 'Okay - when you need it badly enough, give me a shout.'

I did not hesitate. 'Betty, my two ears are about to pop off from the pressure - you better go full steam ahead.'

Within minutes, a young nurse arrived with her 'insemination' kit. 'This won't take long,' she said. 'Just relax, and it will be over before you know it.'

I never felt so imbecilic. I closed my eyes and pretended I had just hit the tape after winning the Olympic 400-metre final.

'Try to hold everything inside you for at least five minutes and you will move quickly,' she said, packing sheets all around me and turning the bed into a veritable moat.

I waited and waited - but still nothing happened. My inseminator threw an occasional weather eye in at me, and after an eye-watering half-hour, asked if I had had any joy.

'No sign of any one of the quads yet,' I replied.

'If nothing happens very soon, I'll talk to Betty,' she said.

Betty arrived shaking her head. 'Everything must have turned to concrete in there.'

'Not at all, Betty. There's a savage volcano gurgling inside of me.'

'That's for sure, but there's no way out yet. Hold on and I'll give you another enema.' As she went to work, she added, 'This time you must really try to keep it inside - otherwise it won't do any good.'

Betty was an elegant woman in her early thirties, with the brownest eyes I had ever seen. As she proceeded with this delicate chore, I closed one eye and half-closed the other. I was curious to know what was going on. Soon she straightened up. 'You're getting good at this enema business,' she said, as she gathered her kit and departed.

Time moved on. The minutes turned into hours, and still the volcano did nothing but rumble painfully. I crammed in as much dinner as I could, and the pressure grew even more. By the time supper arrived, the thought of food was sickening. I decided to abandon theoretical physics and ate nothing.

All during that evening and night, no visitors were allowed except Andy. He was amused at first by my discomfiture, but decided not to linger when he realised how serious it was. Before leaving, he remarked, 'You remind me of the cows at home long ago at the beginning of spring, after they would be let out in the clover fields. Some of them would get constipated for a while, and then all hell would break loose. You definitely would not want to be standing at the wrong end of the cow.'

I took the maximum dose of sleeping tablets, but slept very little. Early the following morning, the big matron heard me groaning and decided to take matters into her own hands, as it were. 'An enema will fix you,' she snarled.

'Enemas are useless, Sister. I've had two already, and they just don't work.'

Of course, it was a bad mistake to tell the battle-axe her job. Before I fully realised what was happening, I was attacked and even hurt by this powerful all-in wrestler. The episode had unpleasant connotations of rape - and I was the victim. When her mission was complete, she pranced away without a word. I waited and waited. Nothing happened.

The turmoil now was so severe I feared imminent physical damage. The only consolation was that the pain in my lower spine and the numbness in my legs had vanished. My own diagnosis was that some kind of caesarean operation was inevitable, but when Betty returned on duty, I found out otherwise. 'I just cannot believe that nothing has happened. The enemas can't stay in long enough to do their work. The only thing is manual extraction,' she said.

'Any way you wish, Betty - and the sooner the better,' I moaned.

Betty donned plastic gloves, while I, quite unable to believe what was happening, was put in the 'delivery' position. She set about her task earnestly. I knew something had to be done to break the log-jam - but as Betty set to, I knew I would never, ever tell anyone of my unimaginable humiliation.

Time moved at a strange pace. I was presumably on the way to Heaven, but was still in hell. I did not know whether to stare into Betty's brown eyes or close my own. Should I stay silent, or should I talk my way through it? Every few minutes she would pause for a break; we would chat for a few moments - and she would begin over again.

'You have a tough job,' I ventured, in a feeble attempt at small talk. 'No money would suffice for what you are doing now.'

Betty shook her lovely head and said, 'Yeah. But how about the satisfaction I'll have when I see the relief written all over your face later on?'

This 30-odd minutes was possibly the most bizarre of my entire life. Most of the time, I felt so embarrassed I could only laugh. Occasionally Betty would join in and say, 'If you don't let me concentrate, I'll ask Matron to take over.' This woman's amazing dedication convinced me, if ever I needed convincing, that nursing is truly a vocation.

Finally after much ado, Vesuvius erupted. Life was wonderful once more. The previous hours were something I hoped I would never again have to endure. The calm after the storm was blissful, but reality soon beckoned. The pain in my back and legs was as acute as ever, and my right leg was as stiff as a ramrod. Solid foods would be off the menu for a long time. Soup, mashed potatoes, jelly, and tea would be my near-liquid staples. I had found the perfect slimming regime.

11 Alarums and excursions

Treatment at 11am became a daily routine. Apparently, I would spend six or seven weeks here before going to a different hospital for surgery. Each day became a dreary carbon copy of the one before, the monotony broken only by my visitors. Andy called every day and never failed to cheer me up. Brendan O'Reilly, a great friend from my athletics days, called several times. Well-known as a sportscaster and singer, the six-foot-five-inch Brendan was a big hit with the nurses. Jean's sister Ellen breezed in quite often, keeping the hope alive that Jean herself would arrive sometime. Old friends and not so old maintained a continuous chain of support as I channelled all my energies into fighting the dreaded disease.

One fateful day I asked Dr Hollywood why the pain in my spine had become so acute.

'I've been wondering about that,' he said. 'It seems to me the radiotherapy has softened your vertebra sufficiently for something to press against your spinal chord. I'll organise a myelogram.'

The following morning, after radiotherapy, I was wheeled in my bed to the operating theatre. I was told I would get a local anaesthetic; fluid would be removed from my spine and replaced with coloured dye; the spine would then be filmed, and the spinal fluid replaced. The procedure seemed fairly innocuous and would provide diversion for an hour or two.

My problems began while I was being transferred from bed to operating table. Two male attendants aided by at least three nurses endeavoured to raise me. As soon as the minutest of pressures was applied to my body, a rapier penetrated my spine. I panicked and startled everyone by roaring, 'Stop, stop, or my spine will snap!' Something was dreadfully amiss in my spine - as if I was about to become totally paralysed.

There was general consternation. I wondered briefly had I turned into an obnoxious monster; perhaps my mind was playing tricks on me. But it seemed imminent disaster would befall me if I did not vehemently dissent.

'I'm sorry, folks, but I cannot let anyone touch me until the surgeon arrives,' I said in deadly earnest.

We waited in awkward silence until the surgeon appeared and ordered a type of hammock which elevated me onto the operating table after several painful minutes. I was slowly turned on my left side and given a local anaesthetic. Soon the surgeon was ready to begin. He made several attempts to insert a large needle between two of my vertebrae so that the spinal fluid could be extracted. But my unnatural lie prevented me from straightening my left leg; consequently, I could not flex my spine. An impasse had been reached; perspiration dripped from my brow; I pleaded for iced water. Soon the freezing sponge had relaxed me sufficiently for the operation to proceed.

The operation was over in 20 minutes, and I was allowed to rest before my journey back to the ward. Dr Hollywood arrived to supervise my transfer into bed. The hammock was very carefully placed under me, and eight people began to lift me. My shoulders moved a fraction, but as they did, the dagger-like pain struck. I panicked in a way I had thought impossible, roaring and screaming like a maniac. I gripped Dr Hollywood with one hand and a nurse with the other and warned them both not to move me. More and more ice was being sponged onto my brow. Someone gave me an injection.

'That will relieve you,' said Dr Hollywood.

Everyone appeared to be waiting for me to fall asleep; I remained stubbornly awake. Soon, another effort was made to transfer me. Once again, the slightest pressure made me scream insanely.

By now the surgeon had left the hospital; young Dr Hollywood was the most senior medic in the building. All his efforts were hampered by my vice-like grip on his hands. I felt that by gripping him, I would not be so readily dropped onto the lower bed and have my spinal chord snapped irreparably.

I remember getting a second injection, and then another. Then Fr Andy loomed over me and put hot oils on my forehead. I remember being in an ambulance. When I woke up, I was in the intensive-care ward of a strange hospital.

The realisation that I was in new surroundings startled me, but I was relieved that the trauma of the operating theatre was over. Here, each patient was sectioned off in a separate cubicle. I quickly noted that I had no pain whatsoever, and that two drips were attached to my arms. I was strangely, though pleasantly, alone with my thoughts.

Questions began to flow through my mind. I had no idea where I was. It was even dark outside. 'Something must have radically gone wrong after the myelogram,' I told myself. I decided to conduct my own investigation. I tried to move my toe; to my infinite delight, I could do so with consummate ease. I tried to straighten my right leg, but failed. I deduced that at least nothing radical had gone wrong. I summoned a fellow in a white coat and asked where I was.

'How are you feeling now?' he asked without answering my question. 'Quite well, I think.'

'That's great,' he said. 'You were brought here to the Richmond hospital yesterday. There was some worry about you at first, but now everything has apparently stabilised.'

'Why was I brought here rather than left in St Luke's?'

He pondered for a few moments, as if choosing his words. 'Apparently you scared the life out of everyone up there, and we're much more equipped to deal with emergencies here. All is well with you now, so try to get a little sleep - it's still the middle of the night.'

I counted lots of sheep, then polystyrene tiles on the ceiling, but the novelty of the situation, coupled with the absence of pain, made sleep impossible.

Even before the sun rose, Dr Hollywood paid me a visit. 'Delighted to see you smiling,' he said.

'I feel so good right now, I'm almost scared it won't last.'

'Unfortunately, that's true,' he replied. 'One of those drips is a painkiller - it will be removed later.'

I apologised for all the commotion and consternation of the previous day. He explained that they had found a splinter of bone from the diseased vertebra protruding into my spinal chord.

'I suppose that means an operation soon,' I said.

'Yes, that's something I was hoping to discuss with you,' he said cautiously. 'As soon as everything has stabilised here, you will come back to us in St Luke's for two to three weeks. Then you will be transferred to either St Vincents or the Mater, where an orthopaedic surgeon, Mr Shunor, and a neurosurgeon named Rayloe will perform two operations on your spine. The first will be an anterior fusion, the second a post-anterior fusion.'

I paused to digest what he had told me, and said, 'Doctor, tell me honestly, am I ever going to get out of all of these hospitals alive? There's a limit to the amount of torture a body can take. I can tell you that I am absolutely worn out. I was never sick in my life, and now I have to endure several months more of anguish with no guarantee that I will ever get out alive.'

'McSweeney,' he said, looking me sternly in the eye, 'You have one great asset, and that is your ability to fight. It's from now on that the battle commences. I am in there with you, so you better not let me down.'

'Whatever fight was in me is all well gone by now. Honestly, if I had any sense in the world, I think I would throw in the towel this very minute.' I lay back with a sigh. I felt snookered in the game of life - as if fate was using me as a guinea-pig and I had not a snowball's chance in hell of survival.

Immediately, I regretted taking out my frustration on young Dr Hollywood, who was very much surpassing the call of duty in my interests. 'I'm sorry, Doctor, for acting the bastard, but these are not some of my best moments. I very much appreciate all that you are doing for me. Perhaps when I get my faculties back I'll see things differently.'

Later that morning Fr Andy, whose clerical collar was a passport to visit anyone almost anywhere, arrived with his usual cheerful greeting. Once again, his genuine concern renewed my resolve to go on living and fighting; my negative thoughts receded. He convinced me that things would soon improve: 'When I was called to St Luke's yesterday, I thought you wouldn't reach this place alive. Now you're back to your old self again. You're more indestructible than old Nick himself. When you survived yesterday, you'll survive anything.'

Andy then told me there had been some drama at my parents' home in Castletownroche the previous night. Apparently my mam answered the phone and was told by a St Luke's doctor of my myelogram misadventure. Since she had been led to believe that I was attending a more orthodox institution, she now jumped to the conclusion that I was close to death.

Later that day, Mr Shunor and Mr Rayloe gave me a brief, cursory examination. They scarcely spoke to me, but conversed with each other in artificially-superior tones. Mr Rayloe's polka dot dicky-bow was an immediate turn-off. Both men appeared to believe that I could be cured only by their brilliance. Within seconds of them entering my life, I felt insignificant. I did my utmost to be courteous, but all my attempts to initiate rapport were rebuffed. As they were leaving, Mr Rayloe stared vacantly in my direction and, in his highly-polished mid-Atlantic accent, said, 'I thank you so much.'

I lay in bed distraught and speechless. My self-confidence had been cruelly dented. But these two gentlemen were now my only passport back to the outside world. Had I been unduly sensitive or even paranoid? Surely the purpose of their brief examination was to interpret whatever they had seen on scans, X-rays, and reports. Perhaps these two were consummate professionals, and their seeming lack of humanity was the norm. I could not help thinking, though, that if one of them employed a civil engineer, like myself, to design even an outside toilet, he would expect the unfortunate engineer to be a great deal more client-friendly than they had been with me. I was now terribly confused and scared.

The vacuity of 'I thank you so much' taunted me for hours. Why, I repeatedly asked myself, had I been thanked? I had not been asked any questions, nor even been given the opportunity to say anything. Indeed, I had been treated with nothing but disdain. My unproductive musings eventually gave way to amusement when I recalled the postcard I had seen somewhere of a sexually-frustrated Pink Panther summing up his loveless plight: 'To all the virgins of the world, thanks for nothing!'

As the day progressed, a few friends were allowed to visit me, in single file. For once, I was pain-free, and their presence helped to distract me from my woes, as well as from the sophisticated hardware all around me in this intensive-care ward.

The following day I was taken aback by the visit of a new team of medics. Again, I felt like an academic project. As they left, a young, good-looking woman stayed behind and asked if I would answer questions for her thesis on various diseases. Glad of any diversion, I agreed.

I learned in the context of this latest examination that Messrs Shunor and Rayloe had for some reason decided against operating on me. I was now thoroughly frightened. My overtaxed brain could not even begin to comprehend what was happening. I did not know what to do or say; I just closed my eyes, thought about Heaven, and prayed and prayed.

Later that day the morphine drip was removed and the pain crept back. The dagger cut into my spine; my legs grew numb; a burning itch skinned the soles of my feet. And all the time, I still could not straighten my right leg.

Two days passed slowly - and it was time to go back to St Luke's. It almost felt like going home. When the ambulance crew arrived, I gave precise instructions on how I should be moved. They wheeled me to the front door, from where I could see the open doors of the waiting ambulance. We paused in the door, because it was raining outside. But when it became evident the rain was not about to stop, my helpers put a plastic cover over me and continued. Slowly and carefully, I was raised from the wheeled trolley and moved toward the ambulance. As soon as a few raindrops fell on my face I shouted, 'Stop, stop!'

'Sorry, but we're doing our best.'

'Ye are doing just fine,' I shouted. 'It's the rain and the breeze on my face - I never felt anything so beautiful. Please hold on for a few minutes. This is Heaven!'

The trip across the city was enlivened by my driver and his lieutenant, who both spoke only about athletics for the entire journey. They were avid marathoners, eager for advice. The attendant kept his hand firmly on the guard-rail enclosing me. Meanwhile, my eyes never left the small window behind my head, through which I could see the upper stories of the buildings moving by.

One street was traffic-jammed; the driver sounded his siren, and we began to jink our way through the scattering traffic. Then my companions laughed simultaneously. 'Some old woman in her Morris Minor has panicked and won't budge,' said the driver. 'I'd best talk to her.' The old lady was eventually persuaded to allow the ambulance driver to shift her vintage chariot, and soon we were on our way again.

Leaving the ambulance, I asked for a second baptism from the precious elements. Again, I wallowed in the invigoratingly cool wind and those gloriously refreshing drops of rain.

Soon I was being whisked along the familiar corridors. My old bed awaited me, and my good friend Dr Hollywood was on hand to transfer me into it. With the agonies of five days before indelibly etched in my memory, the transfer was again extremely painful and frightening.

As soon as Dr Hollywood left, I was besieged by patients and staff. Evidently, my hysterics in the operating theatre had alarmed the entire hospital. Speculation was rife as to whether my spinal chord had severed or not. With the passage of time, the significance of that afternoon would become much clearer. Indeed, I would eventually conclude I was extremely lucky to have any sensation at all in my legs - however painful they might be.

I was glad to be back with my friends in St Luke's. A routine was soon established, and a pleasant sense of normality settled on me. A mobile telephone enabled me, when I had screwed up the courage, to resume contact with the outside world.

Jean was top of my list. Ellen continued to delight the entire ward with her stunning good looks and sense of caring. My greatest fear was that she had been visiting me more out of a sense of duty than out of interest on Jean's part. How thrilled I was when a phonecall revealed Jean was coming to stay with Ellen for the weekend and would call to see me!

My first day back in St Luke's was also my birthday. As the lights were dimmed that night I got a wonderful surprise: I was awaiting my painkillers and sleeping pills when the huge room began to brighten from the lights of more than 30 candles. The nurses, who had bought a large, iced cake, began singing *Happy Birthday*. I was amazed and delighted. After the singing and the blowing out of candles, the cake was sliced and distributed to my 40-or-so room-mates. All joined in the singing and the congratulations.

Presently, I was given a less pleasant surprise. An old-timer from the West of Ireland, who had one ear missing, came to thank me for the piece of cake. We chatted briefly. Then, as the 87-year-old was about to go back to his bed, he turned toward me and asked, 'By the way, what age are you today?'

'What age would you think I am?' I stupidly asked.

He returned to my bedside, leaned close to my face, and conducted a quick scrutiny. 'Ah,' he surmised, 'you have a youngish face. I suppose you're about sixty.'

I was shocked. In his honest appraisal, I was almost twice my real age. I recalled that my visitors, without exception, always greeted me with the same words: 'You're looking great.' Such compliments were, no doubt, well intended. But I noted that no-one ever admired me thus when I was well and looking my normal, 'beautiful' self. Now I realised for the first time that my spartan, anti-constipation diet had combined with all the physical and mental trauma and inactivity to play havoc with my features. Still, I did not worry unduly; I fully realised I was fighting a war and not taking part in a beauty contest.

Friday evening eventually arrived, and Jean walked in trailing a heavenly aura. I gazed at her, and for a moment we were both speechless. She took a bottle of freshly-squeezed orange juice and a pile of chocolates and sweets from her large bag. Then, with a deep breath, she said, 'You're looking great - considering everything.'

'Thanks for being honest with me. In fact you're only the second person who has hinted the truth.' I told her about the old man who thought I had celebrated my 60th birthday. She laughed heartily, and all of a sudden we had reached a new level of intimacy.

'Well, what do you expect?' she said. 'Anyone totally confined to bed loses weight. The important thing is that your treatment is going well, and you could not be in a better place.'

'I do hope you are right, Jean.'

'Of course I am. Before you know it, we'll be bopping around the floor in Papillons, doing that dance we never had.'

'I sure hope so.'

Much too soon she departed, with the promise to return the following day. A quick but tender kiss on the back of my right hand and she was gone. I was over the proverbial moon that she had visited me, even if disappointed that she had not stayed longer. Her physical presence, coupled with her confidence in my future, were wonderfully therapeutic.

Within moments of Jean's departure, Marilyn appeared, all freshly-painted lips, sparkling eyes, and shining teeth. I thanked my stars she had not arrived 30 seconds earlier. Ordinarily, I looked forward to her visits, but now they were tending to complicate everything. Among other things, she had apparently told some of the nurses she was my 'girlfriend'.

She sat beside the bed, placed her handbag and apple-tart on the bed-spread, and remained there until visiting time ended. Meantime, Fr Andy arrived, but for once could scarcely get a word in - Marilyn dominated the proceedings. One of the nurses, aware of what was happening, approached the bed, and with a big, sarcastic smile said, 'Oops, sorry! I forgot your girl-friend was here.'

In the background, Andy smiled and made the sign of the Cross. Then he winked and said, 'See you tomorrow.'

Languishing in hospital, I was delighted to see anyone calling, but Marilyn was placing me under a new kind of strain. She had a heart of gold, and yet she was the first person I had seen Andy take instant irritation to. Even the nurses were not eager to have her around. Of course, I wanted her to keep calling, but not if it was going to complicate my budding relation-ship with Jean.

The following day, Jean arrived shortly after dinner and sat on 'Marilyn's chair'. She was much more relaxed than on the previous evening. I relished every second of our long conversation. While we spoke, Andy walked in. Jean jumped up from her chair: 'Sit down, Father - I need to stretch my legs.'

'Stay where you are, my dear,' said Andy. 'Last night that Marilyn one prevented me from even saying hello.'

'So that was Marilyn,' smiled Jean with mock suspicion.

'Marilyn?' I said innocently.

Jean looked at Andy, and they both smiled. 'Ellen described her to me. I was thinking that was her I passed in the corridor.'

Andy looked straight at me and said, 'Well, I'll tell you one thing - if I ever see her in here again I'm never coming back. She'll frighten everyone away. She hogged the bedside last night and no-one could get a word in edgeways.' Andy, of course, knew how much I had looked forward to seeing Jean; he also knew that Marilyn was just a friend. His outburst was cleverly calculated to make Jean feel entirely welcome.

The following day Jean dropped in again before returning to Cork. Already, I felt, a bond had developed between us. She had given me another reason to fight, and I sensed she would stand by me come what might. In any event, I was incredibly fortunate, at this difficult time in my life, to have gained her friendship.

The days moved along slowly in St Luke's, but never uneventfully. My predominantly-liquid nourishment ensured constipation would not be a problem. I became a dab hand at using the 'pigeon', developing a technique so subtle that it was almost impossible to detect. One day, however, my efforts proved surprisingly fruitless. Initially, I didn't worry. And even after several abortive attempts the following day, I remained confident I would easily perform under cover of darkness. All of a sudden, however, pressure began to soar. Panic lights flashed from my kidneys. Unbelievably, I suddenly felt as distressed as I had done in the throes of constipation. In desperation, I called a nurse; she immediately summoned a doctor. Ten terrifying minutes elapsed before a young female doctor arrived, placed her hand on my stomach, and immediately said, 'I'll have to insert the catheter.'

'What's that, doctor?' I quickly asked.

She held it up. 'This is the bag which collects the urine, and this is the attachment with the little inflatable ball at the end. When this tube is inserted into your bladder, the urine can filter through the telescopically-opening sphere.'

'How does the tube get into the bladder?' I asked, hoping she would not state the obvious.

From her kit-bag she took a syringe with a monstrous needle attached. 'I'll give you a local anaesthetic in the penis and insert the tube up through it into your bladder,' she said without batting an eyelid.

I did not know whether to laugh or cry. This seemed even more embarrassing than my constipation episode. 'Doctor, I'm sure that if I have fifteen minutes to myself there will be no necessity for that javelin you are waving over me. Believe me, you have given me the ultimate incentive.'

'Stop acting like a baby. You've gone well beyond the point of no return. The catheter is your only way out,' she said briskly.

'Please, Doctor, give me a break! I'm still a single man. The last thing I need is to have that rapier poked into my private parts. It may be difficult for you to comprehend, since we are built differently. But I'm now certain that it's unnecessary.'

She laughed, then scratched her chin as if weighing the pros and cons. 'Okay - you have exactly fifteen minutes and not one second more, and if that container is not overflowing, I will come at you like a raging bull.' We both smiled as she reluctantly gathered up the offensive weapon. I pushed and squeezed and grunted and groaned. I imagined I was at the Niagara Falls and the Hoover Dam. I could hear rain teeming down from the skies and taps overflowing. The perspiration running from my forehead tasted like salt on my lips. My pyjamas became soaked with sweat. It was all to no avail. Pressure was building up inside my head; I felt on the verge of hallucination. Soon I was praying my lady physician would hurry back.

She arrived to find me in a kind of frenzy. 'Get it over with as soon as you can,' I begged. Soon the unthinkable needle was being driven through that part of me which God never ordained for such abuse. I put four fingers from my right hand into my mouth and bit tightly, so that this new pain might somehow cancel out the other. After a few minutes, the anaesthetic began to take effect, and the long, transparent tube burned its way into my bladder.

'That's it. Just lie still and relax and you'll be fine,' said my attacker as she fixed a yellowish bag onto the side of my bed.

I looked her straight in the eye for the first time and said, 'Thank you, Darling. But let me tell you something - I'd hate to be one of your boyfriends.' She did not answer; she just winked and walked out.

I lay in terrible pain for ages, but nothing happened. Finally, fearing something had gone wrong, I called a nurse. She raised the plastic bag from its pouch and said, 'Look, you're doing fine. You're up to the litre mark already.' The pain had not yet abated - but I was content for the first time in a couple of days.

This was an experience I never wished to go through again. Why it had to happen in the first place was a mystery to me. I must be taking in something I apparently should not be. Or perhaps inactivity was to blame. In any event, I had now lost all interest in both food and drink.

My last two weeks in St Luke's passed in bearable physical pain. Fear of the unknown and uncertainty about the future were my greatest difficulties. Still, every one of the marvellous staff made each day as comfortable and pleasant as possible. My family and friends, Jean, and Fr Andy - who visited every day - were all an unfailing source of strength and encouragement.

12 The Messiah cometh

The day before I left St Luke's, a tall, athletic, handsome man with greying hair called to see me. 'Hello, I'm Dr Walsh - Martin Walsh. How do you do?'

So this was the man they called 'The Messiah'. Within moments, I began to understand why; he had won my complete confidence. When he told me it was he would operate on me, my initial surprise quickly turned to joy.

'Tomorrow, you will be taken to Cappagh hospital, where you will relax for a couple of weeks. Then you will be transferred to the Mater, where we'll first do an anterior fusion. We'll carry out the post-anterior fusion approximately a month later.' We spoke for only ten minutes, but I was so impressed, almost overawed, by his gravitas and palpable intelligence that I decided to ask none of my usual questions.

'You will need every morsel of your strength,' he went on. 'You have a great deal in your favour. You are young, strong, and a non-smoker. And all those thousands of miles of running should stand to you during the recovery period. I'll see you again in Cappagh and inform you further about operational procedures.'

When he had gone, I lay back pondering this latest development. Suddenly, tears filled my eyes. But they were tears of jubilation. I wanted to make my tremendous good fortune known to everyone. A half-an-hour before, my great worry was that either Rayloe or Shunor, or both, would be on my case. Now, by the grace of God, I had 'my kind of surgeon', ready, willing, and able to harness his immense skill and knowledge to my cause.

Soon, I was bidding adieu to St Luke's - and to the greatest nursing and medical staff imaginable. I was again strapped in the rear of the ambulance, and again took almost childish delight in the sight of house-rooves and trees flying by the small rear windows. After a half-hour journey, I was wheeled into my new surroundings.

13 Countdown to Cappagh

By now, assuming everything had gone according to plan, the tumour had been totally burned from my spine, and all that remained of my fifth lumbar vertebra was a piece of jelly. I was still in great pain, despite the constant diet of supposedly powerful painkillers. I sometimes wondered if these much-vaunted painkillers worked at all; the only evidence of their effect, as far as I could see, was that I was now often dozy.

On my second day in Cappagh, one of the nurses sent her uncle to see me. I was deep in thought when this patriarchal figure, complete with beard, loomed up and towered over my bed. 'Fanahan,' he simply said.

'Yes, Sir,' I replied, hoping he would tell me who he was, but embarrassed that he was clearly waiting for the sign that I recognised him.

Finally I said, 'I'm sorry, but you better blame the drugs. I'm sure I should know you, but as you can imagine, I'm not feeling myself these days.'

'Ah,' he laughed, 'sure that's a dirty old habit anyway.'

It took me several seconds to get the joke. I had no idea who this stranger was, but his hairy appearance and ready wit suggested he might be a messenger sent from Heaven to lighten my gloom.

'I'm a little disappointed you don't recognise me,' he teased.

'You'll have to give me some clue.'

'We're both engineers. We both ran in the Olympics.'

'More, more,' I pleaded.

'Both of us graduated from American universities.'

'It has to be the tablets.' I was now acutely embarrassed.

'How about if I told you that between the two of us we held the national 440-yard and 400-metre records for about forty years?' he said, with a grin on his partly-hidden face.

'Well, I had your photograph on my bedroom wall for surely ten years. You were, and still are, one of my greatest heroes. Jimmy Riordan, I'm delighted to meet you,' I said with great excitement.

I got a huge hug from this lovely man whom I was meeting for the first time. We spoke at length of our several common interests, but it was his sense of humour which gave me the greatest thrill. 'Jimmy,' I said, 'open my bedside locker, uncork one of those bottles of whiskey I got as presents, and have a few swigs.'

'I'd love to, but I haven't touched a drop in five years. Alas, I have well exceeded my quota on this galaxy.'

Jimmy stayed for more than 30 glorious minutes. Then a senior nurse asked him to leave, since I was forbidden to have long conversations. Meeting this longtime hero was a powerful tonic. His embellished athletics stories were classical. As he left the room he turned and said, 'McSweeney, you will survive all right. You have too much in common with myself not to.' I was not entirely sure of his meaning, but I took it as being a sort of layman's blessing from a newfound friend.

Andy, as usual, called every day. On the evening of my last Sunday in Cappagh, he arrived sporting an even larger smile than usual.

'My God, the rain after mass did me the greatest favour ever!' he said, barely containing his laughter. 'That sly sacristan of ours, as you know, is the greatest thief in the country. He has been swiping pound notes from the collection box and right from under my nose ever since I came to the parish. But I could never nail him, though I watched him like a hawk. At the end of mass each Sunday, the boxes would be overflowing with pound notes, but when the counting would begin on Monday, most of the notes would be missing. It's not easy to fool Sheahan - but I was at a total loss. I even wondered at times if I was doing the man a grave injustice.

'Anyway, today the bishop concelebrated mass, and when we were about to walk from the church to my presbytery for dinner, the rain was pouring down. The quare fellow was graciously escorting the two of us, when without thinking, I took the folded umbrella from his hand and raised it over the bishop's head. Lo and behold, twenty or thirty crisp pound notes showered down on the bishop's head! Your man took off rather quickly.'

As the day approached for my transfer to the Mater hospital, I was surprised to learn that Mr Walsh would be operating on me with the assistance of a vascular surgeon but without a neurosurgeon. Fr Andy discussed this information with Kay O'Leary, a very dear mutual friend and a brilliant nurse for whom I had designed a large nursing home. She was reportedly shocked - and insisted on travelling from Bantry to Dublin to discuss the matter with Mr Walsh.

'I'm pretending to be your aunt back from the States and am anxious to know why a neurosurgeon will not be in attendance,' she told me. 'The vascular surgeon's primary function is in controlling blood-flow. If it's a question of money, I will gladly pay five, ten thousand pounds - whatever it costs. It seems to me that for such major surgery a neurosurgeon should be assisting.' I was thrilled that such a busy person would travel a round-trip of 400 miles on my behalf.

After meeting Mr Walsh, Kay came to me with unexpected news: Mr Walsh had explained to her that a neurosurgeon was unnecessary, and she was quite happy with his reasoning. In fact, and as I was to learn later, he could not obtain the necessary assistance, and so had to work alone. But of course, neither he nor Kay dared tell me as much for fear of increasing my anxiety.

A few uneventful days passed before Mr Walsh called. After a brief but pleasant conversation, he said, 'You will be transferred to the Mater Misericordiae hospital this evening. A week from today we will perform the first of two operations on your spine. The first will be an anterior fusion through the stomach. The second, a month or so later, will be an anterior fusion from the rear.'

I asked what would happen during the first operation.

'I'll remove the front section of your L5 vertebra - where, incidentally, the tumour was positioned. I will then bridge this cavity with a section of bone from your hip.'

I took a deep breath and said, 'Where will my intestines be when all of this is happening?'

He just smiled and replied, 'We are in this together. I will really need all your help.'

'Of course, Doctor. I'll be doing my very best. In fact, I think I'm looking forward to it.'

'This is really your Olympic Games final, and you must fight like never before for your gold medal. Fortunately, you are young and don't smoke. And you are very strong from all the years of rigorous training. Now we will see how mentally tough you are.'

I felt contented with my medical lot for the first time in ages. This would surely be the most difficult trial I would ever encounter, but I felt elated and confident to have this very congenial gentleman as my lancer.

As soon as he strode from the room, I felt an extraordinary surge of adrenalin. The competent aura emanating from the great man made me eager to face these seemingly horrific operations. Deep down in my psyche, I looked forward to the day I would look Mr Walsh in the eye and say to him, 'Thanks for saving my life!'

When visiting time came round, I related my story to Fr Andy. He shook his head, almost in disgust. 'You should never ask these doctors anything. They always play God and tell you what you don't need to hear, and so add to your worries.'

'Not at all, Andy. It worries me for sure. But if I'm totally in the dark, I worry even more, and my over-active mind begins to play morbid tricks on me.' We debated along these lines for a time and finally agreed to disagree.

Later that evening, a mobile stretcher arrived, and I was bidding adieu to strangers I had made friends with two weeks previously - simply because our medical predicaments overlapped - and now would probably never meet again.

Once again the uneven streets of the city were both pleasurable and painful. Things were now beginning to happen quickly, and a certain excitement was being generated in my mind.

14 Mother of all operations

The Mater Misericordiae - Mother of Sorrows - appeared huge; at least the corridors were endless. I was delighted to be placed in a ward with five other patients. As I was painstakingly put into a corner bed behind the door, I well knew my incarceration here would last several weeks, and was glad not to be isolated in a lonely private room. The ceiling was 15 or more feet high; this was obviously an old wing.

My first encounter with the head nurse, Sister Lucia, was her robust greeting: 'Where in the name of the Lord do you expect me to store all that junk?' She sounded very much in earnest.

'Sister, I've spent almost three months in four different hospitals. Virtually everything is a sentimental present that I just have to keep.'

Under loud protest, but with a twinkle in her eye, she put a student nurse sorting out my several bags of 'rubbish'. Soon most of the confections were sent to the children's ward. Unwanted clothes were earmarked for the St Vincent de Paul organisation - or possibly the rubbish bin.

It was obvious to me that my new domicile was an integral part of a high-powered surgical conveyor belt. Almost every day someone was wheeled to the operating theatre and returned a day or more later depending on the severity of the operation. Nurses whizzed in and out at an alarming rate. The young students moved as if their jobs were in jeopardy; each seemed to be under the direct scrutiny of a qualified nurse. The qualified nurses, in turn, had to impress the matron. She, despite her awesome power, was anxious to please the doctors. The doctors deferred to the surgeons. As for the surgeons, they had no superiors - quite simply, they were regarded as gods.

There was a lovely old man in the bed next to me. Pat came from a tiny farm in County Longford and radiated innocence and unworldliness. His apparently simple lifestyle made him very special in my eyes. Each of his four daughters would visit him at different times each day. Their unashamed affection for him impressed me profoundly - especially since I had grown up in a household of five boys and no girls.

Old Pat's 20-acre farm was scarcely able to sustain two cows and a few calves, so he supplemented the household income by delivering the post on his bicycle. Early one morning, alas, a drunken driver had smashed into poor Pat and broken his hips and legs so badly that he would spend more than a year in hospital. His colostomy bag did little for the decor, but he was such a beautiful person I would not have exchanged him for anyone else. He never stopped psyching me up for my operation. Always praying, he would constantly say to me, 'Well, God willing, we'll all be home safe and in good health soon.'

Next to Pat was a man from Donegal who had barely survived a horrific road accident. He had been in a coma for weeks and had several broken bones.

Across the room was Gerry, in his mid-twenties. He and his then-girlfriend had been touring France on a motorbike five years previously. They had stopped for a rest at the side of the highway, when a car skidded into Jerry and smashed his right leg. Each year since, he had spent about six months in hospital hoping the next bone graft would take. This time, he feared that his leg would be amputated, yet his irrepressible good humour was an invaluable morale-booster in the ward.

In the centre bed was little John, who had fallen from the rear of his father's tractor while rolling a field ten years previously. The heavy roller dragged over his legs and spine; only his face escaped. He had spent most of the ten years since in hospital, but could now move along in a wheelchair. Scoliosis, or spinal curvature, had set in. Mr Walsh was to operate to correct it.

One bed, opposite me, was reserved for short-term accident victims.

December 18th arrived: the day before my first operation, the anterior fusion. Three efficient but giddy student nurses began scrubbing me from head to toe. Judith Brogan issued the orders to the two equally pretty blondes, Maria and Susan. But the removal of whatever bacteria lurked on me was not the only thing on the minds of the three lassies. They were aware I regarded Jean - the sister of Ellen, whom they had met a few times - as my girlfriend. And they were intrigued as to why Marilyn always introduced herself to them as my girlfriend. 'She almost sits on top of you in the bed. We can hardly get near you at times,' said Judith.

'No. And that good-looking priest that calls to see you doesn't seem to think much of her either,' said Susan.

I explained that I regarded Marilyn as a dear friend, but that her fondness for me was becoming claustrophobic, especially with the increasing likelihood of my two 'girlfriends' meeting as Christmas approached.

'It would be best to write to Marilyn and tell her the truth - otherwise you could risk losing Jean,' said a very concerned Judith.

I had been thinking along those lines myself, but Marilyn had been extremely kind to me, and I did not want to hurt her. 'I wish there was an easy way to tell her,' I moaned.

'If you like, we could help you to compose a nice, pleasant letter which would probably sound much less severe than a fellow would write,' said Susan. They finished my ablutions and promised to return with their tactful feminine composition after work, at four o'clock.

The letter they drafted was much different to what I would have written. It was so subtle I wasn't at all sure Marilyn would get the message. I also feared she would suspect I had not written it, which might complicate things even further. I had so much on my mind, though, that I copied it almost verbatim. When I had finished, Maria gleefully sealed the envelope and even insisted on supplying the stamp. When she left to post it, I felt I had one less complication in my life. And at this critical time, anything that lessened my anxiety was very welcome.

Andy arrived in full priestly garb and, after he had regaled me with his latest joke, said, 'I hope you don't think I'm being negative about tomorrow, but it's usual to administer the last rites before major surgery.'

'Andy, you know I like to cover all possible eventualities. If you can put in a word on my behalf with the Man Above, then that's great with me.'

He produced a small golden cask and donned his stole. Then, almost miraculously, my wild, outgoing, and jocose Andy was transformed into Fr Sheahan the seriously devout priest. He began a ritual prayer. The language was alien to me, but his profound sincerity shone clearly through every sacred word. He then carefully placed his right thumb into the cask and made the sign of the Cross with oils on my forehead and chest. Immediately,

I felt a strange spirituality descend on me. By the time he finished, I felt ready to accept whatever outcome my imminent operation might produce. Soon though, I was back to my normal self, very much thinking of staying alive.

Andy, especially at such times, was the greatest friend anyone could wish for: the perfect mediator between this world and the next. He was always eager to do anything humanly possible to ease my burden. Ever cheerful and humorous, he had a natural flair for making light of the most serious disasters.

Supper came and went, but that dreaded fasting sign had been placed at the end of my bed. My visitors had been asked to leave early; I was told to rest as much as possible.

A nurse entered with a foreign-looking gentleman, pulled the curtains around my bed, and disappeared without a word. The bronzed man introduced himself, but his name quickly slipped my mind, because I thought I was staring straight into the face of Colonel Muamar Gadaffi. At least his voice was kind and friendly.

'I am your anaesthetist. I need to ask you a few questions.' He posed a myriad of routine questions about my medical history. When I had assured him I had never had a serious sickness, we chatted about other things.

'I don't think you're from this neck of the woods,' I ventured.

'Africa,' he replied after some hesitation.

'Oh, great. What part?'

He hesitated again. 'Libya.'

'You sure have Colonel Gadaffi's head on your shoulders,' I said, curious to know how he would react.

'Thank you very, very much,' he said with a broad smile. 'That is a great compliment to get from you.'

In fact, the colonel was at the very bottom of my popularity stakes, but I had recently seen him on television articulating his world-view and had been amazed by his apparent intelligence. And since my life was now partly in the hands of this gentleman who looked so much like the scourge of the USA, I decided it best to contain my admiration for Ronald Reagan. 'In his Green Book,' I waffled, 'he states - if I remember correctly - that both the capitalist and communist systems are a mish-mash of good and bad, but that a combination of the best aspects of each would produce the ideal world.'

'That is absolutely true,' he replied earnestly. 'The colonel is a real genius.' He proceeded to instruct me on the colonel's philosophies in greater detail. I held my peace, and we soon struck up a warm friendship. I thanked my stars I had seen that particular television programme; otherwise, I might be facing my operation with less confidence.

As he departed he turned to me, his voice quivering with passion: 'What kind of man would bomb innocent children asleep in their beds, especially since no-one ever threatened him? He even blew the roof off my parents' house.' He was referring, of course, to one of my heroes, Ronald Reagan, but I dared not risk a confrontation.

'I shall see you early in the morning - and do have a good night's rest,' he said with the utmost courtesy as he walked out the door.

I took a deep breath and pondered about major operations, about Ronald Reagan, about Muamar Gadaffi - and hoped I was about to awaken from a bad dream. But the reality of things was all too apparent. Just then the registrar, Padraic Murray, who was fast becoming a friend and confidant, breezed in and delivered the inevitable pep-talk: 'I'll be in there with you in the morning. Mr Walsh is the very best there is, so it'll be very much up to you to get in and fight like never before. When you come to, you'll be in the intensive-care ward for a few days, on a special rotating bed called a Stryker frame. You'll be strapped onto this contraption - it's a bit like a surfboard - and you'll stay on it until well after your second operation. Every two hours you'll be rotated through 180 degrees onto another 'surfboard' to prevent bedsores. It won't be easy, I can promise you.'

'Padraic,' I interjected, 'there's no need for any more of this psyching-me-up. I know exactly what I'm going to do; I have worked out my game-plan. As soon as I open my eyes in that intensive-care ward, I am going to pretend I'm in the competitive situation I always enjoyed the most: I am being handed the baton on the anchor leg of the 4 x 400 relay and am five or six metres behind the leader; I am feeling strong and confident coming into the home straight; I have reached the point where I know I am going to win - then, that glorious feeling that every athlete fantasises about is going to be stretched to minutes, hours, and as many days as it takes.'

'That's my man!' laughed Padraic, sharing my intoxication and, in his exuberance, delivering a comradely slap that almost dislocated my shoulder. 'See you in the morning. Good luck!'

The senior night-nurse, Mary Long, arrived with the usual painkillers and sleeping tablets. She was a delightful, diligent person, another integral part of this fabulous 'relay' team that was building up around me. 'Just think, you'll probably be able to straighten out both your legs when we see you back here in a few days' time. I'm sure the pressure on your spinal chord will be relieved, and you'll have taken the first big step back to full recovery.'

'Did you say first step, Mary?' I uttered longingly.

She kissed me on the forehead and smiled: 'You'll be asleep soon. All the best tomorrow.'

Within minutes I was unconscious. The stronger-than-usual sleeping tablets coupled with the frenzied anticipation had drained all my energies. The next thing I knew, the fateful morning had arrived.

The nurses went straight into action so quickly that I had little time to brood. I was shaved, and washed from head to toe. An oversized stretcher was wheeled in. Before I was transferred onto it, 'Colonel Gadaffi' arrived and said, 'I will give you a little injection - it will help to relax you.'

After a few minutes, I was carefully transferred onto the mobile buggy. Soon I was being wheeled out into the corridor, with the good wishes of old Pat and all my room-mates in my ears. I vaguely remember talking to 'the colonel' in the operating room - then I lapsed into oblivion.

Six-and-a-half hours and eleven pints of blood later, I was taken to the intensive-care ward. Eventually, I opened my eyes, but saw only a thick haze. I oscillated between consciousness and unconsciousness for an indeterminate period. The more I regained awareness of where I was, the more I wanted to sleep.

I tried to evaluate my situation, but found myself in an insubstantial quandary, unable to fully comprehend or believe the horror of it all. I only knew I was as near to a living hell as could ever be imagined.

The pain and panic were indescribable. I really felt I was about to die at any moment. I counted time in fractions of a second, unsure if I would survive to draw my next breath. I feebly asked myself what if anything I could do to help myself, but feared that if I expended the tiniest amount of energy, even in thought, the extra demand on my system would be instantly fatal. My harsh, cacophonous breathing seemed to be over-vibrating my whole body, so I began taking shorter, less strenuous breaths.

As my breathing eased, I gradually gained the confidence to slowly open my eyes. Even before I could properly see anything, the effort of opening my eyelids was agonising. Soon, my entire landscape comprised tubes, wires, and noisy television monitors.

The overbearing scenario was too frightening, so I quietly closed my eyes and attempted to muster up my great - as I had thought - willpower. Within moments, the fear of dying overpowered me. I became alarmed that I might pass into the next world without even realising it.

I gently opened my eyes in the hope of clinging to the real world. The more I saw, the more I wondered would I be better dead. All the visible evidence, on top of my physical distress, suggested some funeral director must soon be invoked.

Whoever said self-preservation is the strongest of human instincts was incontrovertibly proven to be correct. I felt humiliated, scared, and isolated in depths of unimaginable terror. I felt at every moment that I was about to breath my last; and each of these moments seemed to linger for an eternity. And yet, all this time some tiny part of my psyche was telling me I was definitely not ready to meet my Maker. This trivial sentiment grew slowly; my courage began to improve; after a time, the will to survive was developing into a passion.

I eventually discerned some person in white sitting at my right side. A male voice said some words to me, and even though they did not register, I felt somewhat assured for the first time. I then realised that I was strapped to this very narrow and lofty bed. I was too frightened to even attempt to move any of my limbs.

My confidence began to grow - until the attendant made to leave the room. I panicked utterly, terrified that if left on my own for any time I would be dead when he returned. I began screeching - or trying to screech - with all my feeble might. What happened next I don't recall. I was plunged into an abyss of mental and physical delirium.

Time moved along, but I was incapable of measuring it. Several hours, probably days, later, I found that three intravenous needles were attached to each of my wrists; four tubes were siphoning the bleeding from the bandaged scar on my tummy and side into pint-sized bottles; about ten heart-monitoring suction pads were attached to my chest; a dreadfully uncomfortable tube was extracting bile from my stomach out through my nose; and a catheter was inserted into my plumbing department. Over my head were bags of blood and various other concoctions, while daunting oscilloscope-type television screens were monitoring my various bodily functions.

The more conscious and alert I became, the more evident my physical plight loomed. I still felt too weak to even contemplate a positive approach, but my instincts were telling me to hoard every morsel of strength to stave off the seemingly-imminent beck from Satan or his Foe.

Suddenly someone appeared in front of me dressed as a spaceman. I was startled - then happy to see Fr Andy's face looking down on me.

'How are you feeling?' I think he asked.

'Don't touch me, don't touch me!' I hissed, dreading he would lay a priestly hand on my forehead or shoulder and that even such gentle physical pressure would toss me over the precipice and into eternity.

Andy said very little and was allowed to remain only briefly. But his timely visit gave me new confidence to sit out this savage hurricane.

Some time later, a doctor entered my room, which I now noted looked like a glass-enclosed isolation cubicle within the intensive ward. He asked if I was in pain. Unable to say a word, I signalled Yes. My message was received if not loud at least clear. He immediately attached one of my intravenous needles to a morphine sachet and increased the flow rate.

He returned at intervals, and each time he did I pleaded in frantic sign language for more morphine. He made a few adjustments. The vibrations from his voice became less irritating. But I continued to insist that the pain was unbearable. After a few further adjustments, the agony abated. The relief was blissful - but would be very temporary.

'Your Stryker frame will have to be rotated every two hours to prevent bedsores,' my gracious anaesthetist told me. 'It will be quite distressing, but you will get used to it.' As he talked, I discerned a number of nurses crowding into my glass cell with an awkward-looking 'surfboard'. Quickly they began detaching the bags of morphine, saline solution, and blood from their positions above me and refixing them somewhere onto the bottom of my new bed. The new 'surfboard' was then placed on top of my body and vigorously bolted, first above my head, then below my feet. Now I was the meat in a very tight sandwich. I began to panic and groan, but before I could communicate with my tormentors, I was rotated through 180 degrees - from looking at the ceiling to facing the floor.

I was shellshocked. A few seconds ago, it had seemed that the sound of normal voices was the ultimate in torture. Now I was cruelly and ignominiously spun upside down. They then unscrewed the bolts holding the sandwich together, and raised the original mattress from my back. Then they replaced the drips back onto their original perches.

My body vibrated with pain. The inverted position disoriented my mind; I began to lapse into unconsciousness. Alas, time spent in the sleeping state has no correlation in conceptual duration with time spent in the conscious state, so it seemed as if I were constantly in this inexplicable turmoil.

Time stood still. But, too soon, the nurses returned with the alternative section of my 14-inch-wide sandwich board, and the gruesome assignment of returning me to my original position commenced.

When first rotated, I was innocent of the complications. This time I was less relaxed, and the trauma was even more extreme. The entire manoeuvre, I estimated, lasted about 15 minutes.

Now all the paraphernalia of my space-age hermitage within the intensive-care ward were starkly visible to me. It was not a pretty sight. Bleeping dots and lines were flickering up, down, and sideways on the many oscilloscopes all around me. I pondered the function of each one, and prayed like never before that I would survive this horrendous onslaught on my very existence.

My 'morphine medic' appeared again. 'You're coming along fine,' he said confidently. I knew then I was becoming more alert and conscious of my bizarre environment. I began to believe I was going to at least survive the traumatic hangover of the operation. My immediate challenge now was in enduring the two-hourly rotation of the Stryker frame.

The more lucid my mind became, the more questions it began to formulate. What did Mr Walsh find when he opened me up? Had the cancer spread? Were they giving me all this morphine just to ensure I would remain semi-comatose for the remainder of my days? I thought of the several people I knew who had been opened and then immediately closed up because nothing could be done for them. Was I one of those unfortunates? Myriads of such queasy thoughts perplexed me.

At least, the threat of immediate death had now receded. Irrespective of the news of my operation, which I would doubtless soon receive, I was lucky to have survived this far. I was strangely elated at not having parted this world in the company of my white-coated minder - a stranger whose face I had not even seen. And even if the prognosis turned out to be certain death, I now knew that, with Andy's help, I would be able to make peace with my Maker. This was something I had hitherto purposely avoided because of its defeatist or negative connotations.

Bizarre notions occupied me during those interminable hours and days in intensive care. How could healthy humans ever even contemplate ending their lives for any reason whatever? How could intelligent people smoke cigarettes, when the advice on the package mentions the word cancer? Why are millions of people allowed to starve to death when there is more than sufficient food to prevent the calamity? Why? Why?

In this context, formerly insurmountable personal and even global problems all had glaringly-simple solutions. But all I craved was to remain on in this precious world for as long as possible. My greatest fear was that Mr Walsh or one of his assistants would enter my glass capsule at any time and spell out or hint at the news that every cancer patient dreads. The mental and physical tension was relentless. But there was absolutely nothing I could do except relax as much as possible and pray and hope and wait - and wait.

Time dragged on - and I was delighted when my 'minder' told me my brother was being allowed to see me. The usual 'spaceman' arrived, but behind the mask was not any one of my four brothers, but a sports reporter from one of the tabloid newspapers. Something told me this guy was much more interested in my obituary than in my wellbeing.

Suddenly, all my defensive instincts were aroused. The second-last thing I wanted was unsolicited publicity. I decided, despite my helplessness, that the joke would be on him. Summoning up every morsel of malice, I stared nervously at the human scavenger, as if the very sight of him were going to push me over the edge. I began to screech roguishly and, as far as my physical constraints would permit, shook my head like an imbecile. The startled hack was quickly and unceremoniously ushered from the room by my minder, who had just realised that he had been deceived. When my minder returned, he smiled at me - and I winked back at him.

My brief battle of wits with the contemptible journalist elevated me physically and mentally. I was now ready to encounter reality again - and it was approaching time for me to return to St Agnes's ward. In fact, I told my minder as much.

The nursing staff began to disentangle me from the various monitors. The dozen or so suction pads were gently and carefully plucked from my chest. I was surprised that the removal of large chunks of hair from my chest was painless. The reason was that the morphine had numbed my senses.

The switching off of the monitors and the computers ushered in a blessed, but ironically deafening, silence. I was allowed time to adjust to my new and more normal environment. Eventually I gave the signal that I was ready to return to my old ward.

Then began the long and painful journey. As the wheels of the Stryker frame began to turn, the vibrations went through me like daggers. I moaned and groaned involuntarily all the way and roared like a spoiled child as I was jolted into the lift. Finally I was steered into St Agnes's, to the applause of John, Jerry, and old Pat.

For a few strained moments, no-one uttered a word. Unspoken questions about my operation hung heavy in the air, but nobody wanted to say the wrong thing. Finally, old Pat said aloud, 'We're all delighted that you are well and back here safely, thank God. How are you feeling?'

In a feeble voice I replied, 'To tell you the truth, Pat, I am absolutely knackered.'

'Oh, my God!' said Pat, sounding shaken by my blunt response.

'He'll make it through okay,' laughed Jerry in the far corner. 'There's still some devilment left in him.'

It was great to be 'home' again, but the pain was once again threatening to overwhelm me. I was getting a morphine injection every four hours, as well as painkilling tablets, but felt as if they were having no effect whatever. I was surprised, too, at not having seen Mr Walsh since the operation. When I enquired, I was told he was due in the ward at seven the following morning.

When the great man arrived I said, 'Doctor, there's something radically wrong - the pain at the left side of my hip is beyond belief. Then, strangely, I have no pain whatsoever along the incision across my tummy.' He smiled and began to examine the wound. He seemed pleased enough, but to my dismay, was saying very little. I just had to have some answers. I had to know the truth.

'How did things go during the operation?' I asked with bated breath.

'Fine,' was the brief reply.

'Then what has gone wrong over here?' I pointed to my left hip.

He thought for a moment, then in his soft but authoritative voice said, 'I told you that you must be tough. Hang on in there - it will eventually begin to ease. I can assure you that if you saw how much bone I had to take from your pelvic bone for the graft, you would understand. I must explain that our bodies are ingenious masses of divine technology. When a bone is broken in the normal fashion it will mend without undue stress. But when a healthy bone has a section severed from it mechanically, then that is an entirely different scenario. Evidently nature, or perhaps Providence, never legislated for such desecration; thus the unnatural pain.

'I'll ensure you receive the maximum dose of morphine for a few days. You will get through all right. By the way, we both got a touch of pneumonia after the operation - I even had to spend a few days in bed.' He gave me his usual positive smile as he left the room.

I was in such mental turmoil that I neglected even to say thanks. But the man was so perceptive that I really did not have to say anything; he knew how grateful I was.

One of Mr Walsh's utterances echoed thousands and thousands of times around in my head. He had said everything went 'fine' - and that was a huge beacon of hope. If I had been opened and quickly closed up again, he would hardly have expressed himself thus. His comment, too, about the unnatural onslaught on the healthy pelvic bone gave me new confidence. Almost instantaneously, the pain eased a little.

15 The Christmas spirit

Life was good again, and Christmas, only five days away, was surely something to look forward to. My next operation would not be for at least a week after that. I was becoming more relaxed and was learning to cope with the pain, but the rotating of the Stryker frame was always an ordeal. Every two hours, day and night, I was cruelly spun from facing directly onto the floor to looking up at the ceiling, or vice versa.

Friends were allowed to visit me singly and for only a short while. I was secretly amused that everyone reacted to me in an almost identical manner. When I was on my back and could see them directly, they would gape in amazement at the paraphernalia surrounding and attached to me. Then their eyes would meet mine, and they would courteously lie through their teeth: 'You're looking very well.' When in the prone position, I had a tiny mirror attached to the Stryker frame and adjusted so that I could see the door clearly without rotating my head. Then the real expression of horror was clearly visible. A few visitors were so startled that they meekly disappeared without ever announcing themselves.

I was continually trying to find the optimum method of being rotated. I had the same three student nurses - Judith, Susan, and Maria - turn me by day and had discovered that by tightly wedging my legs with several pillows between the two 'surfboards', I could keep my body fixed and rigid throughout the rotation. This way there was minimal stress on the most vulnerable part of my anatomy: the section of my spine that had been delicately grafted together by a piece of bone from my hip. The very slightest torque exerted on that area would put shock waves through me that would blow the lid off any Richter scale.

During the day these three lovely lassies had lovingly perfected the 'spin'; the super night-nurse, Mary Long, with the help of just one student, was equally proficient. Unfortunately, Mary alternated weekly night-shifts with Marsha, whom Matron had told me was the greatest nurse in the entire hospital. It was inconceivable that anyone could possibly be more caring, efficient, and endearing than Mary. So I eagerly awaited Marsha's arrival.

At precisely eight o'clock Marsha glided into the ward. This five-foot-nothing wizard did not look in my direction or anyone else's. She looked toward the ceiling and sniffed the air like a dog.

'Very stuffy in here - open the windows,' she said aloud but to herself. I was startled. Perched high on top of my 'surfboard', I was permanently cold, even with six sheets and a blanket on top of me. Besides which there were three or four inches of snow on the ground and an icy wind howling outside. It made no difference to Marsha; she pulled and dragged the weighted ropes that hung from the two huge windows.

'Nurse,' I said, as pleasantly as I could, 'I wish you wouldn't open the windows - I feel quite cold as it is.'

'Put some more clothes on you and have some consideration for the other patients,' she snapped.

I could not believe my ears, but managed to reply calmly, 'Nurse, the only bedsores I have are on the tops of my two big toes and are caused by the weight of the clothes I already have on me. No-one has ever complained about the heat - just ask any of the boys.'

She did not flinch, but continued as if I had never said a word. Soon, an arctic gale was whistling through the ward. She then turned on her heel and hurried out the door, sniffing the air and muttering, 'Ridiculous!' She had not once looked at me.

'Pat,' I said, 'she is a strange character and not exactly the ministering angel I was expecting.'

'Oh,' said old Pat, 'Matron says she's the greatest nurse in the hospital.'

'She's the greatest for sure - the greatest cow I ever came across in my life,' said a laughing Jerry in the far corner.

'May God forgive you, Jerry!' said old Pat, while I attempted to laugh for the first time in several weeks.

Marsha returned after half-an-hour and looked at me for the first time. 'I'm going to turn you now,' she said boldly. Involuntarily, I began to tremble.

'Fine, Nurse,' I said, trying to sound as reasonable and co-operative as I could. 'But you'll need the help of a student nurse - Mary always does.'

My diplomacy, or lack of it, fell on deaf ears. 'Don't you tell me my job! I'm nursing for more than twenty years,' she snapped.

She swept out of the ward and returned almost immediately with the 'surfboard'. She dropped it unceremoniously on top of me and began to frantically bolt it down on me at either end. 'You must wedge three pillows between my legs to keep my entire body rigid,' I insisted. She did not utter a word; it was obvious she was becoming more worked up by the moment. Having devised the most comfortable method of rotation with the other nurses, I intended having my instructions followed precisely. But since I had still more than a dozen tubes and drips attached to me and could scarcely raise a finger, I was almost totally at her mercy. 'Stop, stop!' I cried out in desperation. 'I'm not ready!' She grabbed me like a sumo wrestler, and with a flick, released the safety-latch on the Stryker. The memory of what followed will be seared into my memory for the rest of my natural existence. Beneath the Stryker were two small vertically-adjustable platforms. One held the food tray, the other the bedpan. Disastrously, one of these had not been lowered, and while in mid-spin, the Stryker was stopped with a tremendous bang. My legs plunged down between the pair of 'surfboards'. Containers of blood and saline solution were tossed to the ground by the impact. It seemed in that instant the greatest catastrophe and the most unprovoked humiliation I had ever suffered. I thought the bone graft in my spine had burst or else my spinal chord was severed.

Though I was virtually paralysed and temporarily stunned, a vicious monster - which I had never known existed - began to erupt from within me. I had doggedly weathered the traumas of the operation, only for this alleged Florence Nightingale to throw my entire future onto the precipice. And since the curtain was drawn around my bed, all that could be heard without was the sound of metal on metal. I decided I would not go down without a fight. In a fit of growing malice, I began to roar frantically. 'Help, help, help! My spine is smashed! Please, someone help!' I screamed with maximum fervour. My outburst produced an amazing chain reaction: all my fellow patients panicked in sympathy and began screaming as loudly as myself. Marsha made several futile attempts to swivel me back to the original position, but was not strong enough. All she could do was stand dumbfounded as several of her colleagues rushed in and carefully returned me to the supine position.

A doctor examined my legs. I was secretly elated to find that for the first time since the myelogram disaster in St Luke's, a couple of months before, I could fully straighten my right, 'good', leg. I was also able to move all my toes a little, so my spine was intact. I asked if I could relax for 15 minutes or so before being turned again. 'Of course, you can,' said a much chastened Marsha. I lay on my back for a short while and told myself that since I had apparently come unscathed through this latest episode, I had clearly progressed since my days in the intensive ward.

Marsha returned minus her former bluster. 'How are you feeling, Fanahan,' she asked caringly.

'Glad to be alive, Nurse,' I replied sarcastically. She took a deep breath and then continued about her work as if nothing had ever happened. Later that evening I asked her if she would close the window. She did so without demur. Ironically, the excitement with Marsha was to help me cope with the two-hourly rotation on the Stryker; it hurt every time, but I knew it could never again be as traumatic.

Early the following morning a nurse came on duty and enquired how I was feeling. 'Strange that you should ask,' I replied. 'To tell you the truth, I haven't a pain in the world.'

She rushed from the ward and within moments was back with a young doctor, who immediately took a blood sample. 'You need some blood - I'll be back in a while,' were his only words.

He returned in 30 minutes with two containers of blood and attached one of them to a drip. 'You're quite ashen,' he told me. 'It will take the greater part of twenty-four hours for you to return to normal.'

In boredom I watched the crimson fluid drip - slow, regular, and hypnotic as a metronome - into one of my intravenous tubes. The hours passed, and in direct proportion to the amount of blood entering from the two containers, my face lost its ghostly pallor, and the pain returned.

Letters and Christmas cards were arriving in bundles, and I was inexorably drawn into the Christmas spirit of the hospital. The younger nurses were the most excited. Several were openly confiding in me their romantic plans for the holiday. All this diversion helped me cope.

On Christmas Eve Fr Andy was even chirpier than usual; he seemed delighted to note the real improvement in me. 'You can't beat the power of prayer,' he smiled. 'A week or so ago it seemed you were headed for the knacker's yard. Now you will be eating Christmas cake in a couple of days' time. Prayer has to be the answer. I have my two knees worn to the bone from bombarding the Man Above - and He always comes up trumps.'

I had known Andy for most of my life; he was one of my very closest friends. But I still found it hard to reconcile Andy the fun-loving extrovert with Andy the deeply religious and faithful priest.

'Tonight is Christmas Eve, and when midnight mass is over I just might be tempted to indulge in a wee tipple,' he said with a large grin. Again I was reminded of Andy's preaching by example. Five months earlier, when I was first struck down, he had told me that as a personal sacrifice he would not touch alcohol until Christmas Day. I knew that this would be much more demanding on him than any amount of prayer.

The often lonely life of the celibate priest can induce a fondness for 'liquid nourishment'. Andy loved the occasional binge. Once, twice, or on special 'feast-days' during the month, he indulged in a 'night out' with the boys ‑though never if priestly duties beckoned the following morning.

'We could easily be tempted to have a small celebration with a bottle of wine tomorrow evening in here, and maybe even sing a song or two,' he said as he was leaving. I had a strange feeling that this Christmas Day in the Mater might be a little more boisterous that usual.

Christmas morning dawned like every other morning. All my fellow patients had snored, or emitted other sleep-related noises, all night. But being turned every two hours made it almost impossible for me to sleep. At precisely six o'clock I was washed and shaved; then I had my 'six-o'clock twist' on the Stryker. It being the festive season, I decided it would be appropriate to begin taking food again. I sipped some tea through a straw; it tasted strange but very good. I ate a little bread - cautiously, because it tended to clog-up as it reached the tube in my trachea. Such minor discomfort wasn't going to deter me, however, as long as it marked a step back to normality.

Dinner-time arrived, and I was looking forward to experimenting with some further morsels. Eating on the Stryker was unorthodox; it was best to be prostrate. The little one-foot-square platform underneath was raised to the desired level, and the food-tray placed thereon. For this Christmas dinner I requested one slice of turkey, a small slice of white bread, a glass of milk - and a slice of Christmas cake, which I did not really expect to eat. When dinner arrived my appetite departed, but I decided to persist, as I had a full two hours ahead of me in the face-down position. I slowly opened the sachet of salt and shook the tiniest amount onto the meat. I rarely took pepper, but this time decided to do so - just for the novelty. As I shook it, it provoked a violent sneeze. The pressure on the enormous scar across my tummy was horrendous. I could not believe what I had allowed to happen. After carefully averting every potential sneeze since my operation, I had now, in a moment of stupid carelessness, apparently blown my stomach apart.

For a few moments I was in a blind panic. Then I decided to assess the damage by the expression on old Pat's face. He seemed very much unconcerned and said, 'God bless you!'

Thinking Pat's eyes may have deceived him, I slowly slid my left hand toward my stomach, expecting to find my intestines blown through the stitches and hanging the four feet or more to the floor. I searched ever so carefully, but to my astonishment and delight, found everything in place. With that sneeze, however, went the last vestige of my appetite.

Soon after supper, Andy arrived with two of his friends. I was surprised to see him wearing his full priestly garb and a glazed look in his eyes I had not seen for several months.

'What a session we had last night!' he moaned, shaking his head ruefully. 'As soon as midnight mass was over, Mick and Larry and myself hit the hard stuff in a big way. It went straight to my head. I had to go for a ten-mile run before mass this morning to clear the senses. Then, having said three masses, and given three of my best-ever sermons - I think - it was back to Mick's house for dinner. I can tell you, we have had quite a rough evening too.'

Larry McGuinness interjected: 'Andy, the coast looks clear. I think I'll bring in a few scoops.'

He returned with a black refuse sack containing three six-packs and a bottle of Bacardi. The chat and the jokes began to flow. Andy and his friends were settling in for a night of song and booze, and I was enjoying every second of it.

As the evening progressed, the jokes became more hilarious and ribald. The beer and the Bacardi were beginning to dwindle when I remembered I had received two bottles of whiskey as presents. 'They're in the bottom of my locker,' I said in a tone that was deliberately less than convincing.

'Like hell they are,' said a doubting Larry.

'Who in their sane minds would give a virtual non-drinker whiskey, especially in your condition?' added a shrewd-sounding Mick Dunne.

All three stared at me drunkenly. 'Hang on, lads,' slurred Andy, 'McSweeney would surely not tell the good priest a lie on this holiest of days.'

Larry was nearest my bedside locker and began rummaging through the mountain of junk I had accumulated. 'Jaysus, manna from Heaven! He's telling the truth.'

'We must celebrate this with a wee song,' said the delighted Andy, as he launched into *Silent Night*. The title of the song was to be the only silent part of what ensued. Andy's powerful and melodious tenor reverberated through the hospital, and before he had reached the end of the lovely hymn, staff, visitors, and patients from other wards were cramming into our ward. He sang another couple of songs, but then decided that the virtual stampede was beginning to endanger the patients. 'The old throat is getting very dry and it's getting late - we better call it a night,' he said.

The nurses took their cue from Andy - and eventually we were reduced to Andy, Larry, Mick, and four nurses. 'Before we go you must give us a few verses of *Daniel Morgan*,' said Andy to Mick Dunne. 'These broadminded lassies wouldn't mind at all.'

Mick was greatest man I ever knew to consume whiskey. He had spent his entire working life in a distillery and had not passed up the chance to familiarise himself with the product. Now, in his twilight years, he had written poems, ditties, and recitations for every occasion. *Daniel Morgan* was especially suited to a mature and inebriated audience. I had laughed myself to exhaustion the few times I had heard it, but was never in a fit state to memorise very much. And Mick had stubbornly refused all bribes for a copy of the lyrics.

'Mick,' I said, beckoning him closer to the Stryker, 'I want to ask you a special favour.'

'My good man,' he chanted, 'ask and thou shalt receive.'

'Mick,' I said, as earnestly as I could, 'you are fully aware, I'm sure, of my predicament in here. No-one can say if I'll ever get out alive. If you give me the words of *Daniel Morgan*, I will at least go to my reward with a smile on my face.'

Mick did not flinch. Nor had I expected him to. This was a case of 'ask and thou shalt not receive *Daniel Morgan*'. Not I nor anyone else was getting his hands on Mick's special party piece, irrespective of circumstances.

He cunningly sidetracked me: 'I have a nice short recitation which I know Fr Sheahan and the beautiful nurses here will enjoy. It's a short little ditty on a theme dear to all our hearts - the subject of love.' Andy called for some hush, and Mick cleared his throat: 'This is appropriate, believe it or not -

'
> *The love of a beautiful maiden,*
> *The love of a staunch, true man,*
> *The love of a baby unafraid,*
> *Have existed since time began.*
>
> *But the greatest love, the love of loves,*
> *Even greater than that of a mother,*
> *Is the true, genuine, infinite love,*
> *Of one drunken bum for another'.*

Visions of romance quickly gave way to laughter. Andy, as always, laughed loudest. When the laughter abated, one of the nurses said, 'It's ten o'clock, one full hour past visiting time. We have to invert the Stryker, so it's best you all head home. If Sr Lucia knew what was happening, we'd all lose our jobs.'

'Carry on girls - it's early yet. We'll relax out in the corridor,' said Andy, endeavouring to sound as sober a possible.

The curtains were drawn, and I was turned once again like a chicken on a spit. Mick, seeing me for the first time upside-down, was startled. 'That's the most gruesome act I ever witnessed in my whole life. It must hurt like all hell.'

'The only thing that would ease the pain would be a blast of *Daniel Morgan,*' I replied, as if in total earnest. For the first time, he appeared to weaken. I got an inkling I was about to get my wish. Andy launched straight into *Sancta Lucia;* as always, his audience were enraptured. In my prone position, I was able to reach for my tape-recorder and conceal it with a book on top of the meal platform. When Andy reached the crescendo and all eyes were on him, I furtively depressed the record button.

'Andy,' I said as loudly as possible from my bizarre vantage point, 'how about my noble call?'

'Of course - just name it,' he said.

'You have exceeded all expectations in making this great feast day both memorable and enjoyable for me. How about getting Mick to recite a few of those D Morgan verses?'

Andy got to his feet with some difficulty and put his hand on Mick's shoulder. I knew then I would get my request.

Mick stood up and staggered backward. 'Remain seated, Mick,' shouted Andy, 'or you'll knock McSweeney off his perch.'

'No, no,' smiled the big fellow. 'It's vitally important to be standing when reciting or preaching - as you should know. Or did they teach you nothing in the seminary?'

'Quit the kidding, Mick. A little bit of hush please, everyone! On you go, Mick!' said a very merry Andy.

The towering figure cleared his throat, assumed a solemn pose, and began to introduce his masterpiece.

'Ladies and gentlemen, this recitation contains a few minor expletives which might offend less mature people than yourselves. I am confident, though, that you broadminded nurses will enjoy it. Admittedly, a few of the words are open to interpretation, for instance the word 'tool'. This could as easily be a hammer or chisel as anything else. In the good old USA the word 'fanny' means what you sit on. And I believe the word 'cock' can refer to a male hen. Anyway, the whole ditty is just an innocent piece of fun. I surely do not intend to offend anyone. Okay, here we go - '

There was a hush of anticipation. Mick had set the stage perfectly.

This is the tale of Daniel Morgan, who had a small wee sexual organ,
(general laughter)
He gave the girls a dreadful shock when they beheld his tiny cock,
 (more laughter)
He laboured hard to find a cure, he poulticed it with fish manure,
He tied it up with bits of string, but still it was a small wee thing.
T'was half-an-inch when fully reared, and lying down it disappeared,
T'was just by chance they called him Danny; a half-inch less, they'd
have called him Fanny.

Everyone, including the nurses, was by now screaming with laughter. Andy and Larry were kneeling on the floor in convulsions. I was holding my sutures with one hand and biting the index finger on the other to prevent injury.

Now Danny read in the Daily Mail of things called 'falsies' that were for sale,
Women bought them with small breasts and wore them underneath their vests.
Danny said , 'Amn't I a fool - why don't I make a big fake tool?'
He worked all night upon his chopper and wound up with a great big whopper.
Twelve inches long and made of plastic - 'twould stretch a fanny like elastic.
No other fellow had a chance when Dan was at the local dance.
Lying there beneath his pants, it was like an elephant's.
But what a shock Dan had in store, one night while dancing round the floor,
Poor Danny stopped and loudly cursed, he felt his strings and strappings burst.
Before poor Dan could reach his seat, his tool went dangling at his feet.
His partner said in dreadful shock, 'Excuse me, but your cock's fell off.'
Dan could not face the scene thereafter, the wisecracks and the scornful laughter.

And all the girls that Dan had dated, were sad to see his tool deflated.

There was now pandemonium. Everyone was hysterical. People were again crowding into the ward from which so much hilarity was emanating. For a while the stone-faced Mick was unable to continue. I looked at old Pat beside me, and he put the sign of the Cross on his forehead. Scared my cassette tape would run out, I shouted as best I could, 'Quiet, quiet! On you go, Mick.'

'Last verse,' said Mick. 'And perhaps it contains some consolation for someone...

Now any of you who are like Daniel Morgan, and have a small wee sexual organ,
Remember, though it's only wee, it's always good enough to pee.

Mick had concluded, but the laughter was still ringing when Sr Lucia burst in through the door. Some 'concerned' visitor had phoned the convent, and Sr Lucia was not too pleased at being disturbed on Christmas night. I could not see her face, but her voice told the whole story. 'Get out of here!' she bellowed with all her might.

Mick, Larry, and the nurses retreated without saying a word, but Andy attempted his usual diplomatic role: 'Sister, I must apol - apol - apol - apologise on behalf of my friends and myself -'

'Get out of here, Father! Get out! Out!'

Andy realised that a dignified retreat was the only option. He looked at me directly in the mirror of the Stryker, gave a President Reagan salute, and staggered out the door.

Sr Lucia came to the side of the Stryker: 'What unusual friends you have!'

'You cannot begin to imagine, Sister, what those guys have just done for my morale.'

'Morale!' she said, shaking her head, but doing her utmost to conceal a smile. 'What in the name of the Lord has befallen the clergy? This place smells like a brewery.'

I was on a high. I had just enjoyed one of the most entertaining

Christmas nights of my life. I had tasted at least two hours of normality for the first time in two horrific weeks, and the other conscious occupants of the ward were equally elated. I was totally exhausted after the exertions of the shindig and would have loved a long and peaceful sleep, but constant pain coupled with the discomfort of the Stryker made it seemingly impossible. Soon midnight rolled along, and once again it was time to be rotated onto my back.

Several 'spins' later, we were well into a very busy St Stephen's Day. Visitors arrived thick and fast, inducing a lively atmosphere in the ward. My brother Joe and his wife, Mary, arrived from London. Joe's feigned bravado belied his obvious shock at my emaciated condition. 'My God, Fan, you've really been through the mill!' he said open-mouthed. After a pleasant chat, they left with a promise to return later that evening.

Since I was forbidden to receive phonecalls, all messages had to be relayed by some member of the staff. About dinner-time, Sr Lucia approached laughing heartily. 'Some girl just phoned with a message for you. Just for fun, I told her I was sick and tired of relaying messages from girls to you. That took the wind out of her sails.' Sr Lucia imagined she had done me a service. But in fact it was Jean she had rebuffed - as I was to find out several days later. If I had known it at the time, I might not have received the news so calmly.

16 New Year revolutions

For my first dinner I sampled some jelly and tea. They tasted strange, but were garnished with the delightful tincture of normality. As I finished, a neighbour from home, pretty Deirdre Cooke, peeped in the door. 'Hello, Fan. It's me. Can I come in?' She gave me a kiss on the back of the neck. 'I was told you were inside the door on the left, but I've been looking at you for the past few moments and did not recognise you with your long hair. You're looking great, though.'

I rotated my neck as much as I could and said cruelly, 'Deirdre, that's the first lie you ever told me.'

Poor Deirdre blushed: 'You are alive, and I know you will survive, and that's all that matters.' She then told me that a large contingent of my neighbours back at home had chartered the entire carriage of a train and were waiting to see me. Sr Lucia gave strict orders that I be visited by a maximum of two at a time, each pair to be limited to three minutes.

It was great to see so many familiar faces, but I was exhausted by the time the last pair left. Sr Lucia had made a wise decision. While I was thanking her, my brother Joe, his wife, Mary, and another brother, Pat, arrived. Sr Lucia threw her hands heavenward: 'Jesus, Mary, and Joseph!'

Joe's immediate response was, 'No, Sister - it's Pat, Mary, and Joseph.' Sister laughed and allowed all three to stay.

Much later that evening, when visiting was over, Dr Padraic Murray told me that a former international team-mate of mine would be spending a few days in the bed opposite me. Presently, I saw reflected in my little mirror the world indoor mile record-holder, Eamonn Coghlan, with his two legs extensively bandaged, hobbling into the vacant bed opposite. He had been savaged by a dog while training and was in obvious distress and pain. When the doctors left, I enquired from my inverted position what had befallen him. When Eamonn realised who was on the 'spit', he rolled out of bed and hopped on one leg across the room.

Having just returned from New York, he was totally unaware of my plight. When I had briefly recounted my story, he brooded for a few moments and said philosophically, 'Are not all our problems relative? There was I in the bed thinking my world was at an end, since my running career may be cut short by the wounds inflicted by that stupid dog. Now I see you in this dilemma, and my problems don't seem so dreadful after all.

We chatted at length about our many exploits both on and off the running track; it was a great diversion for both of us. After a while Eamonn was told to return to bed in preparation for an operation the following morning to determine the extent of his injuries.

The next day, while Eamonn was being prepared for the operating theatre, Mr Walsh arrived. He was apparently happy with my progress. 'You will be ready to undergo the post anterior fusion soon.'

'Doctor,' I said, 'start today if you wish. The sooner this is all over the better.'

He chatted with Padraic and some of the other surgical staff present and suggested, 'How about the day after tomorrow - New Year's Eve?'

'Great, Doc! One of my big ambitions is to ring in the New Year in an intensive care unit.'

'Just like the previous time, an anaesthetist will see you tomorrow,' Mr Walsh said.

'I hope it's the colonel. He was excellent the last time,' I said with tongue in cheek.

'Colonel who?' asked a mystified Padraic.

'Colonel Gadaffi,' I said as straight-faced as I could. The penny dropped - everyone knew who I was referring to.

I asked Mr Walsh what precisely the operation would accomplish. He explained that he would approach the fifth lumbar vertebra from the rear and affix a rectangular section of stainless steel to the vertebrae above and below it. He would then remove the remainder of the L5. He also said that an extra sliver of bone already taken from my hip would be inserted to encourage solidification of the spine.

'How will you attach the stainless steel to those two vertebrae?' I foolishly asked.

'I will have to drill holes in those vertebrae and then, by means of stainless wire, attach the metal to the bone,' he replied almost casually. I realised there and then that I was gleaning information that could be more a hindrance than a help. In future, I would be more reticent in my enquiries.

Later that day Eamonn arrived back, still unconscious, from the theatre. Later we learned that his several leg wounds had responded to treatment and that, apart from a tiny metal plate inserted in a broken index finger, he had suffered no permanent damage. 'My indoor season could be in jeopardy, but at least I'll be out of here by tomorrow,' he said with relief in his voice.

'Eamonn,' I replied quite seriously, 'nothing would aid my recovery better than to hear that you had gone back to the States and set another world record - for me.'

He looked at me hard for several seconds - and eventually said with some fervour, 'I will.'

Fr Andy arrived with the exciting news that he and two priest friends were going on holiday to South America on January 5th. 'It will be good to get away from all this rich food. I have this pain in my stomach that won't go away.'

'Nothing a few tequilas won't cure,' I said.

'I hope you're right.' he sounded unusually serious. He then began to psyche me up for the next operation.

'I was going to ask Mr Walsh if this one would be as severe as the first, but I was afraid in case he might say yes. If it's as bad, then I'm afraid I'm for the boneyard,' I said.

Andy delivered his usual tirade about the futility of quizzing medics: 'Never ask these doctors anything, especially before an operation. They will never give you anything to be cheerful about. It's much too easy for them to bury their mistakes. The one and only thing to do is to be as positive as you can and say a few prayers in the hope that all will go well.' Andy was a great believer in 'what will be will be' and reliance on the Good Lord's benevolence. 'I'll offer tomorrow morning's mass for your speedy recovery - and see you in the intensive care unit. Best of luck!' he said as he left.

Later that night a Pakistani anaesthetist approached. 'It is I who shall be putting you to sleep before your operation tomorrow morning. I have very many questions to ask you.' When I told him that I had never been sick in my life until now, and that I had been interrogated similarly prior to my first operation, he said, 'That is very good. I shall see you, so, early in the morning.' After two weeks on the Stryker frame without, as far as I could remember, a wink of sleep, the very thought of being knocked out was delicious.

New Year's Eve followed an almost identical format to the morning of my first operation. I had fasted from the previous night. The nurses washed and shaved me. But this time the anaesthetist did not arrive. A nurse gave me a 'special pill', which I was told would relax me. Soon I was being steered once again along the the lengthy corridors, into an elevator, and then along some more passageways until I was placed in a room adjacent to the main operating theatre.

I could sense the momentum beginning to snowball. Competent nurses rushed to and fro. The sight of all the medical hardware again made my heart pound.

My Pakistani anaesthetist greeted me with a smile and a regal curtsy. I asked him if I could speak to Mr Walsh, but he seemed reluctant to arrange it. Then Dr Padraic Murray arrived on the scene in a spacesuit; he nodded in the affirmative when I directed the same question to him.

Mr Walsh soon appeared, he too virtually unrecognisable in moon-walking outfit, and leaned in my direction. I felt somewhat foolish, but resolved to say what I had intended to say. 'Doctor, when you open me up, make sure you check the route of my sciatic nerve. I believe all my problems stem from that area.'

Everyone but the Pakistani seemed hugely amused. He flashed his big black eyes in my direction and said, 'A civil engineer - yes indeed, you do sound like a civil engineer. Now relax your arm, please, and you will be asleep shortly.'

I took one last fleeting glance at the world about me, then closed my eyes and began praying with all my might: 'Please, God, please, don't let me die in my sleep.'

Four-and-a-half peaceful hours and six pints of blood later, I again woke up in intensive care, aware even in the twilight zone between sleep and consciousness that this had been no normal slumber. Before opening my eyes, I tried to assess how I felt relative to when I emerged from the previous operation. At least, the raging fever was much less in evidence.

When I finally summoned up the courage to look around me, I found myself facing the floor. The Stryker, the pain, the tubes, the pads, the needles, and the frightening noises were just the same as before. But my mind was not in the same panic. Nor was my 'minder' of the previous occasion in attendance. I concluded with some relief that my life was not in imminent danger.

This, I told myself, was surely the greatest possible New Year's Eve present. Just then I heard a chirping of happy female voices. I turned my head and saw four white figures hugging each other. It was the stroke of midnight; they were ringing in the new year.

I lay in seclusion in my private little corner, feeling relatively well and trying to speculate on my future for the first time in six months. The monitors and the oscilloscopes bleeped relentlessly over my head, but I kept telling myself that now I could see the proverbial light at the end of the tunnel. I knew that if the cancer had spread, Mr Walsh would have told me so and not bothered to operate a second time. My spirits soared. I began to make all kinds of plans. I thought of Jean - and wondered if she would be part of my new life. I convinced myself that this was the greatest New Year's Eve of my life. I dreamed of future New Year's Eves and smiled at the exaggerated accounts of this experience I would relate. Then I wondered if I might be indulging in reckless optimism.

A nurse approached and whispered, 'How are you feeling, my dear?'

'Ma'am,' I replied, 'I never felt so good in all my life.'

She smiled at such an unexpected reaction. 'You have been lying on your front for several hours, so it would be best to put you lying on your back for as long as you can endure it - otherwise blisters will set in. It will be very difficult, because you will be lying directly on the wound.'

'How large is the opening?' I foolishly asked.

'About twelve inches, but there are four draining tubes inserted into your back, and you will have all your weight directly on top of the wound.'

'Give me about ten minutes to get myself psyched up, and then I will be ready.'

I thought I had learned to endure the always-painful rotation of the Stryker, but when my entire weight landed on the freshly-sewn scar, I roared in unbearable agony. Then, grimly conscious that I had to remain in that position for some time, I pushed my fists into each side of my spine to ease the weight on the incision. Unfortunately, my hands were restricted by the various tubes and drips.

'Please try to squeeze pillows under my ribs at each side of the wound,' I groaned in desperation. After painstaking manipulation, this ploy helped quell the torture slightly.

'How long must I stay in this position?' I grunted pathetically.

'As long as you can,' someone said.

'Why not put some powder on my chest and give it a quick massage? Then I'd be able to stay longer on my tummy,' I suggested.

'You'd make a great nurse,' laughed one of the girls. 'That's exactly what we're going to do.'

'You're so much more alert this time,' said one of the nurses.

'I honestly don't remember seeing any of you in here the last time. The pain in my hip overshadowed everything then. It was still the first sensation I got when I awoke this time - but it's not quite as bad.' Surely, I thought, I would never again have to endure as much pain as I had then. I was now taking my first real step on the road to recovery.

Fr Andy arrived and was amazed to see me in such good spirits. 'I'm as sore as all hell,' I said, 'but infinitely better than the last time. I thought then I was going to kick the bucket. I can handle the pain now. I suppose it's the cancer I have to worry about from here on.'

'All of us have cancer cells in us that could flare up at any moment,' he said consolingly. 'The whole world is only surviving from day to day. Sure I still have this pain in my side; you never know what that could be. Anyway, we'll see how I get on in South America. I'll call tomorrow evening before we go.'

The following day a nurse hurried into the ward. 'News is coming in of a huge gas explosion in the middle of the city. All hospitals are on emergency alert. If you feel up to it, Fanahan, I'll transfer you back to your ward.'

I was shocked. My first reaction was to ask if the one other patient in the ward was being transferred as well. When I was told he had had a heart transplant, I immediately volunteered for the move.

I lay on my stomach for the journey back to St Agnes's and survived it reasonably well. My old cronies gave me another rousing welcome. 'How are you feeling this time?' asked old Pat.

'Much better than the previous time anyway, Pat.'

'I knew it. I prayed for you all the time,' he said with genuine sincerity.

'You're a real saint, Pat,' I told him. The lovely old gentleman nodded as if to say, 'I hope you are right.'

It was great to be back in St Agnes's. I could not remain on my back for more than 15 minutes, so I began to spend between two and three hours on my front. Everyone was probably getting tired of me bragging about my lack of pain. But then Dr Padraic Murray told me he was worried I might get addicted to the heavy doses of intravenous morphine. 'You will have one less tube in you from now on,' he told me. 'We'll give you an injection of morphine every four hours instead.'

'The less tubes the better,' I replied.

Within a few hours a mysterious chill began to possess me. It felt like the coming of an arctic storm. The shivering cold was at first numbing - then it turned to raw pain. It was hell all over again. Lying on my face, I could barely tolerate it, but lying supine, with all my weight on the thick gauze protecting the long incision, I was in the same agony as after the first operation. The only consolation was that now I had a long respite when facing the floor.

The four-hourly morphine injections were having so little effect that I began to wonder if the correct serum was being used. Then, when I took my weight off the wound, the inhuman pain from the desecrated hip-bone sought the ascendancy. I began finally to comprehend and accept that I was in a condition where pain was the central element, and where grim endurance was the best recipe for an expeditious escape. I decided, for better or worse, to exclude the word pain as much as possible from my vocabulary and to put much of my faith in time, the great healer.

Constipation once again reared its ugly head. The devouring of large doses of codeine coupled with the long spells prostrate were doing the damage.

When Fr Andy called in en route to South America with Fr Dan and Fr John, my bed was screened while I lay on my back trying frantically to force a bowel movement. I would dearly have enjoyed a long chat with my three friends, but I simply had to ask the nurse on duty to delay them for a few minutes. After more than half-an-hour of fruitless effort, and with perspiration pouring from my forehead and the wound on my spine screaming for relief, I asked the nurse to fetch the 'ironing-board' and turn me over.

The three clerics were in high spirits after visiting several watering-holes on their way to the hospital. Fr Dan and Fr John were dumbfounded when they saw my long sweat-drenched hair and my bizarre position on the Stryker.

'We must rush, Fanahan. Peru, Argentina, and Brazil are beckoning. I just hate to leave you here in this mess, but at least when we return you'll have most of this travail behind you, and you'll be learning to walk again. I'll try to be back to see your first step,' said Andy.

All three gave me their blessings and then rushed for the airport. I felt sad saying adieu to Andy. He had called to see me every day for the past three months - and never failed to lift me physically and spiritually.

The following day, to my great surprise and delight, Jean walked in. I had had no contact with her since before Christmas. And though she was always on my mind, the operations, the pain, and the big C had dominated. I could not be certain if I had a future - or whether Jean would want to be a part of it. But I was blissfully happy that she had travelled so far to see me.

She was obviously pleased at my progress - and yet she was somehow not her usual vibrant self. Before she left, I asked if something was bothering her. After some coaxing, she told me about the blunt rebuff to her pre-Christmas phone-call. I quickly explained to her about Sr Lucia's offbeat sense of humour. I also made so bold as to tell her she was the only girl I really looked forward to meeting, and that the others were just platonic friends. I was thrilled that she seemed pleased with my reply. I felt a bond developing between us for the first time. My heart began to quicken, and I made a resolve to get out of hospital with all possible speed. Despite all the pain and worry, it was wonderful to have a real goal to dream about and perhaps look forward to.

The following morning, Dr Walsh called with his usual large entourage of assistant doctors and nurses. 'How are you feeling this morning?' he asked.

'Much better than after the first operation, Doctor. How did things go from your end. Did you find anything exciting inside?' I cheekily asked.

'Everything went as expected.'

'Great,' I replied. 'I can straighten both legs and move all my toes with ease for the first time in months. What happens now?'

He paused for a moment before speaking. 'In approximately ten days you will be taken to the plaster room and a fibreglass cast will be moulded to your torso. This will allow you to sit at an angle of forty-five degrees for about a week - to adapt to a more upright position for the first time. Then you will be fitted with a straight body-cast, and after a while you will learn to put all your weight on the graft. Then you can commence walking again.'

'Sounds great, Doc,' I said excitedly. 'But how long do you think it will take me to walk?'

'That is very much up to you. It will not be quite as easy as you might imagine. I should think months rather than weeks. Before you go to the plaster room, Mr Kearney will speak to you. I will see you next week.'

'Many thanks for everything,' I replied.

When he left, I took my usual deep breath and began to assess my status. I felt well contented with what I had heard - and began to think about my rehabilitation. Once again I felt a surge of excitement and optimism.

That evening one of old Pat's daughters told me she was going to knit an Aran sweater for me and went on to describe the various patterns. Later I amused myself by sketching an impression of my ideal sweater, entertaining myself with visions of proudly walking out in my own 'creation'. My dreams were to be brutally short-lived.

17   Second death sentence

Dr Padraic Murray, whom I had come to regard as a confidant, entered and pulled the curtains around the Stryker. 'I have some news which I feel you should know about,' he said quietly.

I froze to the bedclothes; it was obvious this news was not to be good. 'The cancer is still in me,' I thought. 'No, no - it just has to be something else.' Padraic looked at me with sympathy written all over his face.

'Get it over with - you might as well tell me now,' I said with a great lump in my throat.

'The oncology people will come to see you in the next few days and will tell you that when the front section of your vertebra and the tumour were taken out during the first operation, tests revealed that the cancer was still alive. I don't know the full significance of that, but I think you should be prepared for the news.'

I was stunned beyond belief. Padraic tried his best to console me - but the rest of the conversation was a haze. Finally, my tears flowing uncontrollably, I asked him to leave the curtains drawn around me.

I was so shattered I was unable to think. All I knew was the phrase that kept racing through my mind: 'I am definitely dead now.' Tears flowed freely down my face. I tried to think, but there was nothing to think about. I knew there was no way out this time. I had often heard it said that when a cancerous tumour was exposed to the atmosphere, it spread rampantly. I felt cheated - by whom I did not know. All the medics, including Mr Walsh, had done their utmost. But now, having withstood all the mental anguish and physical torment, I was destined for that awful hole in the ground.

I wanted Fr Andy to come and salve my broken spirit, but he was somewhere in South America. Once again I tried to imagine a possible escape route, but there was none. Death was unthinkable - but very definitely this time it was beckoning me. There were no mistakes. All the evidence was in the laboratory. The loneliness and isolation were stifling me.

The agony was beyond comprehension.

In the deafening silence I could hear Pat's daughter talking outside the curtain. I pulled the drape slightly open, and poor Pat looked at me with great sadness in his eyes. Obviously, he had overheard the news. He did not say one word. 'It's all over Pat,' I said.

He immediately put the Sign of the Cross on his forehead and in a daze said, 'May God bless you.'

I dropped the curtain and let the tears flow directly from my eyes onto the floor below. Pat's daughter Brid then put her head through the opening and said, 'You'll be all right. There has to be a mistake.'

'No, Brid - there's no mistake this time. The cancer was alive when they opened me up, so there is no chance whatsoever. By the way, Brid, you can forget about the Aran sweater - I won't be needing it.'

She stood there speechless. I felt that it was unfair to burden someone I scarcely knew with my problems, so I said, 'I'll rest for a while now. Take care of your dad, and please say a prayer for me.'

I lay in a stupor not knowing what to do. Eventually, the head night-nurse, Mary Long, slipped into my dreary cell. She had been briefed by Padraic. 'I'm very sorry. I'll do everything I possibly can to help you.' Her smile was full of warmth and sympathy. We stared at each other - neither one of us knowing what to say.

I uttered the first coherent thought that entered my head: 'Your husband is a very lucky man.'

'He's a civil engineer - the same as yourself,' she said, glad of the chance to divert my attention to everyday matters. We chatted for possibly an hour and spoke about everything except cancer and the next world.

Eventually I got the courage to ask, 'Where do I go from here, Mary? Or is this room the end of the line?'

'Fanahan,' she said with consummate compassion, 'I honestly don't know. Nothing definite has been decided upon yet. I'm sure, though, that you'll go back to St Luke's for more radiation.'

'How soon will I be going there?'

'I presume they'll have to wait for the graft to set before you can be irradiated.'

'Christ,' I gasped, 'what a catch-22! No radiation until the bone-graft solidifies, and that in a perfectly healthy body would probably take twelve months. By then I'll be dead and buried.'

Before she returned to her normal duties, Mary did her utmost to encourage me, but in all the circumstances, words seemed wholly inadequate. My brain was once again bursting out through my skull. Thousands, myriads of fevered thoughts streamed through my mind. It occurred to me more than once that I would be better dead - and that quickly.

Mary returned: 'Are you feeling any better now?'

'How I wish I could say yes,' I replied. 'But my situation is so hopeless. There's no escape this time. Six months ago I had an identical experience - when I was first told I had terminal cancer - and it was a difficult pill to swallow. Back then I could not accept that my time here on this earth was terminating. Now I know it's over. How I wish it were done quickly!'

Mary began to philosophise: 'Life on this earth is paradise for some of us - some of the time. But this world can be a cruel place as well. It's easy for me to talk, but it's so important for all of us to live out every minute of every day. You've often heard it said that there is only one certainty in this life, and that is that each and every one of us is going to die someday. This is not an easy subject to talk about, but I do hope you have a strong belief in God.'

'I believe in God for sure, Mary, but I don't want to meet Him for a long while yet. Wouldn't it be great to die in a car crash, or make some other such sudden exit.'

Mary gazed at me long and hard and eventually said, 'I suppose you're right. I never looked at it that way before. I'll put you lying on your back for as long as you can endure it, and then I'll rotate you again and give you some real good sleeping-pills. One thing, though, you must promise me - never give up hope.'

Mary rotated me with the help of one of the student nurses.

'Susan will massage your chest and shoulders to increase the blood-flow, which should enable you to sleep for a while longer after we turn you on your back later.' Young Susan Heffernan had a wild glint in her eyes; obviously, she was unaware of the seriousness of my plight. She opened the buttons of my pyjama-top and gently rubbed lotion on me. She began massaging boldly, as if we knew each other intimately. She then began telling mildly double-meaning but somewhat appropriate jokes. Neither my sense of humour nor my memory was functioning particularly well. I kept asking myself whether I was having a delightful dream or was in the throes of a nightmare.

'I hear you have lots of girlfriends. I bet they all like your hairy chest,' she said cheerily.

'Oh, I don't know,' I said, entering into the spirit of flirtation. 'One thing is for sure, though, Susan - there isn't a guy in the world could say no to a beautiful blonde like yourself.'

The banter continued for the fifteen-or-so minutes of extraordinary mental and physical therapy. Eventually she called Mary to rotate me and give me the sleeping-pills.

'This is by far your longest period lying on the wound,' said Mary.

'The blonde magician made me forget all about the pain,' was my honest response.

The cumbersome 'ironing-board' was bolted down, and the drips, blood-bottles, and other attachments were fastened to the Stryker. Soon I was lying comfortably on my well powdered and massaged chest. Susan then made to pull the curtains that had screened me since I was given the killer-blow. My first instinct was to stay in my cocoon; but I would sooner or later have to face reality - I told her to open them.

Before she left my side, Susan whispered, 'As soon as you get out of here, we are definitely getting married.' It occurred to me then that she knew my predicament all along - and her undoubtedly unorthodox bedside manner had been calculated therapy. Anyway, it was all in good fun. Very soon I was having my first real sleep in three weeks.

I awoke six hours later, feeling less stressed than for some time. But, as ever, reality dawned all too quickly. Old Pat stared at me, obviously resigned to the inevitability that I was going to die. 'I have been praying for you all night,' he said. 'May God bless your soul!'

'What the hell am I going to do now, Pat?'

'Oh, please don't mention that bad word. Just pray to Almighty God. He always takes care of His own, and I know He will take care of you.'

Jerry spoke up from the other corner: 'Never give up hope - there's always a chance.'

'You're right, Jerry. But it's not looking too good for me this time around.'

As the morning dragged morbidly on, a rather pedantic gentleman of the cloth approached. 'I'm back on sabbatical from Africa; I like to visit patients when I have some free time. How are you today?' He spoke as if ignorant of my condition.

I welcomed at first the diversion of telling him my story, but I soon developed the impression that he wanted to be my 'saviour'. I told him my friend Fr Andy had given me absolution and anointed me on three different occasions. It made no difference - he kept on zealously trying to help me. I began to feel claustrophobic to the point of virtual panic.

'Father,' I said in some annoyance, 'these hours and days are the worst of my life, and I very much appreciate you being so caring and helpful. I realise that I will be meeting my Maker in the not-too-distant future, but to tell you the truth, I am still not ready to meet Him. I have my own way of talking to Him, and at this point, I still don't want to get too familiar with Him. That does not make any sense to you, but I feel I must do things my way, for now at least. I hope you understand. If you call in a few weeks time, I'm sure I'll be much more grateful for your concern and guidance.'

This pious gentleman was only trying to help. He found if difficult to fathom my attitude. But he eventually got the message, and left with a promise to call again.

As soon as he exited, I began to wonder had his arrival been a well-intentioned set-up or just a timely - or perhaps untimely - coincidence. Perhaps it had been instigated by some of the medical staff. It seemed all too ominous: the logical follow-up to the news Padraic had given me. Sr Lucia knew Fr Andy would be three weeks in South America. I could only conclude that this priest was sent to me because I would not be around when Andy returned.

The terror of imminent death was incredible agony. Fate had again trapped me in a corner from which there was no escape. My brain tried to explode within my head, and my body shivered with agony. No-one who had not endured this ordeal, not even Willie Shakespeare himself, could ever have captured this ordeal in all its grimness. Nor was there any earthly dictionary equipped to describe it.

All the loose ends were now being tied up. I would soon be pumped

*My grandmother Bridget (centre) with
her sisters, Ann (left), and Frances*

Young, free, and healthy - the author aged ten

*At the World Student Games, Turin, Italy, 1971. From left, Fionnbar Callanan, Brendan
O'Regan, Frank Murphy, John Dillon, Donie Walsh, and myself*

Munich bound - wearing the Olympic blazer in 1972

Where's the posse? - winning in Louisiana

Rounding into the home straight - in a 400-metre heat at the World Student Games in Italy 1971

Wedding party - Sean Kyle, Maeve Kyle, Yvonne Coghlan, and Eamonn Coghlan flank Jean and me on our great day in March 1988

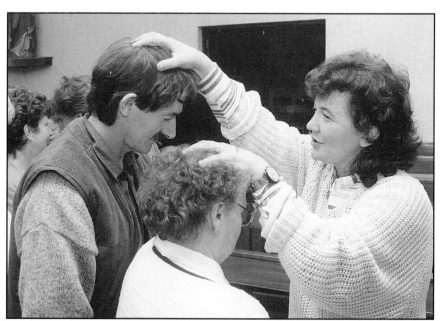

Healing hands - I meet one of the Medjugorje visionaries, Visca, on her visit to the Holy Trinity Church, Cork, in June 1994

The lilt in the kilt - my great friend Fr Andy in full cabaret dress and (inset) I tickle the ivories while he carries the tune

Young Andy, aged two, and Fanahan Beag, nine months, in 1993

Little Andy proves a handful at four months old in July 1991

With Mam and Dad in Castletownroche in 1993. The back garden at home is Dad's pride and joy

Jogging in Cork in the Seventies, with my faithful friend Prince carrying the spikes

At full stretch - in the Grange/Fermoy singlet at Banteer Open Sports

John Dillon (no 14) and I battle it out over 880 yards at an international meet in Crystal Palace, London, in 1973

With the great Eamonn Coghlan at his new home in Porterstown, Co. Dublin

My friend, mentor, and fellow golf-addict Ger Canning in typically relaxed pose

Brothers all - Kevin, Joe, Pat, myself, and Terry with dog Jessie in 1962

Faithful five - Joe, myself, Pat, Terry, and Kevin at my wedding

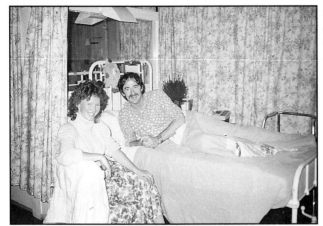

Momentous occasion - Jean's first visit to St Luke's hospital, October 1986

Christmas night 1986 in the Mater - from left to right, Jerry McGuinness, Larry McGuinness, the patient, Fr Andy, and Mick Dunne

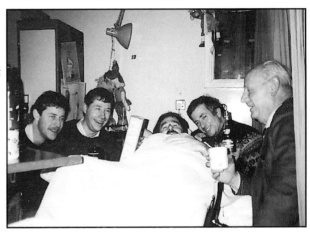

Nurse Susan Heffernan, Fr Andy, and myself, Christmas night 1986

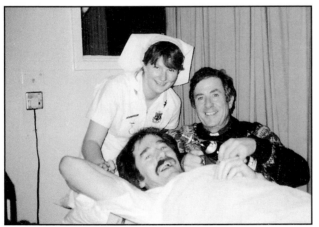

full of morphine to minimise the physical pain, but the mental torture would still have to be endured alone. As I wallowed in these morbid thoughts, a young doctor entered. 'I need to take a bone-marrow sample for Mr Kearney,' he said earnestly. 'Do you mind if I begin right now?'

He carried a large briefcase and a large lamp. I decided to close my eyes and let him get on with the job. Soon the heat from the lamp was driving perspiration down my face. I got an injection in my breast-bone, from where I presumed he was going to extract the marrow. I usually liked to know exactly what was happening, but this time I just did not care. Very soon an instrument resembling a hand auger was drilling a hole through my breast-bone. My rib-cage seemed about to cave in under the pressure. 'Easy, Doc,' I would plead occasionally.

'Shouldn't be long now,' he would invariably murmur.

The audible chipping of the bone continued until eventually he said, 'Good, success at last.'

When he had enough marrow, he diligently cleaned the tiny wound and placed a small band-aid thereon. He then dropped the creamy fluid between several pairs of glass plates. Instantly the words of my brother Doctor Terry, three months previously, came brutally to mind: 'If this type of cancer had progressed into your bone-marrow, you would be dead before the cancer could be killed off.'

It was eerie looking at the liquid that would correspond to the final nail in my coffin. For sure, it was impregnated with millions of cancer cells; it would provide the ultimate confirmation Mr Kearney needed to write me off. When eventually the young doctor left my curtained-off compartment, I felt relieved for my sake - and his.

Evening time arrived, and I was a little surprised that no visitor called. Again my addled brain began to speculate: maybe it was hospital policy to debar visitors from someone who had just been given 'grave' news. Yet again I was suspiciously analysing every word and gesture of every medic and visitor that entered the ward. Any unusual action I interpreted as endorsing my fatal prognosis. Since I was spending less than half-an-hour on my back and about four hours on my front, facing the corner, most of my scrutiny was laboriously done through the small mirror attached to the Stryker.

This constant surveillance was driving me ever deeper into dementia.

A nun's habit appeared in my mirror and approached. I double checked the shoes in case it was the devil himself in disguise. I had always greatly admired these women of the cloth, who shunned the 'pleasures of the world' and dedicated themselves to the poor, the sick, and the downtrodden. Still, I was not ready for another lecture on the next life or the goodness of the Man Above. Before I had time to utter a word, a pleasant voice said, 'I am a sister of Margaret O'Mahony. She gave me some home-made brown bread for you.' Margaret was the wife of my good friend Eamonn. I had met another of Margaret's sisters - also a nun, domiciled in the USA - but never this lady, who had spent her time teaching the poor in Africa. It was obvious that she knew little of my condition. I grasped eagerly the chance to talk to someone about something other than cancer. She was a fascinating person and a very good listener. I would have talked all night, but finally she politely said, since she was undoubtedly bored beyond distraction, 'You look tired, so I won't bother you any longer. But I'll call again next week.'

She had barely left when I had another timely diversion. John Michael Carson, whom I had not seen in months, nonchalantly strolled in and weighed up the situation. When he spoke his voice was droll. 'You may think you are hard done by being in here with cancer - and you are. But it is nothing to what I went through a few months ago. Before I got married, I went on a last fling - if you know what I mean - to San Francisco. I had a wild night or two with a couple of fun-loving girls over there. It was only when I got home that the proverbial hit the fan. Everyone here was talking about the aids virus. When the penny dropped, I felt pains breaking out in every part of my body. Whenever the word aids was mentioned on the radio, the pains got worse. I was facing the most horrible death imaginable. I could see myself lying all alone in a hospital bed with none of the lads calling to see me for fear of being branded as my boyfriend. I eventually decided to go to Dublin for tests. I stopped several times at the side of the road, with the most terrible pain between my legs. When the tests were done I had to wait a week for the results.'

By now I was laughing uncontrollably. 'I think I have an idea what you were going through alright.'

'You have no idea what it was like - I even went unbelievably religious for that whole week. Of course, when I got the all-clear I was back to my old ways within hours. I have come to the conclusion that we are no better than the animals,' he said with a mixture of disgust and relish. Then he wished me a speedy recovery and disappeared out the door.

Poor John Michael's saga amused me. And even though it was undoubtedly based on fact, it was probably dramatised by the shock he got when he saw the emaciated hippy on the Stryker. The consolation for me was that someone I knew had gone through a nightmare more terrifying - if that were possible - than my own.

As the evening progressed, I felt I had to communicate my tale of woe and despair to someone very close. Jean immediately sprang to mind. I had not written a letter for several months (apart from the Dear Marilyn - which had been composed for me), but decided that to do so would be at least therapeutic. Being prostrate in the Stryker was no real hindrance. With shaking hand, and in a barely legible scrawl, I wrote:

My Dearest Jean,

I feel as if I must talk to someone now and you must forgive me if I am unfairly throwing the burden of my latest news onto the person that means more to me than anyone else. Today I'm really back in the wars again. Now that the pain is abating from the second operation, I am being told that the big C was still alive when they tested whatever they took from me during the first operation, so now I am in deep deep trouble.

This morning Mr Walsh told me that I will have a plaster-cast put around my torso in about ten days time, but in the same breath he told me that before then a Mr Kearney would visit me. Today the young in-house doctor, Padraic Murray, who I have become quite good friends with, told me to be prepared for a visit from Mr Kearney of the oncology department who will tell me that the tests done after the first operation revealed the bad news.

From here Padraic thinks that I will be eventually returned to St Luke's, but I believe that I cannot be radiated until the bone grafts have solidified, and that will take several months. So things do not look good at all. After all the pain and anxiety I've been put through in so many hospitals during this past six months - and now I hear that it is all in vain.

Jean, I hate to burden you with all the grim news but I feel I must at least thank you for all you have done for me in recent times. You calling to visit me in the Regional hospital was the greatest thing that ever happened to me. You could never imagine how much your visits and getting to know you meant to me. The plans I dreamed of every night for the two of us (please don't laugh) gave me the hope and the confidence I needed during my worst periods - to keep my sanity. For those many glorious moments I will be eternally grateful.

It's five in the morning. I began scribbling while facing the floor. Since then I have been turned twice. Everyone around me is snoring, so I will close for now and will keep you up to date on what's happening. Still keep up the prayers.

Love Ya,

Fanahan.

This was the second draft of my letter to Jean. Some way through the first feeble attempt, a big wet tear dropped straight onto the paper, and I had to begin again.

I put the letter in an envelope, but I was still undecided if I should post it.

The following morning one of old Pat's daughters called to visit him, as they all did every day, and I asked her if she would post my letter. She had scarcely walked from the ward when my scrupulous conscience began to bother me; I asked one of the nurses to intercept her. It was too late; the letter had been quickly dropped into a post-box near the hospital. I felt guilty about my selfishness in burdening with such a gruesome and morbid tale of woe the one girl I had ever dreamed of marrying. My only consolation was that for the first time I had told her she meant a lot to me.

Padraic called later that day. I told him that since the drains had been removed from the incision in my spine, the pain was now concentrated mainly in my buttocks. He immediately investigated and said, 'All the morphine injections have taken their toll. From now on it's best to put you on oral painkillers.'

The tablets were much less effective than the injections, but after a few days the pain had become bearable. The twelve-inch incision was being washed and treated twice daily. According to the nurses, it was healing well.

18 Painful progress

The days grew uneventful and boring. Each and every agonising moment, I continued to scan the movements and actions of everyone who entered the ward. Visitors now tended to stay only a short time. Each tried to help - but now there was so very little to talk about or hope for. In fact the word hope seemed obsolete - and without hope anything and everything is meaningless. I was now just the sick encaged lamb awaiting the slaughter. I wished it were all over quickly, yet paradoxically could not accept the fact that I was going to die.

A few moments of the morning of 7th January 1987 were to utterly change the scenario. I was lying face down on my narrow platform, patiently awaiting death, when the efficient footsteps of a team of medics resounded from the tiled corridor. Within seconds the curtains were drawn, and a suave, dicky-bowed gentleman stood beside me with his entourage.

'Not another bastard with a polka-dot dicky-bow,' I thought to myself, remembering the obnoxious Shunor and Rayloe.

'Hello, I'm Mr Kearney from the oncology department.' Though I had never met him, I knew exactly who he was. My executioner had arrived.

Surprisingly, he looked pleasant and cheerful. But I knew that one of his duties was to be the bearer of death sentences almost every day of the week. Strangely, I pitied him in his melancholy assignment and decided to ease his task somewhat. 'Doctor,' I interjected, 'I found out the cancer was alive when they opened me up the first time. All I want to know is how long I have left?'

He seemed genuinely surprised. 'Yes, Mr McSweeney, the cancer was alive - but plasma cytoma is particularly resilient and usually survives for up to three months after radiation therapy. My department is pleased with your progress, so when you are strong enough to return home you will be under the care of a most eminent oncologist, Dr Paula Cotter in the Cork Regional hospital. The best of good luck to you!' He turned on his heel and briskly walked from my enclosure. Someone made to open the drapes, but I asked that they be left closed for a while. I needed time to come to terms with what had happened.

I lay with my hands under my face and filled them with tears. Too much had happened too quickly. I was breathless as well as dumbfounded. When I had regained composure and towelled my face, I reached for the curtain to my right and said, 'Pat, did you hear what the cancer doctor told me?'

'No, honestly, I did not hear a word,' he said gently.

Aghast, I asked him sharply, 'Did you not overhear someone talking to me a few minutes ago.'

'To tell you the truth, I did not hear a thing,' he meekly said.

I thought I had completely lost my mind. 'Pat, call a nurse quickly! Nurse, nurse, nurse!' I was beside myself, roaring like an imbecile.

Immediately, my three fellow-sufferers took up the chorus. 'Nurse, nurse, nurse!'

Suddenly, Nurse Eva McDonogh was looking down on me with her beautiful brown eyes. 'Are you all right?'

'Eva, did the cancer doctor come in here a few minutes ago?'

'Yes, he did.' She sounded entirely genuine.

'Are you absolutely sure,' I asked with bated breath.

'Of course I am. Wasn't I standing right beside him.'

'What did he tell me?'

'He said you'd be under the care of some lady doctor when you return home, and he was pleased with your progress,' she said cheerily.

I took a couple of deep breaths. 'Eva, you're a lifesaver and an absolute darling.' Straining my neck, I looked directly at her for final confirmation. The tears of delight in her eyes were the perfect authentication. She gleefully swished the curtains from around the Stryker, and as she hurried off to diligently attend to the rest of her flock, announced to the whole ward, 'What a great day today is!'

The atmosphere Eva had generated was incredible; everyone in the room was very much confined to bed, but it felt as if we all were floating on air.

'Can ye possibly imagine the consequences for me of the news I just got?' I asked philosophically.

'I'm not very religious,' said Jerry from the far corner. 'But that news is the closest I've ever been to seeing a real-life miracle.'

'I think it would be nice now if we all recited the rosary,' said old Pat.

'There's no good in tempting fate,' joked Jerry. 'We cannot possibly get anymore out of Your Man Above today.'

I was so excited I felt like running out into the street and telling everyone about my good fortune. The fact that I could scarcely move my toes seemed irrelevant. All of a sudden, I could forget about the big hole in the ground, coffins, and the Hippy with the beard. Now there was a possible future to speculate on. Above all, there was Jean. A life with her was something I could at least dream about.

She would have to be told immediately about my change of fortune, especially since she had probably received my tragic letter. I summoned Eva - much less dramatically than before. Her first greeting was, 'I have some more very good news for you.' I was to have my first plaster-cast fitted the following day - meaning I had just one more night, after more than a month, to endure the Stryker frame. I asked her to phone Jean and tell her about my reprieve.

Dr Padraic called and shook my hand vigorously. 'I suppose my initial news scared the life out of you,' he said.

'Yeah, but it's an ill wind. If you hadn't deflated me, I couldn't possibly be on such a high right now. Just think how great I feel.'

Padraic again explained that the first cast would have me sitting at an angle of 45 degrees. After ten days, I would be fitted with a straight cast. 'Then it will be up to you. As soon as you are able to walk on crutches, you will be on your way home,' he said with a smile.

'How long should all this take?' I asked with tongue in cheek.

'Well, your operations were unique, to say the least. Still, if the grafts have solidified sufficiently to withstand your upper-body weight, you could be going home within two to three months. You may have to go to a rehabilitation hospital for extensive physiotherapy, but at least you will have a goal to aim for. From then on, everything will be very much in your own hands.'

My spirits were sky-high, but the prospect of a further three months in confinement brought me nearer to earth.

The following morning, as I was being wheeled on the Stryker frame from St Agnes's for the last time, all my room-mates cheered me on my way. I was taken to an X-ray room adjacent to the plaster room. A beaming Mr Walsh greeted me. He had several helpers with him, including Dr Padraic. Clearly, this was no routine assembly.

They quickly began the task of transferring me from the Stryker to the X-ray platform. My sheet was used as a hammock; four men at either side raised me with infinite care. Padraic directed the manoeuvre and talked me across the most scary couple of feet I had ever traversed. My spine felt as slender as a match-stick. The graft seemed about to snap at any moment. When I was settled on the X-ray machine, Mr Walsh asked me how I was feeling.

'Pretty good, Doctor,' I fibbed shamelessly.

When the first set of internal photographs were taken, I was turned on my side for a profile. The silent pain I had to endure during this ordeal was immense. I was petrified that the graft would sever and that I would have to face the scalpel all over again, but I took consolation in the fact that Mr Walsh was looking on and appeared unperturbed.

After 15 long minutes, I was transferred back onto the Stryker and wheeled into the large plaster room. I asked Padraic to position my head near the sink, for fear my stomach might not withstand the unfamiliar elevation of my torso.

'Mr Walsh is pleased with the X-rays, so now let me see how tough an ex-international athlete is,' joked Padraic.

I told myself that if one more person told me to be strong, I would surely faint. But I firmly gripped Padraic's strong shoulder as several pairs of hands began to raise me according to my explicit instructions.

'You can get sick into the sink whenever you wish,' Padraic said. Strangely, that assurance, coupled with the knowledge that he was well exceeding his line of duty by participating at all, gave me new confidence.

Soon I was enjoying a new perspective on the world. As I was raised, pillows were stuffed behind me. With surprisingly little discomfort, I approached the magic 45 degrees.

'How are you feeling?' inquired the director.

'Great. Keep on going until I say otherwise,' I said with some confidence. Everyone laughed. They were obviously willing me on. Soon, I was almost vertical.

'Come on, you're almost there,' said an excited Padraic.

'Will this mean I get out of here sooner?'

'Almost for sure,' was the reply.

The sensation of being vertical was as exciting as was the novelty of seeing everyone for the first time from a normal perspective. But I felt as if perched precariously on a tightrope over Niagara Falls. Mr Walsh nodded to a nurse, Liz; she and some colleagues immediately began to wash me with warm, damp sponges. The massaging motion on my skin was heavenly. Then I was dried, and large chunks of cotton wool were placed over my lower back and the freshly-ointmented wound. Then Liz rolled gauze bandages all around my torso. Soon I was mummified from my neck to the top of my pelvic bone.

'In ten to fifteen minutes the fibreglass mould will have solidified, and you will be on your way back to your ward,' Padraic said. During this entire 'fitting', my head remained crystal clear, but a strange burning itch attacked my two legs.

Soon, I was carefully eased back to the horizontal and wheeled on the Stryker back to the ward. There awaiting me was the glorious sight of a conventional bed. But first I had to endure another tedious transfer from the high-level Stryker to the much lower and wider single bed. The feeling of the soft mattress and the sight of the dreaded surfboard being steered from the room were sensations to be truly savoured.

Later that evening, Padraic called. 'We had a most successful morning in the plaster room,' he said. 'You really surprised us all by forgoing the first cast. All going well, you have shortened your stay in hospital by the greater part of two weeks. In a few days time - possible Monday - we will have the physiotherapists stand you out on the floor. I must warn you, though, that regaining your balance and learning to walk again will be much more difficult than you imagine. But I am delighted you are on your way.'

I thanked Padraic profusely for all he had done. Thorough gentleman that he was, he simply said, 'Not at all. I enjoyed every minute of it.'

That weekend was the most pleasant I ever spent within the confines of a hospital building. I was free of drips and tubes, and looking forward to my first normal sleep in more than a month. My fibreglass barrel was no bed of roses - but I could easily live with that. The freedom of my new bed was particularly invigorating.

A letter arrived from Jean. She was delighted to hear the great news from nurse Eva. A postcard from Fr Andy in Peru said the food and booze were having an adverse effect on him. He was having to spend much of the time in bed.

Each day grew shorter and less boring than the one before. The sleeping tablets knocked me out from eleven at night to at least six in the morning. It was wondeful to be a 'normal' patient again; I prayed for the arrival of the physiotherapists.

About ten o'clock on Monday morning, a slim middle-aged woman approached. 'Good morning. My name is Mrs Kilduff.' Her badge said she was chief physiotherapist. She began a series of questions, probing to see if I was mentally and physically ready to take my first step. I exuded such confidence that she tended not to believe me. 'It will take several weeks before you will be able to walk without the help of an attendant, and several months without crutches,' she advised, repeating almost verbatim what Dr Padraic had told me.

'Then the sooner we begin the better,' I said.

She returned after half-an-hour with two youngish female physios and Padraic. One of the younger women lay down on the side of my bed and demonstrated how to sit up. It looked easy; I was ready to move.

I was first turned on my side, and while Padraic sturdily grasped my upper body, Mrs Kilduff carefully lowered my two legs over the side of the bed and onto the floor. I felt dizzy and weak, but the sheer weight and pain of the body-cast were what most alarmed me. A yellowish pus from the wound on my back had seeped onto flesh made tender by the pressure of the cast on the incision at my left hip; the skin had annealed to the cast and was being torn by my sitting action. Almost at the point of collapse, I asked for some ice-water, which helped enormously to cool my forehead. I then took a few deep breaths and regained composure. I knew it was vitally important to make a positive start.

Someone suggested I wait for a few days - seemingly, my face had turned ashen - but I insisted I was ready for a long walk. 'Just a few steps will be good progress for today,' someone cautioned.

Padraic grasped me firmly by one arm; Mrs Kilduff held me by the other. One physiotherapist held a walking aid directly in front of me, while two others knelt onto my bed to give me maximum support from behind. 'Up, up slowly,' everyone urged in unison.

Within moments, I felt like a newly-delivered giraffe calf; I had attained an almost inhuman altitude. I grabbed the top of the walking aid, but found that the tortoise-like shell around my torso prevented me from standing erect. I was falling backward, my feeble legs unable to sustain my weight for more than a few seconds. The blood rushed to my legs, which felt as if they were at boiling point. I tilted forward onto the walking aid in the hope of improving my balance, and then tried to take a step with the help of at least five pairs of hands. Alas, I was unable to budge. I once more imagined I was entering the last 100 metres in the final of the Olympic Games 400 metres. I could hear Coach Bob Hayes and Coach Sean Kyle roaring from the stands: 'Drive those arms! Raise your knees!' I had no idea what was happening. I shuffled and pulled, and then heard someone say, 'That's enough for today. We'll lift you back into bed.' I fought against the urge to faint. Then I found myself back on the horizontal.

Disappointment eventually gave way to clear thinking. I was glad to be lying on my back again, but it appeared it would definitely be several months before I would be mobile. Padraic called later and asked how I was feeling.

'Honestly, do you have to ask? After my lack of performance, how could I be anything other than dejected?' I said sombrely.

'Dejected?' he said. 'We were all amazed you were so strong. The graft withstood your weight remarkably well, and of course, you took your first steps. I really thought it would be several days, even longer, before you would travel as far.'

I was pleasantly surprised. I then wondered how successful I really was. 'By the way, how far did I travel - to the nearest yard?'

'Well,' said Padraic with a smile, 'you travelled exactly three feet, and that rounded off to the nearest yard comes to...'

I told him about the damage the cast was causing to the skin at the top of my hips. I also asked if a massage would help my roasting legs before I ventured on my second trip the following day. 'Are you attempting another walk so soon?' he asked rhetorically. It was beginning to sink in that perhaps my prospects were brighter than I had imagined.

Student nurses Judith Brogan and Maria Egan duly arrived armed with bandages, ointments, and creams. They were both genuinely excited at my progress. First they began to examine the damage caused by the cast on the top of my hips. Having cleaned and covered the sores, they set about injecting life back into my legs. They took a leg each and massaged to the point of exhaustion. The sensation of life returning to my extremities was not only invigorating - it gave further hope of recovery.

With new courage, and knowledge of my limitations, I looked forward to my second excursion. Getting onto my feet proved just as difficult as the first time. When finally I had myself as upright and balanced as possible, I again tried with all my might to shuffle forward. Unfortunately, the task was just as difficult as before. I still had no sense of equipoise whatsoever. Overpowering pain hindered every action. I was again at the point of collapse, but knew that every inch yielded would set me back a mile. After several precarious, agonising, and dizzy moments of shuffling, I was throbbing with soreness when I returned to bed. Half-conscious, I asked someone how far I had travelled. 'About twice as far as yesterday,' was the sweet-sounding reply.

The following day was even better. I reached to the door of the ward and back, a distance of about eight yards. I almost got to look out into the corridor. The pain and the exertion were as great as ever, but the sense of achievement was the spur I needed to set further goals.

On reaching the corridor the next day, I was overjoyed. My concentration was so great I could scarcely see what was happening around me. Every ounce of energy was channelled into the forward shuffle. There was no time to inspect the decor of the corridor or observe those around me.

Another day, and I was still labouring painfully on the corridor - but was now much more aware of my surroundings. I was saddened to see that every visitor who passed by stared at me pityingly. As I neared the point of exhaustion, a crotchety old woman stopped and stared piously into my face. Towering shakily above her, an emaciated Jesus-like figure, I must have looked like death warmed up. She blessed herself with an exaggerated Sign of the Cross. No doubt her intentions were good - she thought her intercession might help my cause. As she continued to gaze mournfully at me, I stared at her devilishly and said, 'Thank you, Ma'am, but don't give up on me yet. I bet you could easily be in Heaven before me.' Flabbergasted, she hurried away.

I had managed a few more shuffles when a nurse ran into the corridor. 'There's a phonecall for you from Tennessee. I'll transfer it to the phone in the corridor if you can take it.'

The three physiotherapists steered me to the open kiosk, and while I frantically held onto the walking aid, two held me erect, and the other held the receiver to my ear. It was Eamonn Coghlan. He had called to tell me he had won his first indoor mile easily, in three minutes and 54 seconds - a fabulous time. During the few moments in which Eamonn excitedly related his good news to me, I totally forgot my pain - for the first time in many months. When I later realised this, I knew I just had to be on the road to recovery.

The following day, I ventured almost half the length of the corridor. The pain and the effort had diminished little, but I was travelling farther each day, and my confidence was growing. As I slowly moved past the ladies' toilet, I spotted a wall-mirror. Curiosity and perhaps a little vanity prompted me to ask my minders if I could see myself for the first time in a real mirror. The pale, tortured face, the scrawny neck, and the long greasy hair reminded me of no-one I knew. The concentration-camp appearance demonstrated graphically what it meant to be a cancer victim. I uttered an oath. Mrs Kilduff quickly cut in: 'What do you expect after all you've been through? From now on you'll be improving every day. In a couple of months you'll be as good as new.' I stood there staring into space. The horror of what I had been through was indelibly written across my face. Once again, my mind was plunged into brutal turmoil.

Mrs Kilduff shouted at me to concentrate on returning to base. I managed to struggle back - but in a most distressed state. Back in bed, I was again tormented with imaginings. Why were all my friends so dishonest with me? Why did everyone keep telling me I was looking healthy and well, when the mirror revealed the horrific degradation of my face? It was clear the cancer was still alive in me. But what was I to do? I came to the conclusion that if I must die, I would prefer to expire at home than in this faraway city. I must try even harder on my daily marathon!

Friday morning arrived, and Mrs Kilduff asked if I would like to try aluminium crutches. I was fearful at first in case I might suffer an accident that would impede my progress, but my apprehension quickly turned to delight when I realised that I could travel more quickly and with less effort than on the walking frame. A new world was unfolding. Having been propped up by my three fabulous physiotherapists as far as the corridor, I travelled half the length of the corridor and back to bed unaided. Mrs Kilduff was delighted; she said I could repeat the adventure each day over the weekend with the accompaniment of two nurses.

Jean had told me in a letter that she would call later that evening, so I convinced two of the student nurses that I was allowed to exercise under their guidance and would like to attempt a second 'walk'. I motored along the corridor so confidently that just one of the girls walked in attendance. As I neared the end of the huge corridor, Jean rushed by and recognised me only by the long dressing gown I always wore. She stared at me in disbelief. It was several seconds before she could utter a word. 'I can't believe my eyes,' she declared. 'It's unbelievable to see you up and about.'

I did my utmost to impress her, but after all my heroics, I knew it was past time to return to base. 'Jean will chaperon me back to bed,' I told nurse Maria.

'I'd lose my job if anything went wrong,' she said. 'But go ahead and don't pretend I'm behind.'

I looked at Jean and, with tongue in cheek, said, 'Maria must think there's something going on between us.' Jean blushed a little and smiled.

It was the greatest feeling imaginable to be shuffling along the long hallway with the one person in the world I most wished to accompany me. She was enthusiastic, urging me to raise my knees higher and move more quickly. I made an almighty effort - and was close to collapse when I reached my bed.

Jean gave me the usual sack of home-made goodies and my favourite freshly-squeezed orange juice. We had a long, wide-ranging, and entertaining chat. 'I'm secretly hoping to return home much sooner than I even dreamed of,' I eventually told her.

After a couple of hours talking and laughing, she left for her sister's house, saying she looked forward to another 'walk' the following day. I was on cloud nine. Later, nurse Egan gave my still very itchy legs a vigorous massage. Then, having devoured my customary painkilling and sleeping pills, I quickly fell asleep.

Soon after breakfast, I was taken for another stroll. The physical exertion and pain were immense, but it was seventh heaven compared to the Stryker frame, and I was travelling farther each time. I was ecstatic at the prospect of returning home soon, even though no-one had yet hinted at a date.

That evening, Jean returned and brought me on another walk. But she seemed surprisingly reticent and less enthusiastic than during any of her previous visits. We talked and laughed, and talked some more, but I felt compelled to ask if something was astray.

'No, not at all. I could not be happier for you. It's just great to see you on the mend again.' She still seemed hesitant.

'Yeah, but today you haven't quite the same enthusiasm or even smile as you always do,' I insisted.

'Well,' she said, groping for words, 'up to now I always looked forward to hearing good news about your recovery. But this is probably the last time I will visit you in hospital, and though no-one in the world is happier than I am, still, things will never be the same again.'

I quickly interjected, 'Come on! Things seem to be changing for the better, but I still hope you'll visit me when I return home.'

Jean smiled. 'I...I just might.'

On Monday morning, Mrs Kilduff entered. 'I'm hearing all kinds of rumours about you running around the hospital. Tell me, is there any truth in what I'm hearing?'

'I'm pretty happy with the way things have been improving over the past few days. But what I'd like to know is precisely what standard I must attain before you can tell me I'm well enough to return home?'

'Home?' she laughed. 'Did you say home?'

'Yes, of course,' I replied. 'It would be great if you would set a realistic target for me to aim at.'

She frowned, pondered, and assumed an air of authority. 'Okay. When you can sit up and get out of bed unaided, walk halfway up the corridor on crutches, then down and up one flight of stairs, and then return to bed - then I will allow you to go. Of course, Mr Walsh and the oncology department will have the final say.'

I immediately turned on my side - somewhat gracefully under the circumstances - and without pausing to consider what I was doing, I was on the
floor and heading out the door on the crutches. My initial exuberance
induced a dizzy spell. I inhaled deeply as I would before a race. I also cleverly bought precious time by asking all my room-mates to wish me luck.
Soon, my Olympic final had begun.

I reached the halfway point of the corridor without undue stress and
then insisted on tackling the stairway. One of the younger physiotherapists
demonstrated how to negotiate the stairs with one crutch. It seemed simple
enough, but I found my legs weakening and my head spinning again. I
grasped onto the metal railing, and with the aid of one crutch, painfully
reached the bottom of the stairs. I turned around and changed hands.
Surprisingly, the ascent was quicker and easier than the descent. I nonchalantly headed for the bed, managing, with a mighty effort, to cloak my distress.

'How was that?' I asked boldly.

'Couldn't believe my eyes,' remarked one of the younger physios.

'I'll have a chat with Mr Walsh when I see him,' said Mrs Kilduff.

As soon as everyone exited the ward, I summoned Nurse Eva. She had
kept a furtive eye on my 'performance' and said she would search the hospital for Mr Walsh. She came running back within minutes - he would visit
me within half-an-hour.

He duly arrived and greeted me warmly. 'How are you getting along
with the walking aid?' he asked. Obviously, he had not been told of my
progress.

'Doctor, I've graduated to the crutches. But I would just love to know
what progress I must achieve before you'll allow me home.'

He looked me straight in the eye. 'As soon as the physiotherapy
department gives you the green light, then all I will require is to have some
X-rays taken. If I am happy with them, I will be delighted to see you go. Of
course, that is quite some while in the future.'

'So, Mr Walsh, when the physios give me the go-ahead, and if the X-
rays are fine, then you are telling me that I can go home?'

'Why should we keep you here any longer than necessary?'

I thanked him profusely, but even as he left the room, something was
telling me I was still not ready for the long trip home - even if I had deceived

Mrs Kilduff about my fitness. At least, my immediate destiny was now in my own hands. I had managed to con almost everyone into discharging me within two weeks, when it seemed three months might be more appropriate. I decided to relax and spend a few leisurely days recuperating some more.

Later that evening, student nurse Judith took me for my second walk of the day. This time I just went through the motions. I had scarcely moved ten yards from the bed when my legs began to buckle and I had to return to base quickly. Clearly, unless I was psyched up almost to fever-pitch for the effort, I would scarcely be able to get out of bed.

I relaxed and once again began to hallucinate pleasurably about re-entering the good old world which I thought had slipped from my grasp. A welcome diversion appeared in the form of Marsha. She breezed into the ward after her prolonged Christmas vacation, her manner as obnoxiously efficient as before. It was as if the Stryker fiasco had never happened. She sniffed the air vindictively and immediately proceeded to open the large windows. The freezing air bothered everyone, but no-one dared speak up. 'Nurse always knows best' seemed to be the motto. I wasn't too perturbed; now that I was in a regular bed and far away from the Stryker, the freezing air affected me much less.

But Marsha's attitude triggered off something devilish in my own psyche. Just as in my first encounter with her, a wicked urge for reprisal began to take shape.

Later that night, opportunity knocked for me in an extraordinary fashion. The man in the bed at the other side of old Pat had been unconscious for about a month. The only word he had uttered was 'greyhound'. He was constantly kicking all the clothes from his bed, even though he had broken his pelvis in several places, both hands, and one leg - and had several other internal injuries. This used to entertain the rest of the patients, especially when he denuded himself while Pat's daughters were visiting. As he quickly regained physical strength, there was an increasing possibility he might break out of his shackles and do himself further injury.

Marsha entered the ward several times that night and diligently performed seemingly petty chores, but still did not speak to anyone of us. My much rejuvenated faculties were analysing her every move. The more she ignored me, the more I longed to tackle her about her astonishing disposition.

When finally she began to tuck in the 'greyhound man' by just raising the safety barriers at each side of his bed, I felt obliged to intervene. 'Nurse,' I advised, 'that man has regained much of his strength since you were last on duty. Mary Long always props several pillows at his sides and between his legs and straps him firmly to the bed - otherwise he will kill himself if he falls onto the floor.'

She paused, looked at the ground, and pointed a javelin-like finger at me. 'Don't you ever tell me my job!'

While I enjoyed this unscheduled diversion from the boredom of pain-endurance, I still wished I could expose this fiendish madonna. I did not have to wait too long. At about three o'clock in the morning, we were all awakened by a loud crash. I looked across, but could not see the 'greyhound man'. We all shouted, 'Nurse, nurse, nurse!'

Student nurse Judith rushed to my side, thinking something had befallen me. 'Turn on the lights,' I roared.

The grim sight of the unconscious man dangling from the bed while still attached to drips and catheter put Judith running into the corridor for help. A student doctor came to the rescue, and soon the unfortunate patient was firmly secured back in his bed. The young intern thanked us. 'Only for you all, things would have turned nasty for that poor guy.'

An hour later, Marsha hurried into the ward. She checked the unconscious man, but did not say a word.

The following morning, the 'greyhound man's' surgeon, with the young intern and several other doctors and nurses, began examining his patient. From what I could hear, it seemed the surgeon was convinced that the intern was at fault. And I was shocked to observe that the young man seemed too scared to defend himself. Without thinking, I raised my hand: 'Sir, if you wish, I can tell you precisely what happened last night.' I related the entire sequence of events in detail, after which I received a wink of gratitude from the shy young intern. That was the last I heard of the incident.

Later that day, I went for my usual walk in the corridor. I was still finding it difficult, especially sitting up and standing onto the floor with the crutches. The fibreglass tightly embracing my torso was sore and awkward. My tediously itchy and spindly legs were scarcely able to sustain my weight for more than a minute. And my severed hip-bone was throbbing so intensely that it drowned out the sensation from the two monstrous scars across my belly and my back. My bedpan days had come to an end, but the escorted trips to the bathroom were a continuing embarrassment. The fear of a possible calamity on the homeward journey made me wonder if I should not defer my departure until my strength had increased some more.

Fortunately, decisions in large institutions, especially at Christmas, tend to take time. Another week passed, and I was gradually tying up most of the loose ends. Dr Kearney confirmed that Dr Paula Cotter had been told to expect me within two weeks of my returning home. The physiotherapy department were keeping a close eye on me. I still awaited Mr Walsh's return to have me X-rayed.

As the weekend approached, I asked nurse Eva to again summon Mr Walsh. When he arrived, I got the distinct impression that if I put on a good performance I could be on my way.

'Sit up, and I'll hand you your crutches, and walk around the room for me,' he said. I felt sprightly and had two laps of the room done within minutes.

'Do you want me to take a trip up the corridor?' I asked confidently.

'Just relax in bed. We will have you taken for some X-rays, and then we will take it from there.'

That evening, I was taken to the X-ray department. Later, I was relaxing in bed when a friend from back home arrived. Brendan was the guy who had informed Jean's friend several months previously that I was in hospital. But for his intervention, I might never have progressed beyond the stage of idly day-dreaming about her. He was visibly taken aback when he saw me. After a long chat, he asked what was the proposed next phase in my recovery.

'There is a strong possibility I may be going home in the car with you tomorrow. It would be a lot more comfortable than an ambulance.'

Presently, a nurse came to take me for a walk. Brendan was horrified when he fully realised how much weight I had lost. As much as he would love to drive me home, he told me, he was scared stiff I might have some mishap. 'The long road home would kill you. Wait until you're stronger, and I'll gladly come and pick you up - that is, of course, when the doctors release you.'

'I'm hoping they'll give me the green light tomorrow. If you could come here at about three o'clock, I should know by then.'

'I'll be here at three o'clock,' he said reluctantly. 'But you are going nowhere unless some doctor or nurse tells me you are free to go.'

I was intensely excited at the prospect of escaping the cloistered environs of the hospital. Six months of torture were suddenly coming to an end. The more I thought of it, the more my heart pounded. I gulped down the sleeping pills - this was one night I would need them.

Very early the following morning, Mr Walsh appeared. 'I am quite happy with your X-rays,' was his first, welcome message.

When I told him about returning home by car, he thought for a moment and said, 'Great. Just be very careful, and if you should have any problems contact me or the nearest doctor. Otherwise, I will want to see you back here for a change of cast and X-rays in four weeks time.'

I could scarcely comprehend what was happening. I was free at last! Or was I? Suddenly I felt like a caged lion who, when the door is opened, just sits in the corner afraid to leave.

19 Sweet freedom

The idea of leaving the security of an excellent hospital and a fabulous staff and venturing into the cruel world outside was suddenly terrifying. But my better self was telling me that six long months and six hospitals was as much as I could handle - I very much wanted to go home.

Blonde student nurse Susan Heffernan packed the huge amount of belongings and junk I had accumulated. When my two suitcases were filled, she began piling letters, presents, and more clothes into several large plastic sacks. 'You may be leaving,' she joked, 'but we're still getting married when you've fully recuperated.' Susan and all her lovely colleagues had undoubtedly helped me retain my sanity during the most traumatic weeks of my life.

The faces of my room-mates told their own stories. Each and every one was happy for me, but I could so easily identify with how deeply each was wishing it was his turn.

When Brendan arrived, I told him the news. He was still nervous. 'I'd love to drive you, Fan, but I'm sure it would be much safer in an ambulance,' he said stubbornly.

'Go and ask Eva McDonogh, the nurse in charge' I insisted.

He returned after a few minutes, wide-eyed with excitement. 'Jesus, she's the most beautiful girl I ever saw! What's the news on her?'

'Did she say I can go home?'

'I forgot to see if she was wearing a ring,' he said, speaking to himself rather than me.

'She's single for sure, but what did she say?' I persisted.

'Put in a word for me and we are on our way,' he said, emerging from his reverie.

A tinge of nostalgia came over me, but I was ready to go. Then began the arduous task of getting decked out in street clothes. My trousers presented the first obstacle; the coarse material tickled my itchy legs, and the cumbersome fibreglass cast was six inches more than my normal girth - the fly and waistband would never close. Old Pat presented me with an old-fashioned pair of shoulder braces; a safety pin helped bridge the draught in front. A shirt was split from tail to neck, and an elasticated tracksuit top had me looking like Humpty Dumpty.

Brendan began transferring my two suitcases and the ten large black refuse sacks to the front foyer. Meanwhile, Eva walked me from John's, to Jerry's, to Michael's, and finally to old Pat Lennon's bedside as we all exchanged farewells. I shook Pat's right hand while the saintly old gentleman placed his left hand over his tear-filled eyes and, with genuine sorrow in his voice, said, 'I am so glad for you. God be with you! I will pray for you every day, and I do hope you will come back to visit me some day.'

It would have been great if they all could have left with me. I gave one last glance at my empty bed and a last farewell to my friends and headed along the long corridor toward the front foyer.

Just as we were about to leave, Brendan said he had to go back for the last two sacks. I stood alone beside my belongings in the open foyer and waited. Five, then ten, long minutes passed - and he had not returned. I had just travelled the inordinate distance of 100 yards and was beginning to feel weak and queasy. I struggled to the front door. An arriving visitor assisted me into the freezing air outside. I knew I had to attempt to descend the snow-covered steps and lean on the small, granite front wall. I was perspiring and shivering at the same time. I began to vomit - and was terrified that some nurse or doctor would learn of my predicament and summarily order me back to St Agnes's.

Brendan finally arrived. 'I can't find Eva. What the hell am I going to do? I gotta get her phone number!'

'Brendan,' I gasped, 'get the fucking car quick and drive me around the corner before someone sees me. I'm as sick as a dog. You can come back later for my belongings.'

He got the message; within seconds, he was back with the car. 'You'll have to lift me across into the car. There's no way I can stand up from this wall,' I said.

'I'll get someone from the hospital to help,' he said.

'No, no!' I protested vehemently.

Brendan got down on his haunches on the snow-covered pavement, slung me across his back, and like St Christopher, carried me across the road. At last, I was shivering happily in the reclining front seat. He threw my goods and chattels into the boot and rear seats. Soon I was relishing the taste of freedom - of being anonymous amidst the slushy streets of the teeming metropolis. It was joy beyond description.

The four-hour journey took more that six painful, but ecstatically happy, hours. I could scarcely see out the windows from my fully-reclined seat, but the tops of the trees and the rooves of the houses looked wonderful. 'It's so great not to be passing along this road in a timber box,' I boringly repeated to big Bren several times.

The sight of my own house was overwhelming. I had told the doctors I was returning to the care and attention of my parents' home in the country. But I was determined to stay in my own house in the city, where most of my friends and Jean lived. Incidentals such as meals never entered my calculations.

When we arrived, Brendan called my two next-door neighbours to help him transfer me from the car. The house had not been aired or cleaned, nor had the beds been dressed, in months. Danny's wife, Marie, insisted I wait in their house while she prepare my bedroom. As efficiently as any hospital nurse, she changed the sheets and provided the various domestic touches that only a woman can. Soon, I was stretched out on my very own bed. A meal of steak, potatoes, and vegetables, served by Marie, was the most delicious I had ever tasted.

News of my homecoming spread like wildfire. By the time I finished my meal, more than 20 friends had crowded into the bedroom. Everyone appeared to have brought bottles of whiskey and beer; soon the party was in full swing. One slightly inebriated wit commented that the scene was like an old-fashioned wake - except that this time the corpse was alive.

Eventually, Danny took charge and persuaded the revellers that I needed rest and that they should leave forthwith. Marie insisted she would make my meals the following day. Danny urged me to phone him at any time, day or night, if I needed anything.

When I opened my eyes the following morning, I took several seconds to fully realise I was in my own bed. Marie arrived with a splendid breakfast and told me my other next-door neighbours, Victor and Breda, had undertaken to feed me on alternate days. 'You just concentrate on getting better - Breda and I will make sure you regain all that weight you lost,' she told me. Lady Luck was smiling on me; the marvellous care I had received in hospital was being duplicated in my own home.

A local hospital nurse called and informed me she would tend my wounds every week, or whenever necessary. She had apparently been told about me by another neighbour. The real value of good neighbours became fully apparent to me for the first time.

When my parents came to visit, my mother insisted I return home with them. But I was much too content where I was, and when Mam saw the care being lavished on me by all and sundry, she relented.

Later that evening, I phoned Jean. She sounded happy that I was back home, but appeared hesitant about calling. Eventually, when I pointedly invited her, she promised to visit within a day or two.

She arrived with her friend Eileen at a time when there were several other friends present; it was impossible to talk intimately. As she left, I said I would phone her soon.

First thing the following morning, I dialled her number. 'I wish we could have chatted - like when you used to visit me in hospital. I do hope you will call again soon,' I told her.

Sounding shy but pleased, she promised to take me for a drive in her car as soon as I was well rested and physically ready. It would be a diversion, she said, from being cooped-up in my room.

Life now took on a new routine. Splendid meals arrived four and five times every day. A constant stream of friends dropped in. Someone likened my bedroom to the cockpit of a jumbo jet - with television, stereo, telephone, electric blanket, personal computer, and lighting all controlled at arm's length. Every possible comfort was literally at hand. Now, getting back to full health and getting to know Jean better were my prime concerns.

The pain from my severed hip-bone and scars remained intense. The body-cast still made it almost impossible to walk - so trips to the bathroom were hazardous unless some-one was present. My visiting nurse did her best to clean the concealed hip-wound with a forceps and then packed huge wads of cotton wool inside both the top and bottom edges of the cast to make lying down more tolerable.

My immediate challenge now lay in ascertaining the possibility of a relationship with Jean. From the onset of my illness, she had gone well beyond the bounds of duty in helping me. Of course, it occurred to me that - caring and warm person that she was - she would have equally comforted anyone else in my position. I also knew that, in the present circumstances, I wasn't exactly God's gift to womankind. Nevertheless, BP was the only girl I had ever dreamt of marrying. I continued to dream of marrying her. For now, at the very least, I would keep on trying to build on our precious friendship.

20 A friend in need

I had been home a week when the voice at the other end of the phone said, 'Ah-hum-aha-chi!' Fr Andy had arrived back from South America and called into the Mater on his way home from the airport. He was thrilled to hear about my progress. 'I couldn't believe my eyes and ears when I found out you had survived the second operation and walked out of the hospital.'

I asked how he enjoyed his holiday. His succinct reply alarmed me. 'It could have been a wonderful experience, but the entire trip was a nightmare. As soon as I arrived in Peru, my tummy became upset, and I spent most of the time in bed. As soon as I get a few hours sleep I'm going straight into hospital. I'm following in your footsteps.' He sounded seriously deflated.

'Too much tequilas and spicy food,' I chirped brightly.

'How I wish you were right! I'm afraid the game is up. I'm certain I'm in the same boat as Fr Hennessy.' Again he sounded in deadly earnest. I was shocked. Fr Hennessy was a young colleague of Andy's in a previous parish, who had suffered an ignominious death from colon cancer.

When Andy hung up, I reflected on his unorthodox lifestyle. His great love of the priesthood, and his passion for helping the underprivileged, often kept him busy from before seven o'clock in the morning until his arrival home to an empty house, often after a charity show, at two or three the following morning. Ministering to the sick and dying often meant his few hours of sleep were interrupted. The unnatural and even inhuman vocation of the bachelor priest meant that for much of his life he was unravelling, sharing, and enduring the perplexing personal and social problems of too many of his parishioners.

On the occasional fishing or shooting trip or foreign holiday, Andy would recharge his pastoral batteries with large draughts of his favourite brews and generous helpings of rich food. That he had arrived home probably jet-lagged and suffering from over-indulgence in exotic South American cuisine did not really alarm me.

Later that night I phoned him. He told me he was being admitted to hospital that weekend for tests. I now became a little anxious.

Eventually, Jean phoned and asked if I would like a pizza. I would have said yes to arsenic if she had suggested it. She arrived looking much more relaxed than on the previous occasion. She went into the kitchen to make tea and returned laughing at the very many tell-tale signs of bachelorhood. 'I have never seen white cups so discoloured in my life. In fact, your entire kitchen needs to be sterilised before someone is poisoned.'

When I suggested, only half in jest, that she take on the job, she replied that she would love to, but then grew reticent at the course the conversation was taking. She seemed anxious to lend a woman's touch to my house, but politely steered away from involvement.

Wednesday arrived: time for me to get to the Regional hospital to meet the haematologist Dr Paula Cotter. My brother Pat carefully dressed me and helped me into his car. When we arrived at the hospital we were escorted to a door with a sign: Blood Tests. The nurse put the crimson sample into a smallish test-tube, and we were steered in the direction of the laboratory. 'I'll have the results for you in about ten minutes,' said the white-coated attendant. I tried to sit in a chair, but my wide cast would not fit into the bucket seat. After an agonising ten-minute wait, we were given the result sheet. We then set out in the direction of Ward 1A - a distance of about 200 yards.

Ten years previously, as resident engineer here, I sprinted powerfully along these lengthy corridors on rainy evenings, in preparation for the European Indoor Championships. Today I was travelling at a very much reduced speed. As I struggled from corridor to corridor, I became more and more curious about the test results. Eventually, I persuaded Pat to open the envelope. The investigation was all too easy. About 30 different constituents were analysed, and behind most of the computer printed results was one of two letters: H and L. The tolerable limits were spelt out: the extremes - 'high' and 'low' - were very simple to decipher. There were far too many Hs and Ls. 'I'll be back in St Luke's tonight,' I told Pat.

When we reached cancer-ward 1A, I was trembling with fear and exhaustion. We entered the waiting room, where a dozen or more equally ashen-faced people were quietly sitting. I did not attempt to sit down. 'I'm getting sick, Pat. I must lie down. Call a nurse, quickly,' I shouted.

Pat scurried down the corridor, and soon a nurse rushed into the nearest bedroom and ordered a sprightly old man to don his dressing-gown and get out of bed. I lay down in his place and awaited my sentence.

After a long wait, Dr Con C Murphy, Dr Cotter's next-in-command, approached. Smiling warmly, he held my blood-test results in his hand. 'I followed your athletics career with much pleasure,' was his first utterance.

He's going to build my morale before delivering my death-sentence,' I thought, and cut in: 'How are my bloods, Doc?'

He scanned the long list in his hand as if this was his first time looking at it. Finally he said, 'Good - not too bad. Considering the inordinate amount of radiotherapy you have received, I suppose they are as good as could be expected.'

'So where do I go from here, Doc?'

'We would like to see you every second Wednesday for similar blood-tests as today. We will give you mild chemotherapy tablets - melphalan and prednisolone. We will do more extensive tests every few months depending on progress. This will continue for at least two years. Hopefully, the quantity and frequency of the tablets will gradually be reduced,' he said nonchalantly.

'Thank you very much, Doctor.' I felt enormous relief. 'Does this mean I am at least out of the danger zone for now?'

'You must continue on as before. I'd give you at best a fifty-fifty chance of survival.'

I was temporarily shaken, but my mind flashed back to the moments when in the same hospital Surgeon McGuinness told me I had malignant cancer. Then, my chances of survival had seemed to be a million to one against. Compared with that, fifty-fifty or thereabouts now sounded like tremendous odds.

Dr Murphy gave me two plastic containers of tablets. 'Take five of each daily for five days. You may feel a little sick, but you will survive.' I was given a haematology slip and then, as if in a dream, was on my way home.

Back in my own bedroom with an almost fifty-fifty chance of survival, I felt I had the world at my feet. My gracious next-door neighbours
were feeding and entertaining me. Jean was calling to see me every second
day - and each time we seemed to be growing closer. The suspicion created
by the Bell's palsy farce was being slowly but surely buried.

The weekend of Andy's tests arrived. When I phoned him, he sounded as if
his world had caved in - even though the results would not arrive until later
that week. I asked why he was so concerned. He said he had exactly the
same symptoms as Fr Hennessy. Andy had shared a presbytery with Fr
Hennessy and had seen at first hand how this strong and healthy 44-year-old
had wasted away.

'A slight touch of piles aggravated by South American food has
alarmed you,' I told him. I still could not imagine anything seriously wrong
with him.

Wednesday approached, and I had to decide how I would travel to
Dublin to meet Mr Walsh and have my cast changed. Several friends offered
to drive me; Andy offered to collect me from the train station. I finally
decided to travel in the large cab of an articulated truck. The sleeper behind
the front seats seemed to offer the most comfortable ride.

Jack O'Connell arrived early on Wednesday morning with his huge
18-wheeler. Willie Murphy, an old friend, had arranged for Danny, Victor,
and Jack to raise me gently the seven-or-so feet into the cab. Marie prepared
breakfast for everyone. When I had gone through the arduous rigmarole of
dressing, Willie fetched a weighing scales, and they had a contest to see who
was closest to me in weight. Normally, I bordered 190 pounds. I was a long
way from that now, but after four weeks of five-star nourishment, my
armpits were bursting through the top of my cast. Clearly, I had regained
some of my lost bulk. My actual weight, 118 pounds, surprised everyone,
especially me.

They had a hard job raising me into the truck. Marie produced a heavy
woollen blanket, in which they tried to wrap me. But I had an aversion to
being mummified, so Victor got two wooden planks and suggested making
a stretcher by nailing the blanket to the four-by-twos. Marie grew anxious
and wanted to phone for an ambulance - but I was enjoying the fracas.

Anyway, I had long ago lost all love of ambulances.

Victor finally completed the makeshift pallet and was so proud of his handiwork he suggested a trial run - he would be the passenger. Willie and Danny charged along the pavement, with their 'patient' hanging on for dear life. Poor Victor was scared witless - but the newly-patented stretcher was proven to be roadworthy.

Soon I was as snug as a bug in the little bed behind Jack's driving seat. Then, to the roar of the powerful engine and the sound of the deep-base hooter, we were on our way. Five hours later, Fr Andy was on hand with his friends Larry and Mick to welcome our arrival.

Carefully I was manoeuvred from my perch and into Andy's car. Andy looked healthy and seemed as exuberant as ever. Before I could enquire about his welfare, he peppered me with questions about my second operation and my learning to walk again. I wondered briefly had I imagined his illness. When I finally asked how he was, his entire attitude changed. 'I would swap places with you this very minute if it were possible,' he said sadly.

'Andy, do you really believe there is something seriously wrong?'

'I have definitely the same problem as Hennessy - and you know where he is now.'

'When did the problem begin?' I wanted to make sure he was really being serious.

'Seven months ago - July,' he said ruefully.

'Andy, that's the very month I found out I had the big C. Why didn't you tell me then, or the doctors in St Luke's?'

He drove along from traffic light to traffic light with a childlike stare in his eyes. It was a while before he spoke. 'It's very easy to talk when someone else has the problem, but when it's yourself, then it's a very different matter.'

We reached the Mater, and I had to concentrate again on my own problems. Andy helped me with the crutches, and we headed first for St Agnes's. I was astonished at how easily I negotiated the long corridors. Without realising it, I had improved enormously.

My former ward was unrecognisable. Old Pat had been transferred to an orthopaedic hospital; John was recuperating in a nursing home; Jerry had returned home, further grafting having been deemed impossible; the greyhound man had emerged suddenly from his coma to find that all his bones had mended satisfactorily, and he too had been sent packing.

Only the furniture was the same. The six beds, the high ceilings, and the floor tiles - each one of which I felt I knew personally - were all in place. The skeletal frame of the Stryker was parked at the end of the corridor. I found if difficult to fathom that I and my parted friends had endured so much pain and mental torture in that innocuous-looking room just a few short weeks previously.

Lovely Eva was on duty - and was genuinely delighted to see me alive and well. We had a brief but entertaining chat. She gave Andy a sackful of letters and cards that had accumulated. Then we set out for Mr Walsh's department.

A large crowd awaited Mr Walsh, but I was taken directly into the plaster room. There was Nurse Liz, who had put the cast on. 'I'll remove the cast with this rotary saw. You will then have some X-rays taken. Mr Walsh will see you before I put another one on you,' she said.

As she spoke, Mr Walsh, Dr Murray, and the usual entourage entered. Mr Walsh, as always, asked the first questions. 'How is everything with you?'

I tried to be even more upbeat than I felt: 'Great, thanks, Doctor! Considering everything, I'm doing fine.'

'We will remove the cast and have you X-rayed immediately,' he said.

Dr Padraic and another medic held my arms tightly as Liz sawed her way vertically through the front of the cast. When the rigid fibreglass split, it was flexible enough for two strong pairs of hands to wrestle it from my torso. As the huge wads of bandages and cotton wool were carefully peeled off, the direct cause of much of my discomfort became evident; both of my hips were black and blue, as was the upper part of my chest and armpits, from the pressure my increased weight had exerted on the inflexible cast.

Gripping onto the arms of Padraic and some other medic, I was steered slowly into the X-ray room. I felt as stable as the proverbial three sheets in a gale. Like before, it seemed as if the upper half of my body was about to detach itself from the lower half. Fortunately, I was in capable hands. After a painful and nerve-wracking manoeuvre, I was finally lying on the rigid bed. Padraic ordered ice-water, which brought blessed relief, and while I waited for photographing to commence, Liz washed my torso with warm, soapy water.

When the first session of X-rays had been completed, I was turned on my side for profile shots. After about ten painful minutes, Mr Walsh and Padraic returned with the finished pictures. 'The grafts appear to be solidifying satisfactorily,' were the welcome words from Mr Walsh.

'Any sign of tumours or bones being eaten away?' I asked bluntly.

Mr Walsh gave me a large smile. 'Everything looks normal.'

Everyone seemed to think my question had been facetious. But hearing the boss utter those three magic words greatly eased my troubled mind.

Mr Walsh explained with the help of the X-rays precisely what he had done to my spine. The stainless steel rectangle looked as if it measured about six inches by two inches and a quarter-inch in diameter. It was ingeniously fastened to the rear of my spine by several pieces of wire threaded through holes drilled into the rear of the vertebrae. The banana-shaped bone taken from my hip was clearly visible, inserted into apertures gouged out in the front of the two vertebrae above and below the collapsed L5. The entwined pieces of wire, protruding at least an inch, were sandwiched, I was told, between the layers of muscle. This extraordinary scaffolding was the creation of the man they called The Messiah. But for his skill and ingenuity, I doubt I would ever have walked again.

Eventually I was returned to the plaster-room, where my bruises were wrapped with several wads of cotton-wool and gauze before the warm fibreglass bandages were tightly moulded to my torso. Then the warm, watery liquid was pasted all over the soft fibreglass. Within minutes, the silken strait-jacket was solidifying, while all the time I subtly expanded with my index fingers those corners that might pinch and squeeze as I continued to gain weight.

When the cast had set, Liz began examining the spots where sores might develop, and making alterations with her circular saw. Soon I was vertical again and heading to meet Andy in the waiting room. The new cast felt much more spacious and comfortable than the first. It was great to be once more leaving the hospital behind.

We had some time to spare before Jack was to pick me up in the car-park of Andy's church. 'When did you have your last pint,' Andy enquired casually.

It had been almost nine months; the idea sounded like a good one. Within minutes I was propped up in a chair in the Strawberry Beds Tavern and attacking a pint of Guinness. I recalled the Christmas night hooley in St Agnes's with Andy and Mick and Larry, and remarked to myself how heavenly in comparison was this present ambience. Sadly, the tone of the conversation had not changed significantly. Between drinks we spoke about the big C, then Peru, then the big C, then Argentina, then the big C again, then Brazil, then inevitably back to the big C once more.

The entire scenario was bizarre. Normal, everyday topics seemed irrelevant. I was fighting the unspeakable monster; Andy felt he was about to be thrown into the same savage arena. It was only when we had a gallon consumed between us that the conversation improved. The black stuff was quelling the itchiness in my legs. And Andy began to relapse into joke-telling mode.

Too soon, it was time for the long road home; we headed for the presbytery, where the big juggernaut was waiting for me.

Andy insisted on cooking a meal for us before we set out. As we devoured the enormous plates of rashers, bacon, sausages, and black pudding, Andy phoned his parish priest - we needed another pair of hands to help raise me into the cab. 'The fry is the only man to smother the smell of the beer,' he said as he put the phone down. He was right. Fr McDowell never suspected for a moment we had been boozing.

Andy had a great working relationship with his PP. Their personalities complemented each other; they were constantly exchanging witticisms.

'I see Fr Sheahan is trying to get into our very exclusive club. He just hates not to be included in everything,' Fr McDowell quipped when he arrived. It was the first inkling for me that he himself had had a colostomy several years before.

Soon, I was loaded into my lofty bunk, and Jack and I were on our way. Within an hour the effects of the Guinness had waned, and the chilling numbness had returned to my legs. The exertions of the day were taking their toll. I decided I needed another dose of the black elixir. Jack, a shy tee-totaller, somewhat reluctantly stopped at the next roadside watering-hole. He was gone for a good 15 minutes. Then he came running back to the cab with a partially-spilled pint. 'Drink up quickly. I have to return the glass as soon as possible,' he said nervously.

I barely had the glass to my lips when the proprietor rushed aggressively from the hotel and across to the juggernaut. 'It's okay,' I shouted, and explained my predicament.

He apologised heartily. 'I noticed your friend skulking near the door with the filled glass and then making a dash for it. I wondered what the hell he was up to,' he said ruefully. 'Take as much time as you wish.' He returned to his post, and arrived back a few minutes later with two complimentary pints of Guinness. Since Jack did not drink, I had a pain-free trip home.

Home life slowly returned to normality. Marie and Breda continued to feed me sumptuously on alternate days. My nurse called twice-weekly. Jean usually called to see me after school - I lived for her company.

Various friends began taking me to the local hotel almost every night; the three pints of Guinness I consumed there helped greatly to reduce my dependence on conventional painkillers. With two weeks to go before I had to return to hospital for blood-tests, I was now thinking more and more about Andy.

He entered hospital on the weekend and was to get his results the same evening. I was utterly confident he would be given the all-clear. He was as much a health fanatic as myself; he had always led a salutary existence, running or cycling almost every day; and he was a non-smoker. His only weakness - if you could call it that - was the monthly or twice-monthly binge on whiskey or beer. He often bragged about how long he was going to live, particularly since his father was still hale and hearty and approaching the century mark.

He phoned me soon after returning from hospital. 'I was correct,' he said, his voice almost unrecognisable with distress. 'I have it for sure.'

My heart stopped for a moment, but I could not even pretend to go along with what I knew he was telling me. 'You have what, Andy?' I asked nonchalantly.

'The very same as Hennessy - colon cancer. The game is really up now.'

'Don't talk nonsense, Andy. You're a long way from the knacker's yard yet. What's the next move?'

'I'll be going under the knife in a week's time. I'll end up with one of those dreaded colostomy bags.'

'But that's great news, Andy,' I replied with all the false cheer I could muster. 'The sooner you're on that colostomy bag the better. There are hundreds of thousands of people worldwide in that position, and they are all doing extremely well. Don't worry, you'll be fine.'

His reply was subdued and horribly fatalistic. 'Before I went to South America, I knew I was going on my last holiday. I knew only too well I had the identical symptoms as Hennessy.' Why then, I asked, did he not have himself examined long before now. 'It was much too late when I fully realised what I really had. Anyway, when it's your own dilemma, it's a different game altogether.'

When he had rung off, I felt confused and bewildered. For eight months, he had kept me going with almost daily encouragement and spiritual advice. Now the tide was beginning to turn - and I was trying to help the priest. It was all too unreal to fully comprehend. I would not have wished what I had experienced on my worst enemy. But now it seemed to be happening to my best friend.

Jean arrived that Saturday and took me for our first 'official' outing. We travelled to the windy seaside, hoping the salt breeze and the pure ozone would improve my ghostly complexion. It took time to muster up courage to walk along the sand. With the aluminium crutches and Jean as chaperon, I eventually shed my shoes and ventured into the cold surf. Jean's tiny feet were no match for the freezing March sea-water, but to my great astonishment, the cold, sharp shock was inveigling the blood into my spindly legs. I stood like a tripod for several minutes while Jean jogged along the beach. She then braved the icy water and helped me back to the car. The tingling in my thigh muscles persisted, but the new vigour in my lower legs suggested I had found a remedy for one of my most unpleasant symptoms.

On the way home, I suffered waves of nausea, a reaction to the excursion. Jean slowed the car and drove the rest of the way at snail's pace for fear the vibrations would aggravate my nausea.

The following day, Jean called and cooked Sunday dinner for me. We had just finished eating when my parents arrived. My mother and Jean struck up an instant and intimate friendship. They had plenty to talk about, not least because we had all been reared within ten miles of one another. I took a back seat and observed the first encounter between my mother and the first really serious girlfriend I'd ever dated. I was amazed to note the uncanny resemblance; their height and facial bone-structure, even their hair-colour, were similar. When my parents were leaving, my mam discreetly whispered, 'That Jean is a real gem.' When I replied that we were just friends, she seemed disappointed.

Late that night a very depressed Fr Andy phoned to tell me his 97-year-old father had died unexpectedly in his sleep. Burial would be two days later in Annakissa, a small churchyard about an hour's drive from me. I told him I would like to meet him at Annakissa before the burial, but he insisted I should not attempt the journey. My parents were equally emphatic. But Jean would be in school; I had known and loved Andy's father all my life; I felt I had to make the effort - it was the least I could do to reciprocate some of the enormous encouragement and succour Andy had given me before my operations.

On the day of the funeral, I tried for the first time to dress myself unaided. The shirt wasn't too difficult, but the trousers were reluctant to co-operate. Eventually, I spread them on the floor and wriggled my legs into position. Then, with the aid of a specially-converted aluminium coat-hang-er, I managed to raised them into position. Old Pat's braces helped to do the rest. Shoes and socks were out of the question - slippers would have to do. Complete with huge, cumbersome overcoat, I waddled to my car.

Getting into the driver's seat unaided proved almost beyond me. The body-cast ground into my torso, and once seated, I could not raise my spindly legs into the car. I eventually achieved the impossible by dragging at the legs of my trousers. Meanwhile, I had dropped one of my slippers on the footpath; there was no chance of retrieving it.

Dazed and disoriented, I persisted in my crazy quest. I raised my two legs onto the clutch and accelerator pedals and had the presence of mind to attempt to use the controls before cranking up the engine. I tried to change gears - to no avail. My legs would not respond; nor had I the strength to depress the pedals. I then knew that the trip would have to be aborted.

By now the base of my spine seemed about to snap. I tried to get out of the car, but could not move. I lay on my side onto the passenger seat so as to relieve some of the pressure. Eventually, I panicked and began to roar for help.

Marie, my genial next-door neighbour, rushed to the scene and delivered a stern lecture about commonsense. Then, like a ministering angel, she helped me back to my bed.

Later that night, my mother phoned and described the moving funeral ceremony conducted by Fr Andy. Seemingly, his sermon and singing of the hymn *Going Home* had moved the congregation to tears.

When the burial was over, Andy drove directly back to Dublin and entered Blanchardstown Hospital, where he was to undergo his colon operation the following morning.

A few days later, I phoned Andy's parish priest. The operation had been an apparent success. Andy would be in intensive care for a day or two. Fr McDowell would phone me when he had further news.

Two days later my phone rang. Fr McDowell's voice was unmistakable.

'What's the news, Father?' I quickly asked.

'Not good, I think,' was his unvarnished response. He was, he said, reluctant to speculate, but his earnest requests for information had elicited nothing from a very evasive surgeon. 'I was his religious instructor when he was in junior school. Yet when I asked him if the prognosis was encouraging, he declined to give me a definite answer. What bothers me even more is Andy's attitude. He simply refuses to see anyone but myself. He seems to be in another world. He wants to pray all the time, and you know that is not exactly his style. I wish I knew what to do.'

I decided to take the first available train to Dublin. Fr McDowell offered to collect me at the station.

The three-hour journey was barely tolerable, but I consoled myself with the recollection that it would have been quite impossible only one month previously. I had more to dwell on, however, than my own comfort.

Fr McDowell drove me straight to Blanchardstown. On the way, I enquired after Andy. 'It's just amazing,' said the PP. 'He's still refusing to see anyone. Sometimes I feel I'm not too welcome myself.'

When we reached the hospital, Father said, 'Since he warned me not to allow anyone in to see him, you best go in on your own and don't pretend a word.'

I took the lift to the second floor and headed toward room number 32. I had been warned it would not be easy to breach security, but trusted that my crutches and my clearly-invalid condition would see me through. As I passed the nurses' station, a sturdily-built sister stopped me. 'Who, may I ask, are you visiting, Sir?'

'Oh, just a friend - and I have travelled a long way to see him,' I said, knowing well that she suspected where I was going.

'I'm very sorry, but Fr Sheahan is not seeing anyone.'

I looked her in the eye, smiled boldly, and said as if in jest, 'That's the first time a nun ever told me a lie. I know for a fact that his parish priest sees him every day.'

My attempt at banter fell flat. Neither I nor anyone else was going to see Andy - and that was that. I showed her my cast and tried to explain that but for Andy I might not be alive. 'I have the same complaint as Fr Sheahan. I have spent more than six months in six different hospitals. He visited me every day and anointed me three times. I owe him at least one visit.'

'I understand all that,' she said brusquely. 'But you must understand we have rules to keep in here, and it's my duty to see they are carried out.'

She had her job to do - but I was going to see Andy come hell or high water. From my lofty position I looked down on this confident lady who, though much shorter, was surely twice my weight, and spoke with quiet conviction. 'Sister, you will have to forgive my impertinence, but I am now going to walk down the corridor to room thirty-two, and if you try to stop me then I will probably finish up as a patient in the room next to Fr Andy.'

I began to wobble in the direction of room thirty-two. She stood in front and did her best to block me. I pressed forward, telling her to call security - and if Andy did not want to see me, I would leave immediately. When it was clear she would have to physically tackle me to stop me, she ran back into the nurses' station.

I headed for my destination as quickly as I could, which was about half normal pace, and reached room 32 unhindered. I knocked at the door, poked my head in, and uttered Andy's own salutation: 'Ah-hum-a-ha-chi!' He stared at me with obvious disbelief.

He was lying in bed attached to the usual drips and drains. The expression on his face was one of real terror. His usually neat, wavy hair was standing on top of his head, and for the first time it seemed to have a grey tinge. 'How on earth did you get in here?' he asked.

'Young man,' I replied, 'we are in this cancer business together. You got me out of that hell-hole, and now I will get you out of this.' As I spoke, two security guards and my heavy adversary burst in. One wave of his hand, and Andy had given the instruction that everything was in order.

There followed the most bizarre conversation that has ever taken place between two health freaks. We spoke about cancer. We spoke of the mathematical unlikelihood of either one of us ever catching the disease in the first place. We spoke of the seemingly billion-to-one chance of the two of us contracting it at the same time. Of course, I lied to him in telling him that he looked great, as he and everyone else had lied to me. As we spoke, he continually grimaced in pain.

'You saw me at my very worst, Andy, and now you can see how much I have improved. I am now seeing you at your lowest. In a matter of weeks you will be back running marathons, and I will still be hobbling along on these crutches.' I was trying desperately to convince him that his dilemma was no worse than mine.

As we spoke, he struggled from the bed and headed for the bathroom. Here was a small opportunity to bolster his confidence. 'I have very little sympathy for anyone who can walk to the toilet,' I said emphatically. 'I spent three long months confined, constipated, and confused, and here are you running around as lively as a March hare.'

Andy gave a small laugh and then clutched his side with pain. 'I suppose everything is relative,' he said under his breath.

When he came back, I proceeded to expound my theories - correct or otherwise - on cancer. 'Drop the humble potato and damage it, and within a relatively short time decay will set in. Remove the damaged part quickly, and that spud will be as wholesome as any other. That damage turns to cancer quickly - as least as far as the potato is concerned. Or take a brand new Rolls Royce and purposely damage one of its doors. Rust will set in - which is cancer to an automobile. Leave it unattended for a period, and the door falls to pieces. Repair or replace the door, and that car is as good as new. On the other hand, let the rust continue, and the vehicle is on the scrap heap years before its time.' I was now in full flow.

'I damaged my spine and had a repair job done on it. Now I feel as if I am on my way to recovery. You have either a slight congenital defect or you ate the wrong food or drank the wrong drinks. Fortunately, we live in an age when medical technology can successfully treat these problems. So now it's a matter of sitting it out and trusting in that technology and in the Man Above.'

Andy shook his head. 'Your rust theory makes a lot of sense, I suppose. But I've been passing blood for about eight months and, like Hennessy, I have left it too late. I'll be going out of here in a timber overcoat.'

I had done most of the talking; by his own standards, Andy was particularly subdued. I still had to have several casts changed and X-rays taken, which could potentially reveal all sorts of sinister information about my chassis. I had spent almost half-an-hour sitting in a chair, and when I tried to stand up, I found it extremely difficult. I decided to milk the situation for all it was worth.

'Andy, call the nurses' station and get an orderly to help me out of here.'

While we waited, I stared hard at Andy and said with as much conviction as possible, 'Andy, let me tell you something. It's not easy being a cancer patient, but if we don't help each other and fight like all hell, then we'll both be in the manure business.'

Sister arrived and summoned an orderly. Andy began to act like his old self, issuing explicit instructions on how best to raise me. While the orderly held me firmly, I deliberately lunged onto the neck of my small stout foe and roared like a madman: 'Jaysus - go easy, Sister, or you'll kill me!'

Andy's hearty laugh rang out for the first time. I scarcely said goodbye to him as the nun and myself struggled out the door. The orderly then supported me against the jamb of the door as the poor harassed nun raced back for my crutches. I continued with my histrionics until I was well out of sight and sound of room 32, and then said, 'I'm fine now, Sister. Thanks very much.' I then straightened up and marched as smartly as I could to the door of the lift.

As I entered the lift, I was thrilled to hear the bemused sister say to the orderly, 'What a strange character! Thank God I never met the likes of him before.'

Fr McDowell enjoyed my account of the visit and was especially glad when I told him Andy had promised to receive his friends Mick Dunne and Larry McGuinness.

On the train journey home, I smoothed my way by frequent visits to the bar, but had to beware of over-indulgence and its potential for catastrophe. I also had to be reasonably sober reaching the station in Cork - I did not want Jean to notice I was using more than one painkiller.

She was waiting at the station, looking radiantly beautiful. I felt at that moment as though I were the most important person in her life. She hurried over and eagerly helped me from the train, anxious to learn the latest news on both Andy and me. I could hardly take my eyes off her lovely face, silhouetted by each street-lamp we flashed past on the way home. We might have been the two best friends in the world, but my contraceptive fibreglass cast ensured that for at least three or four months we would never get any closer than holding hands. For now, all I wanted was that we would remain friends; for that privilege alone, I would be always infinitely grateful.

The following week I went with Fr Dan Gould to see Andy. Fr Gould was one of the friends with whom Andy had travelled to South America. They had also been in the seminary together, and Dan was anxious to get first-hand information. As we approached the nurses' station, my rotund sparring partner approached. 'I'm delighted to see you. Ever since your last visit, Fr Sheahan has completely come out of his shell and is now the life and soul of the entire hospital.' It was difficult to believe she was the same person I had almost come to blows with a few days before. I was so pleasantly surprised, I scarcely knew how to reply.

We entered room 32 and were greeted by a smiling patient, a man totally transformed from the one of the previous week. We chatted for more than an hour, Andy rattling off yarns and joking as if nothing had happened. His room was a riot of flowers and get-well cards from hundreds of friends and local schoolchildren. Dan inquired about his operation and recuperation, but never once did Andy mention the word cancer. Dan noticed a box of matches on the bedside table and wondered out loud if the man who was always so anti-smoking had been converted to the dreaded weed. Andy grinned. 'Not on your life, but I will explain later.'

Fr Dan was mystified. 'What the hell are you up to, Sheahan?'

Andy hesitated, then raised his dressing gown sufficiently to show the corner of his colostomy bag. 'Well, it's like this. Old Fred here tends to misbehave. So when Fred farts, I crack a match, and then the aroma from the sulphur dominates the airwaves.' That was the best laugh of the day, and it proved that Andy had regained his spirit. Before we left, he said he hoped to be discharged within a few days, and to recuperate down south with his sister Mary and family.

This trip included another visit to the Mater for X-rays and change of body-cast. This was my third visit to the scene of the most painful tribulations of my life, and each visit was better than the last. I particularly enjoyed renewing acquaintance with the man who had performed such a miracle on my spine. Mr Walsh's skill, dedication, and charm gave me all the encouragement I needed to face another month in my strait-jacket. I felt privileged and blessed to have met him.

There was always tangible excitement, even euphoria, among Mr Walsh and his team with my apparent progress. I had again put on more than ten pounds in weight and was bursting out of my month-old cast. 'How many more of these casts will I have to endure?' I asked the great man.

'If things progress as they have done, and I am confident they will, then a minimum of three more should suffice.'

The thought of spending four more months in this mobile prison was akin to purgatory, but the recollection of my incarceration on the Stryker made it seem like Heaven.

'See you in four weeks,' were his parting words.

21 Agony and ecstasy

Back home again, I continued to gain ground. Most of my time was still spent in bed. But I could now get out and visit the bathroom unassisted. My incredibly generous next-door neighbours still cooked all my meals. Jean was becoming more at home every time she visited, even occasionally doing some tidying and cleaning. She would always bring a little surprise, as she used to call it, for me to eat. Most evenings, some of my friends took me to a local pub for liquid painkillers. Soon I began to sally forth at three or four o'clock in the mornings for short walks around the roads near my house, hobbling along on my aluminium crutches bedecked in my long, brown dressing gown.

Every second Wednesday, I was driven to the Regional hospital. It was a visit I dreaded. I would enter the hospital and go directly to have a blood-sample taken. I would then take the blood to the laboratory and wait an agonising ten minutes or so for the computer analysis sheet. I would then go to the nearest bathroom and say a prayer before opening the unsealed envelope and scrutinising the 20-or-so itemised results. When no more than four or five were outside the stipulated norms, I assumed I was in reasonably good shape. I would then walk the long corridors to the oncology department and sit in a smoke-filled waiting-room with about 20 fellow-sufferers. We were awaiting consultation with the chief haematologist, Dr Paula Cotter, or her chief assistant, Dr Con C Murphy. Most of the women in the queue wore obvious wigs; many of the men sported smart caps or hats. Whenever eye-contact was made, a smile was exchanged, but we rarely spoke to each other for any length. Everyone seemed content to stare at the centre of the floor. What we all had in common was too obvious, and making friends with someone did not seem wise - his or her absence on the next visit might be too disconcerting.

When my turn came, I would always asked straightaway, 'How are the bloods, Doctor?' Any reply other than 'bad' was welcome. I would then be given 25 prednisolone and 25 melphalan tablets. Back home, I would head straight to bed, emotionally drained but faintly euphoric that I had at least a two-week reprieve from morbidity.

Andy was discharged from hospital and taken to his sister's house in Emly, County Tipperary. He invited Jean and myself for dinner the following Sunday.

It was great seeing him away from the hospital environment. He was subdued by his standards, and his voice was an octave or two lower. He had lost some weight and was in apparent discomfort. But his sense of humour seemed reasonably intact.

After dinner, he and I walked along the tree-lined driveway in front of the house. Andy was weak and used a walking stick, while I very much needed my crutches. 'This snail's pace is a far cry from the interval training we used to do on the Belfield tartan track a few years ago,' I remarked.

'I still cannot believe what is happening to the two of us,' he replied in his hoarse voice.

'From now on we will both be getting faster. Some day soon we will be back to normal.'

'You may have some chance,' he said, 'but Fred will always be here to remind me of my condition. Anyway, I am down the same road as Fr Hennessy - and we all know where he is.'

'I know you don't really mean that,' I barked. 'How about all that stainless steel in my spine? I may never be allowed to pass through security at any airport, and with the top of my left hip grafted into my spine, my trousers will never hang straight again.'

Andy grinned: 'I suppose we are both now in the hands of God. Prayer is the only answer.'

This insistence on prayer was all very fine - for we would both have been in a sorry state without it. But there was an awful sense of resignation about Andy that I found difficult to deal with and impossible to endorse.

Following my next visit to the Mater for my new and larger body cast, I drove directly to the presbytery. A rejuvenated and smiling Andy greeted me with the old familiar 'Ah-hum-a-ha-chi!'

I stared at him in disbelief. 'It's a definite miracle. You are really back to your old self. How are you feeling?' Before he had time to respond, I dropped one of my crutches and hugged him around the shoulders. 'It's great to see at least one of us getting back to normal,' I said, as if I had no doubt whatever as to which one of us was the luckier.

'Today has been something of a milestone for me,' he said almost apologetically. 'I went to see my surgeon this morning. He said he doesn't want to see me again for three months. It was great sitting into my car and driving away from his surgery. I admit I thought the writing was on the wall at first, but I'm feeling reasonably well again, thank God. How are things with yourself?'

'It's a cruel world for some of us,' I moaned. 'Just like everything else on this planet, it's not what you know that matters, but who you know. You having a direct line to the Man Above has made all the difference. All those years of clean living have yielded the harvest for the holy priest. The poor bachelor boy has to pay for all the sins that are part and parcel of a carefree single life.' `

We talked and laughed for much of the evening. At one less-inspired moment I asked, 'If it were possible to trade places with me, would you consider it?'

Andy grinned and said, 'There is no doubt you will eventually be back to your own self. But to tell you the truth, when the surgeon mentioned about returning in three months, it was real music to my ears. I think I'll just tolerate old Fred and stay the way I am for now.'

I was overjoyed for Andy. Of all the people I had encountered in my time in this aptly-named vale of tears, he least deserved to suffer. He had done an enormous amount of charitable work and innumerable unselfish deeds. He and a few other talented priests had raised two-and-a-half million pounds through their singing and entertaining and given it directly to the needy. Much of his almost-20-hour day was spent in ministering to his flock. Surely, I thought, he merited better from the God he had so unselfishly dedicated his entire life to.

'How in the name of the Lord did the two of us get cancer?' It was not the first time I had put the question to Andy.

'God Himself only knows.'

'I have a theory about my situation, which at least helps me to keep sane in the darkest hours. I got this cancer in precisely the same area that I damaged my spine almost twenty years ago playing hurling. That just has to be more than coincidental. Every step I took during my athletics career was painful, and that pain stemmed directly from that precise spot in my lower spine. Only minutes before I walked onto the track in the Munich Olympics I had to have a strapping German physiotherapist walk in her stockings across my spine to ease the numbness radiating down my left leg. All this abuse cannot have done any good to my fifth lumbar vertebra.'

Andy roared with laughter. 'You do come up with the most bizarre theories. Still, I suppose there could be some truth in what you say.'

I asked if he had any crazy theory about his own case.

'Seeing the route that Fr Hennessy took, all I can conclude is that the celibacy and all this clean living must be to blame. I never indulged in any of those cancer sticks, and as you know, I was always fairly conscious of my diet. Of course, the whiskey probably did me no favours. Yes, the more I think of it, the damn whiskey most surely be to blame.'

Andy began to recount some of the many binges he and his friend Mick Dunne had shared. Our morbid speculation changed to inevitable laughter when he concluded, 'No, no - it could definitely not be the whiskey. It just couldn't be the whiskey - because if that were the case, the arse would surely have been burned out of Mick years ago.'

Andy's humour had again brightened up a lugubrious conversation. We both then decided that, at least for the time being, we had the big C on the defensive. We agreed there might even be a future for both of us. Andy then turned the conversation to Jean.

'The two of you are evidently getting along very well together, and it appears to me that ye have much in common. The more I get to know her, the more I like her. She is a real gem.'

I laughed. 'That's exactly the word my mother used to describe her.'

'I hope ye will be giving us all a big day out in the not-too-distant future. And don't give me the usual bull about you being too young - and you well into your thirties. Tell me, have you asked her yet?'

'Andy,' I replied, 'she is very definitely everything I have ever dreamed about, and I can tell you I would marry her this very day - but there is one small problem.'

'What in the name of God is that?'

'Surely you know. To coin a phrase, I am medically ozone-unfriendly. With one leg in the grave and the other on a banana skin, I would not even consider popping the question. She might take pity on me and say yes. But if I ever get a clean bill of health, then I will be on bended knee. For now though, I will just have to continue as if nursing my old piano accordion - playing the situation by ear and hoping for the best.'

Andy was fertilising the seeds I had set in my mind from the first evening I took Jean out for that momentous meal, before I had entered St Luke's. I was so grateful to the Good Lord for having her befriend me. But it would be many months, even years, before I could even contemplate marriage. It was even possible she might one day tell me she had to consider her own future - and that I could not realistically be part of it.

I could still be grateful for all the mercies that had befallen me since my illness. My operations had been as successful as could be expected. Andy had been given the all-clear for at least three months. I was now mobile, and even though the fibreglass cast was cumbersome and painful, I was quite adept with the crutches.

The weeks passed; I had my fourth, fifth, and sixth casts fitted; my fortnightly blood-tests were reasonably good; my confidence grew with each milestone.

At last the day arrived for the sixth cast to be removed. Nurse Liz Twomey seemed almost as excited as myself. Willie Murphy had prepared the ground somewhat by using a breadknife to cut a four-inch slit near the top to ease the pressure from my ever-increasing weight; an amused Liz completed the dissection.

Mr Walsh arrived with my X-rays and appeared pleased. 'How is everything looking inside?' I inquired.

'Everything seems to be knitting well together,' he smiled as he showed me the near-perfect graft. 'This crescent-shaped white outline is the bone I took from your hip. It is wedged into the fourth lumbar vertebra and pelvic bone. I also put a sliver of bone adjacent to the metal at the rear to speed calcification. In a year or so, the area where your L5 was will be completely filled in with solid bone and stronger than ever.'

Since the chunk of bone he had taken from my hip would eventually take the exact shape of my spine, I wondered if my hip would grow back.

'No, but it's a very small sacrifice when you think that if nature did not operate in this way, you would never walk again,' he said softly.

'Nature is surely a wonderful thing,' I replied. 'Or should I have said that it is God who is wonderful - or perhaps God and Mr Walsh together.'

He just smiled. 'Everything is looking well from my perspective. See you in three months time.'

Liz fitted me with a strong corset, which gave me the support and confidence I needed in the absence of the rigid cast. I was all for attempting to walk without crutches for the first time, but she adamantly forbade it. I asked for my old fibreglass cast as a souvenir, and Liz harnessed it to my back. Soon, I was joyfully heading for my car. The incredible sense of freedom recalled the first day I walked from the same hospital - just six months previously.

I drove directly to Andy's house. He ran to me and began nudging my back with his knuckles to confirm the cast had been finally removed. 'You look like a young roaring lion who has just escaped to freedom,' he said gleefully. 'Your face even looks different. That vacant stare and expression of pain have gone. You have put back most of the weight you lost. Thank God, things are looking up for you!'

When I told him he looked better than ever, he pointed ruefully to his side. 'Right in that spot there is something continually stinging me. I was thinking of going back to see my surgeon. But my appointment is not for another couple of weeks. I'll persevere until then.'

I lost my temper and insisted he go immediately, but he categorically refused. Later that evening we met his parish priest in the church; I told him about Andy's pain. Fr McDowell unhesitatingly backed me up. 'Sheahan, the voting is two to one. I'll phone the hospital. If there is anything amiss, it can be sorted out very quickly at this stage.'

Andy had great respect for his parish priest. And as this was probably the first time this very pleasant gentleman had issued a direct order to his curate, Andy instantly obeyed.

I travelled the short distance to the hospital with him. His attitude had again changed dramatically; he was petrified beyond belief. 'I know exactly what he is going to say. The game is definitely up this time,' he said, his voice very much devoid of its customary lilt.

'I'll still gladly exchange places with you this very minute,' I said.

'I bet you won't,' he replied.

'I'm telling you I will.' Then we both burst out laughing, realising how childish the exchange sounded.

When we reached the hospital grounds he said, 'I better get it over with as quickly as possible.' With that, he jumped from the car and ran directly into the hospital.

I reclined my seat, loosened my corset, and began scratching. Ever since the cast had been removed, the blood seemed to be pumping through my torso as never before. Sometimes, I itched in a dozen different spots all at once.

After not more than half-an-hour, Andy returned looking surprisingly composed and punching his hand in the air. 'You were right. I'm glad I took your advice.'

'What did he tell you?'

'No lesions - just adhesions, which I believe are quite innocuous. Apparently these adhesions are the result of fibrous tissue abnormally joining together, and a blast or two of radiotherapy will sort them out. I'm heading to your alma mater St Luke's for my first session tomorrow.'

He sounded enormously relieved. Only an hour previously he thought he was going to have his death sentence confirmed; now he had been given a reprieve. The frightened stare had already given way to the normal happy smile. But still the conversation dwelt on things morbid. 'Little did I ever think I would be strapped onto that hissing machine, as you used to describe it, in St Luke's,' he said ruefully.

'It banished my tumour, so it will easily take care of your whatever-you-call-ems,' I said confidently.

Back at the presbytery, Andy insisted on making a meal for me before I left for home. While he set about preparing it, I said I would go and tell his parish priest the good news.

Fr McDowell was obviously expecting the worst. When I told him the good news, he let out a huge sigh of relief and ushered me conspiratorially into his office. 'Thank God they did not give him any bad news directly! I'm confidentially told he gave specific instructions never to be given any alarming news. When I phoned his surgeon lately, he was again deliberately vague. I honestly doubt that he has much of a chance.'

I was stunned and speechless.

'Let's go next door and let's both be really excited about his apparent good news,' said Fr McDowell.

I drove home that evening in deep confusion. My dreaded body-cast was sitting pretty in the back seat telling me I had taken another gigantic step on the road to normality. But Fr McDowell's words haunted me. Why was Andy's surgeon so reticent with Fr McDowell? Did Andy's parish priest misinterpret what the surgeon told him? Was Andy really in serious trouble? For that matter, was I myself being told the whole truth about my own condition? What were people saying about me behind my back? Was my apparent progress due more to my underlying physical fitness than to any diminution of my carcinogenic tumour? Was I, after all, in a better or worse state than Andy? There were myriads of imponderables and no clear answers. And there was little to do but continue to sit and wait and hope.

My spine felt extremely fragile and vulnerable in the small, slender corset. Every ten miles or so, I stopped, reclined the seat, and rested for a few minutes; then I continued my personal relay-race all the way home.

My newfound freedom was hugely therapeutic. For the first time in more than a year I looked almost normal; I was also beginning to feel normal. I began to dispense with the crutches for much of the time, getting about on a walking-stick that, ironically, Andy had given me. I now spent as much of the day out of my bedroom as I in it. I began to visit friends rather than have them visit me.

One such friend was Nurse Kay O'Leary. Kay it was who had visited Mr Walsh before my first operation and offered to pay whatever it would cost to have a neurosurgeon in attendance - then came back to me and told me Mr Walsh had insisted no neurosurgeon was needed. Now read on.

I rushed into her house. 'Kay, I have had fantastic news from Mr Walsh.'

'What did he say?'

'The bones he implanted in my spine have apparently calcified well. The lower section of my spine will soon be rock-solid.'

Kay smiled, but did not answer immediately. Apparently engrossed in thought, she shook her lovely head, took a deep breath, and said, 'I am so very glad to hear that great news. You will never, ever be able to fully appreciate what Mr Walsh has accomplished for you.'

'Are you trying to tell me something I don't know, Kay?'

'When I visited Mr Walsh, I argued that when I worked in the United States, spinal operations much less severe than yours always had a neurosurgeon in attendance. He fully agreed - but he said he had been unable to obtain suitably qualified assistance.

'Mr Walsh told me that if he did not operate, you had no chance of survival. If he did, you had at least a fighting chance. You were young, you had never smoked, and you were mentally and physically strong from your athletics days.'

I was confused: 'But you told me at the time, Kay, that Mr Walsh said a neurosurgeon was unnecessary?'

'That was the most calculated lie I ever told,' Kay confessed.

'Well, I'm glad you didn't tell me the truth. I never realised I was so close to being in a wheelchair for the rest of my life.'

'You wouldn't even have been able to sit up in a wheelchair; you would have been confined in a special bed,' she assured me.

'How will I ever be able to thank the man?' I asked rhetorically.

Kay's story was just another instance of the never-ending round of nightmares that cancer patients have to endure. Once again, I wondered what was really going on behind my back. I had no alternative but to live every hour as bravely as I could. The Damoclean sword that hung over both Andy and me was impossible to forget for even one fleeting moment.

Of course, I deemed myself somewhat more fortunate than Andy, since Jean was becoming more and more a part of my life. I longed to be with her all the time. Everything about her delighted me. Her entry into my life had produced extraordinarily felicitous consequences and seemed to me more than mere chance. Why she bothered with me and all my troublesome and morbid complications was a sweet mystery to me.

One Sunday, driving in the countryside, we found ourselves near where Jean was born and raised. 'I would love to meet your mother,' I quipped.

'Sure,' she said, calling my bluff and taking a by-road for the hamlet of Clondulane.

'Just show me the house where you were born and the school you attended. If your mother saw me with these crutches she would probably have a mass said for me.' I was getting distinctly cold feet.

'Of course. I'm not taking you to see my parents for quite some time yet,' she smiled.

We visited the old schoolhouse and a few local beauty spots. As we headed toward a picturesque old farmhouse at the end of a long tree-lined boreen, she steered the car abruptly into the driveway of a very modern bungalow. 'Just a friend's house,' she said with forced casualness.

I was helped from the car and was being escorted toward the house, when a smiling woman in her fifties approached. She looked uncannily like my lovely driver. 'I'd like you to meet my mother,' Jean said cheekily.

The smiling lady extended her hand in welcome. It took me several seconds to free my hand to shake hers, but in those few seconds, I knew I was in the presence of very special people.

This was one of the greatest moments of my life. A voice seemed to whisper in my ear that here were both my future wife and my future mother-in-law. Soon I met the genial father and brothers and sisters. Their genuine and unembarrassed welcome made me feel I was really Jean's boyfriend and not just a semi-paraplegic cancer patient she had befriended out of kindness. I decided to speak openly about every aspect of my illness - and soon got the impression I was the only person present who was not absolutely sure I was going to make a full recovery.

Later that unforgettable summer's evening, Jean and I walked around the tiny village, while she recalled cherished memories from her apparently very happy childhood. I was enthralled as this pulchritudinous creature reminisced dreamily: 'See that field over there - I had one of the most pleasurable days of my young life in there. When I was about six, my dad taught me how to drive the tractor. On this particular day, he let me harrow the field. He had already harrowed the headlands, and all I had to do was steer the tractor around in ever-decreasing circles, which was not too difficult. All my school-mates were standing on the ditch there watching. I felt like the strongest and proudest girl in the whole world.'

Every field and tree and lane held some treasured memory. It was evident to me that I was now with the real Jean Dorgan - and I was totally enchanted.

My heated imagination started to beguile me. Of course, I had to survive cancer and all its horrific works and ravages - and that would be tantamount to winning the lottery. But to some day marry this heaven-sent creature - that would be like hitting the jackpot a second, even a third, time. Talk
about wildest dreams!

Perhaps, I told myself, I was dreaming too much. After all, I was
extremely lucky to have reached this far. I would have to leave the future
very much in God's hands. But maybe it was no harm to cling onto a dream
that made it easier for me to fight on.

The weeks passed, and as my upper body grew stronger, I was able to dispense with the crutches. My fortnightly blood tests continued, the highs and
lows on the computer printout a source of repeated anxiety, no matter how
unconcerned the experts appeared.

Fr Andy attended for weekly radiotherapy in St Luke's. I accompanied him once - my first time returning since my confinement there. The old
building was as pristine and sterile as ever, but to me there would always be
a morbid stench about the place. The staff were what made it bearable. From
lofty consultants to humble janitors, everyone I met appeared to know me
and to be genuinely delighted to see me walking around. Many of them I had
never met or seen before - but my fame had apparently spread following that
dreadful night when my transfer from operating table to bed went horribly
wrong. My unearthly hysterics had made an indelible impression in those
otherwise-quiet surroundings.

I was delighted to meet Dr Breslin, still speeding around in his wheelchair, and my great friend Dr Hollywood, who had done so much for me. I
thanked them again for all they had done to keep me alive; again, the words
seemed woefully inadequate.

I sought out my favourite nurses, in particular Betty, who had gone
way beyond the call of duty when I could not answer the call of nature. She
was in the lecture theatre instructing a class of students. I burst in and
embraced my embarrassed heroine, saying, 'Girls, this Florence Nightingale
should get a Nobel nursing prize for what she did for me when I was a
patient here last year.' I kissed the red-faced and brown-eyed beauty and
walked out.

I then joined Andy in the familiar queue for laser treatment. This time though, Andy was going through the long and winding corridor for his encounter with the radiotherapy machine, and I was happily waiting on the outside. When he emerged and we were walking to the car, I thought warmly of those wonderfully dedicated and caring medics with whom I had just spent a few cherished moments of reunion. Then I took one final glance back at the edifice where my cancer was first tackled, and silently told myself I would be glad if I were never to set foot in the place again.

We turned the corner from St Luke's - and were back to blessed normality. Andy's niggling pain had abated; I was feeling almost human. Andy was for hitting one of his favourite watering holes; he suggested we rope in his two old sidekicks, Mick 'Whiskey' Dunne and Larry McGuinness.

It was just like old times, full of talk and jokes and, inevitably, Andy's singing. As the night wore on, Andy and Mick conspired to try to shame Larry and myself out of bachelorhood.

'Larry is making an idiot out of Philomena for years. And neither would it kill McSweeney to pop the question to that lovely girl who nursed him throughout his illness. I need a few good days out - I may not have too many left,' joked the merry priest.

'Now, now,' interrupted Mick. 'Let's not be morbid. I need a day out too - I'm as old as all of you together. It's I who have not too many days left.'

Andy knocked back another draught of vintage and persisted: 'It's vital to pin McSweeney down on this subject once and for all. We are at least entitled to some indication.'

I stood up from my seat and leaned against the bar-counter as if about to make an earth-shattering pronouncement. 'I can tell you all right now that if the Good Lord Jesus Christ Himself appeared in front of me this very minute and guaranteed me that the cancer was gone and would not return, then I would rush to the nearest phone and - as they say - pop the question. I am not afraid to admit that I have never met another woman in all my born days that I wanted and needed as much as I want and need Jean Dorgan.' Then, as solemnly as I could, I slowly sat down and reached for my pint.

My three friends did not utter a word. They looked at each other as if to enquire was I serious or pulling their legs. After several seconds, I began to giggle. Soon the giggling turned to laughter. None of them still had an inkling if I was serious or not.

I may have confused my friends but I had no doubt myself. Not once did I ever question my feelings for Jean. Never once did I ask any of my friends the usual question: What do you think of her? From the moment she walked into my ward in the Cork Regional, I knew I wanted to share the rest of my life with her. Every time we met after that glorious day - a day which I began and ended believing I had only a few weeks to live - my affection for her was reinforced. I could have told Andy and Mick and Larry that, if it were possible, I would have married her in that pub that very night, with Andy as witness and the two lads as best men. But marriage would have to wait until my health had improved considerably - and of course until Jean accepted.

The weeks passed, marked by blood-tests and mild chemotherapy tablets every fortnight. I was still numb-legged and spending about half of each day in bed, but my spine was growing stronger. I went for my test results every time on tenterhooks. A good result meant further respite; a bad computer readout could spell the beginning of the end. The stakes were infinitely high.

22 Another Last Supper

The cruelty of the outside world where the 'healthy' reside was brought home to me on a number of occasions. When I began to wade through the hundreds of letters that had lain unopened for several months, one missive informed me that the worldwide patent I had secured on my 'almost-totally-efficient-domestic-heat-exchange-chimney' had lapsed while I was in St Luke's - because I had failed to pay the renewal fees. I had spent three years developing this prototype; when my spine collapsed, I was on the threshold of becoming a very rich young man indeed. Now that dream had vanished.

Further proof of the hard facts of life was provided by my friendly bank manager. During my first three months back at home, the key was always in my front door - for obvious reasons. This gentleman entered at least once a week, reminding me of the monies I had borrowed to develop my heating project and the interest that was accumulating by the day. 'I'm only doing my job. You do realise that,' he would always say. Luckily for him, I had two houses. He decided to take the more valuable one.

A few days after I signed away my house, I was told that this automaton's mother had died from cancer the previous year. He was 'only doing his job', but the full weight of his insensitivity descended on me the instant I heard about his unfortunate mother's fate. For a couple of agonising hours - the one and only time during my sickness - I really wished I were dead. I just did not wish to be a part of the same world in which he and his ilk operated.

But this cruel world was a two-sided coin. The obvious goodness of the other side was easily worth all the trauma and evil. Every morning when I opened my eyes, I personally thanked the Good Lord Himself for placing the sun back up in the sky. The blossoming flowers, the leafy trees, the singing birds, everything that was pure and wholesome, was part of the living God. God became so real and present that I sometimes doubted my own sanity. But the evidence was so overwhelming that I decided to enjoy every second of life that remained in me. It was truly great to be alive.

Twelve months elapsed since my release from hospital. I was feeling better and more confident all the time. Fr Andy was back to his old self and claimed to be feeling as well as ever - apart from the inconvenience of 'Fred'. He had resumed his Thursday night cabaret act with the Holy Show. They were planning a tour of Scotland and England, various television appearances, and a tour of the USA.

Jean and I became more intimate by the day. Friends began to ask when were we getting married. Everyone appeared to think we were 'right' for each other - though we had never discussed the matter. Somehow it seemed unnecessary to spell out our feelings for each other. And anyway, my return to good health seemed a prerequisite to any permanent relationship.

One evening just before Christmas, Jean told me animatedly that her flatmate of almost ten years, Ann Sheehy, was getting engaged to Oliver on Christmas Eve. Almost without thinking, I asked, 'Would you like to get engaged on the same day?'

She replied without hesitation: 'I'd love to.'

We looked at each other in amazement. I scarcely realised what I had said. She had not anticipated my asking, nor I her reply. Magically, all the pieces of the jigsaw of our love seemed to fall quietly into place.

An exhaustive search was conducted, and an over-expensive nine-stone sparkler purchased. Then Jean asked if we could bring the official announcement forward a few days, so as not to clash with Ann's Christmas Eve announcement.

We wined and dined, and I quietly slipped the ring on her finger in a city restaurant. She then steered me to a nearby hotel; Ann and Oliver were there, and Jean wanted Ann to see the ring before anyone else did. On the way, I nipped into a phone box to relate my happy news to Fr Andy. He was naturally delighted, but sounded a little strange.

'Where are you exactly now?' was his rather baffling response. Moments later I phoned my parents; to my amazement, my mother asked the very same question as Andy.

Jean and I hurried to the hotel so as to have one celebratory drink with

Ann and Oliver before closing time. As we entered the foyer, I thought I saw my brother Pat in the distance. 'Doesn't he look right stupid dressed up as a priest,' I said with a grin. Then I noticed a friend, Joe Hartnett - also dressed as a priest. Suddenly it seemed everyone was staring at us - and they were. About 200 friends had thrown a 'vicars and tarts' surprise party for me, as I was almost a year out of hospital. Jean was in on the act and had coupled the function with our secret engagement. I was dumbfounded - but so was everyone else when I announced that Jean and I would be getting married on March 26th.

The next three months flashed by. Jean made most of the arrangements. We invited guests from near and far. I asked all the staff from the oncology department in the Regional along to the 'afters'. I was taken aback, though, when Dr Con C Murphy, the oncology specialist, said to me, 'I hope your wife-to-be is aware of the medical situation. I feel you should tell her that your chances of survival are at best fifty-fifty.' There seemed to be no escaping the stark reality of my predicament. But Jean had no illusions. Once the initial shock had abated, the preparations resumed their momentum.

The big day came, and the morning rain gave way to bright sunshine. For me it was a day straight from a fairytale. My parents and four brothers were together for the first time in years. Most of my friends were present. My health was better than it had been for a long time - as was that of the chief celebrant.

I sneaked a look as my beautiful bride made her regal way on her dad's arm down the aisle. My main feeling was one of incredulity: 'Something like this could never happen to me.' Incredibly, my mind flashed back to that fateful night when Surgeon McGuinness told me I had malignant cancer. Back then, my response had been similar: 'Something like this could never happen to me.' This time, however, those words had an astronomically different meaning.

Every moment of the proceedings was precious. Andy presided with both solemnity and joy. Nearing the end of the ceremony, he sang, 'I'll walk beside you.' His powerful and melodious voice raised goose-pimples on my neck. Several guests could not hold back the tears.

During the reception, the symptoms of my illness contrived to haunt me. My legs were numb; my lower back threatened to cave in. The best man, my chiropractor brother, ordered me to bed for an hour and gave me a vigorous massage. Soon my body and spirits were refreshed. Eventually, 'my wife' and I set out on the first leg of our journey to Louisiana and Texas.

Two weeks later, we visited the Grand Ol' Opry in Nashville, Tennessee. It was from there that I phoned Andy in Philadelphia - this much-in-demand cleric had been invited to the city of brotherly love to baptise a newborn baby. The voice at the other end of the phone said, 'Father is unable to take your call right now. He retired to bed earlier this evening and is feeling quite ill.'

When I spoke to him the following morning, he told me his flight across the Atlantic had turned his stomach upside down. 'Something has gone dreadfully wrong inside. I'm afraid the old problem has returned with a vengeance.'

I assured him that I too was feeling lousy much of the time, but he appeared to be in too much of a panic to even begin to take any solace.

When I hung up the receiver, a heavy numbness engulfed me. Jean had just signalled that she was going across the vast lobby to sneak a close-up peep at Dolly Parton, who was leaving with her entourage. Very much out of character, I did not even bother to look; all I could think of was the agony and turmoil my great friend was once again enduring.

A few weeks later, back from an otherwise delightful honeymoon, I called to Andy's house. Dishevelled and haggard, he greeted me with much less enthusiasm than usual. 'I feel as sick as a dog,' was his opening remark. 'I have a pain in here,' he continued, pointing in agony to the left side of his stomach, 'and it is absolutely murdering me.'

'I thought Fred was at the other side,' I cheekily interjected.

'You are correct, but the pain is exactly where that temporary drain was exiting after the operation. Something in there feels just like boiling oil. I have even gone completely off my food - not to mention my drink.'

I told him I was not feeling much better myself, but that marrying Jean had given me a whole new purpose in life. 'I just have to keep on fighting for her as well as myself. I owe it to her to persevere more than ever. If I even talked of throwing in the towel, she would not hear of it.' I added that what 'the holy priest' needed was a good woman.

'Yes - a rich old widow with a very bad cough,' was his more grimacing than smiling response.

I then began to lecture Andy once again on my 'body-rust' theory. 'Any dent, even on the most expensive Mercedes, will eventually turn to rust if it is not attended to. My brother Terry tells me we all have hundreds of congenital defects which rarely if ever surface. Occasionally though, some unintentional self-inflicted legacy of our so-called progressive age can trigger something off. I have no doubt in the world that your surgeon has rectified your little problem. I am convinced too that the hurling injury I received when I was seventeen was the root of my problem.'

The more I spoke, the more I confused both Andy and myself. Eventually, we agreed that neither of us would mention the word cancer for one full month. With that we set out for the local pub in the hope that the Guinness would drown our woes.

Andy was to visit his surgeon a few days later. I phoned to see what news he had received and was astonished at his reply. 'To tell you the truth, I did not have time to go. Later this week, three of the guys in the Holy Show and I are recording a dozen or more songs in studio. We've been flat-out rehearsing all week with a new professional backing group. But I will definitely phone him at the weekend.'

'Andy, you could be committing suicide without realising it. You really are playing Russian roulette.'

'To tell you the truth, Fanahan, I find it impossible to sit into my car and drive to meet that surgeon. If the game is up, then I would prefer not to find out until the very last moment.' He spoke as if he really meant it.

'Listen to me, Andy. Three times you and I thought I was headed for the bone-yard. Each time I had to face the music, and each time was more difficult than the previous one.'

'But how could I hit the high notes if I had been given bad news?' He laughed. I refused to share in his little joke, but made him promise that as soon as he finished in the recording studio he would immediately contact the surgeon.

As the weekend approached, I became petrified to answer the phone in case it was Andy with bad news. When I had not heard from him by

Sunday dinnertime, I decided to phone him.

'Don't ask me if I made that visit,' was his opening gambit. 'I will def-initely go to the hospital tomorrow - the pain is getting worse by the minute. In fact I could not deliver my sermon today, the pain was so intense.' I threatened to bring the surgeon to him that coming Wednesday - when I was due to visit the Mater - if he had not been to see him by then.

I phoned Fr McDowell, who told me Andy was in dreadful pain but was refusing to see his surgeon. 'I'm terribly worried,' he said.

Before I set out on Wednesday, I again phoned Fr McDowell. He informed me that Andy was being admitted to St Vincent's hospital the fol-lowing day.

Later that evening, I met Andy, and my first question was, 'Did you see the doctor?'

'He is sending me to St Vincent's for more radiotherapy. Apparently the adhesions from the scar have not properly healed. Some ingrowth of fibrous tissue is causing all the pain.' He sounded fairly confident.

'That sounds like very good news to me,' I replied, and without think-ing, continued, 'and since you will be going in tomorrow morning, how about on this occasion I take you out for your Last Supper tonight?'

Andy fixed me with a steely eye. 'You of all people checking up on me behind my back! Who told you I was going in tomorrow morning? Everyone checking on me behind my back scares me stiff.'

I told him it was only people who cared who would take the trouble to check. When I had put him more at ease, I said mawkishly, 'Let's go to the same restaurant where we had my Last Supper and at least have one more good night out together.'

'Let's call it a meal. The Last Supper sounds a bit morbid to me.'

'Andy, I'm paying for it this time, and just like you called it the Last Supper for me, I'm calling it the Last Supper for you,' I was determined on setting precisely the same scenario as he had done more than 18 months pre-viously.

It was a cold September night in the city. We parked the car a distance from the Kingsland Chinese restaurant and hurried there on foot, but I could not travel nearly as fast as he. When we reached the plush, dimly-lit restau-rant, a tiny dapper Asian greeted us. 'You would like a table for two - yes, please?' He took us to a table which by my recollection was not far from where Andy and I had celebrated my 'Last Supper'.

'Sir,' I asked, 'would it be possible to sit at that small table near the window?'

'I am indeed very sorry, Sir. But, as you can see, there is a reserved sign on it.'

'I appreciate that. But it is very important that we sit at that particular table.' I was not about to elaborate, especially with Andy present, so I slipped this gentleman what I thought was a generous banknote. He enclosed it expertly in his white-gloved hand, but made no immediate move to grant my request. He seemed to be weighing up the situation; he scrutinised myself - as if trying to decide if this was a dangerous subsersive, a rich eccentric, or perhaps a silly playboy desirous of a vantage point from which to spot likely victims. He then ran his expert eye over the smaller of the two, and appeared satisfied that he was as he seemed: a respectable man of the cloth. With exquisite tact, he inspected the bribe. The vacant expression told me that if I exactly doubled the stipend we were headed to the desired table. I extracted another note from my wallet, held it by my side but within his line of vision, and nodded toward the table. Our weird body language was in perfect harmony. He quietly removed the plastic sign and then, thief-like, plucked the money from my hand. So subtly and quickly had it all happened, I was sure Andy never noticed.

I felt a strange sense of achievement sitting at the exact table where I had once thought I was really having my very last supper. Something told me an anaesthetic was called for; I ordered a bottle of our genial host's best white wine. The meal had scarcely begun when we called for a second bottle. After a while, a slightly drunk Andy began to unburden himself. 'I suppose I haven't a snowball's chance in hell of surviving,' he said mournfully.

'Your joking, of course,' I said scornfully. 'Cancer only kills ordinary folk like me, but you are a better escape artist than the great Houdini himself. You have nothing to worry about. Anyway, the Man Above needs you too much down here - you are doing more for parishioners and charities than the hundreds of old doddering priests all put together. The one thing though that I cannot understand is why you did not have yourself checked when you first began passing blood, rather than waiting the most of eight months. I heard recently that two thousand young women died from a certain type of cancer last year, and every one of them would be still alive if they had been treated in time. Promise me one thing here and now - that you will do exactly what the medics say from today on.'

I realised I was doing all the talking, something that was generally impossible in Andy's presence. All the time I was speaking, he stared vacantly at me as if pondering what possible damage he had inadvertently inflicted on himself.

'These are really desperate days,' he uttered, almost in a trance. 'We always think it only happens to someone else. It's so easy to give advice and consolation then, but when you yourself are the potential stiff, it's a totally different matter.' I laughed loudly at the mention of the word 'stiff', which usually referred to a corpse in one of Andy's hilarious jokes.

We tried to change the subject and enjoy the remainder of the meal and the wine, but it was obvious I was in the presence of a particularly scared and ailing man. Later, we retired to the same pub as we had gone to after my own Last Supper, so as to 'concentrate on some serious drinking'. As I awaited the two pints of Guinness at the bar-counter, I could see Andy in the mirror, leaning against the wall and surreptitiously trying to supress grimaces of pain. When I returned I pretended I had not seen his contortions, but I knew in my heart he had a huge battle on his hands. He tried bravely to be cheerful, and I gladly went along with his pretences. But after just two pints, he suggested we return to the presbytery.

As we negotiated the not-too-busy city streets, I decided to shorten the journey by taking a quite safe but illegal right-hand turn over the canal. Needless to say, an unmarked police car was skulking at that very junction. They pursued us quietly for a few blocks before sticking the hand-held blue-flashing siren on the roof and ordering us to stop.

I looked in my rear-view mirror and was flabbergasted to see a hand-held pistol coming toward me. Andy recognised the gravity of the situation and quickly raised his reclining seat. 'Don't say a word! Let me do all the talking,' he hissed, very much in control.

One Special Branch type came directly to my door. Another two or three took cover behind their car (seemingly, they had been on stake-out following a tip-off about subversives). I slowly lowered my window. But before the enforcer had time to say a word, Andy spoke in the most confidential and sincere voice imaginable. 'I'm sorry, Officer, about that right-hand turn. It's absolutely my fault. I'm rushing home from the Holy Show.

We've had a few beers, and I'm on the half-seven in Mount View in the morning.'

We were both dressed casually, but there was no doubting that Andy was a real priest. The detective played his torch courteously around our faces, and without saying a word to us, walked behind my car. His voice was just audible: 'Relax. You won't believe what we've got - two of the fucking singing priests - and they're both pissed drunk.' The four of them took to uncontrolled laughter.

Presently, our interrogator walked back to my window and looked in my face. 'Father, drive carefully - and you might say a prayer for me sometime.'

'Thank you, Officer. God speed!' was my saintly and terse reply as I put pedal to metal and headed for the presbytery.

We laughed long and loud about our providential escape. 'You would talk your way out of any situation,' I spluttered. 'I can tell you, the big C hasn't a prayer.'

Despite Andy's hearty laughter at our 'escape', his voice still had ominous reverberations. When I later reflected on our hair-raising run-in with the Special Branch, I thought how ironic it was that they were really the only few precious seconds in more than two years when the ever-haunting word 'cancer' was totally absent from my conscious mind.

The following morning, Andy was up early saying mass. I went along, mainly to see how he would cope with the situation. He walked along the aisle to the altar at a pace which by his standards was slow, and then made a bold effort to pretend to the congregation that everything was normal.

Later, as I bade him adieu, I felt I was deserting him. He was having to face the unknown later that day on his own; I was happily headed home to Jean. A few times I had experienced what he was about to endure; I would not have wished it on my worst enemy.

The mystery deepened later that evening, when Andy phoned me and said the doctor had examined him, given him some heavy painkillers, and sent him home with the admonition to rest completely for several weeks.

Back home, I continued slowly to detach myself from the mental clutches of what I had believed was imminent death. I was still unable to attend funerals or read the death columns in the daily papers. But there were tiny indicators that mentally I was on the mend. For a start, I did not have to close my eyes when some funeral cortege came on the television screen. And I was facing the fortnightly blood-tests and tablets with growing aplomb.

Jean was my greatest comfort and joy. Every moment I spent with her was better than anything in my whole life up to then. She was ever good-humoured and happy. And she had an uncanny knack of sensing even the tiniest diminution in my spirits. Always she would go out of her way to convince me that my problems were more imagined than real.

23 The final heartbreak

After a few weeks, Andy returned to the hospital because his tranquillisers were proving less and less effective; he was kept in. I phoned that night and was told he was taking no calls. I then phoned Fr McDowell; he told me he had learned from the hospital that further tests were mooted, but neither radiotherapy nor chemotherapy had been mentioned. I once again became preoccupied with Andy's welfare.

About a week later, I visited him in St Vincent's and and got a dreadful shock. He had obviously lost weight; his fine mop of wavy hair looked greasy and had taken on a pronounced greyish tinge; the expression on his face was one of pain and resignation. He had a tube inserted into his stomach through his nose and a saline drip affixed to his arm. I wanted to tell him he was looking well, but could only ask how he was feeling.

'Just look at me,' he said in patent agony. 'What do you think of all these yokes attached to me? I can tell you that they are only there because my whole system is breaking down.'

I felt obliged to be unfailingly optimistic with him - almost to the point of cruelty - just as he had been with me. An unwritten code had developed between us whereby the healthier one must arrogantly insist that the other had little or nothing to worry about.

'For the love of God, don't sign your own death warrant, Andy!' I said, with little ostensible compassion. 'You have seen me in situations that were infinitely worse than what you are in now, and I am still going strong. You of all people throwing in the towel! Come on, young man, you have got to be tough! I can tell you, Andy, you don't have to die - but you must believe it!' I asked if his stomach was hurting much.

'It has improved a heck of a lot since they inserted this tube. Before then I was in dreadful pain.'

'This is the last place in the world where anyone would like to be,' I mused. 'But we are lucky to be living in an advanced technical era where so much can be done.'

'You are correct about one thing for sure,' he replied with a brave grin. 'This is definitely the last place in the world to be. I can almost smell the Angel of Death.'

I was lost for words. Andy's frame of mind was frustrating all my efforts to cheer him up. I decided to appeal to that side of the man that very few people knew.

'How about bombarding the Man Above with constant prayer? If there is anyone up there - and believe me, I got a peep in that door - then we better start the petitions right now.' I knew that behind the gregarious and sometimes wild facade there lurked a real priest with a genuine and deep faith.

Andy pondered for a minute. 'I'm sure you are absolutely correct, but I just cannot believe I am in this predicament. I do not know what to do.'

I stared at him and continued, 'I know exactly how you feel - physically and mentally. It's like being on Death Row. All you can do is pray to your Maker, obey everything the doctors tell you, and be as positive as possible. Unfortunately, there is no easy way out. You have just got to be tough. I know you will survive - but it is not going to be easy.'

¯Andy gazed at me and into outer space at the same time. 'You truly are a friend in need, McSweeney - but, my God, what am I going to do?'

Two long weeks passed before I could travel to see him again. Whenever the postman called or the phone rang, I prayed I was about to receive good news. But none came.

I called to see him before I went for my own check-up to the Mater, and was more shocked than ever to see how much he had deteriorated. He had lost several pounds but gained the semblance of a beard. His voice was very low and strange, seemingly because the tube inserted into his stomach had irritated his larynx. I was so distressed I was even unsure how to greet him. At least he was still mobile and obviously aware of his physical appearance.

'What's this beard all about?' I asked, scared that the usual, glib 'You're looking fine' might sound brutally phoney.

He told me his electric razor had ceased to function after falling from his hand into the toilet bowl, whereupon I said I would fetch mine from the car. I was glad of the chance to get out of the room and regain my composure. I stared back at the window of room 305 and said silently, 'Sheahan, you are in deep trouble.' I returned with the razor and told him he could have it for as long as he wished. I then set out to see Mr Walsh.

My visits to the Mater were no longer terrifying, not least because my physical strength had improved enormously. I always enjoyed meeting Mr Walsh; his assertive and pleasant manner made me feel like a normal human being.

My total preoccupation on this trip, though, was with Andy. It occurred to me as I left the Mater that in giving him the razor I may also have given him the impression that I could do without it for the short time he had remaining. I decided to buy him one identical to his own and take it to him straightaway. When I went back with it, I knew I had done the right thing. He grabbed hold of it, gazed at the floor, then glanced at me. Before he uttered a word of thanks, I could see he was thinking to himself that I must hold some hope for his survival.

Mick Dunne and Larry McGuinness were seated by the bed. Mick, in his inimitable way, began recalling that crazy Christmas night less than two years previously, when the circumstances had been similar but the roles of visitor and patient reversed. As he recalled that - and many other funny and bizarre incidents - Andy interrupted. 'All we are short now are a few bottles of Guinness.'

Larry disappeared and returned with a large white sack and a smile. 'Clean clothes in here for Fr Sheahan, I told the nurses at the station.'

'Let the party begin,' said Mick, taking a cluster of keys from his pocket - it was no surprise that a bottle-opener was attached. 'Good health to everyone! And may Andy be back to his old self and out of here in a few days!'

Andy, slowly sipping through a straw, seemed to enjoy the impromptu hooley. When a nurse entered, we thought we would all be evicted, but she pretended not to notice the alcohol. Eventually, Larry persuaded Mick to recite *Daniel Morgan,* but before he had completed the first verse, it was obvious he would have to abandon; Andy was suffering agonies every time he laughed. Our little party came to an abrupt end. As we left the room, Andy was already falling asleep.

We retired to the nearest pub for the inevitable 'post-mortem'. 'What do you think?' was the question to which we all wanted an answer.

'With my hand on my heart,' proffered Mick, 'I can say that Andy is the greatest man I ever had the privilege of knowing. I would even say I have a special kind of love for the man. But seeing what I see up in that very sad ward, and taking the doctor's actions into consideration, I think he is in very serious trouble.'

We began asking futile questions to which there were no plausible answers. Why had he been passing blood for eight or nine months and doing nothing about it? Why did he not do exactly what the doctors told him to do? Why had the most positive and assertive man in the world acted so negatively, since he was surely aware of the plight he was in?

Of course, it's easy to recommend equanimity to others, but when the death-threat is to yourself, rationally objectivity is harder to maintain. All we could agree on was that Andy was now in a desperate predicament, and none of us could do much more than offer prayer and encouragement.

The following Wednesday my own blood-tests gave Dr Con C Murphy cause for concern. 'How have you been feeling lately?' was his first question.

'About the same, Doctor,' I replied. 'my legs are still numb, and the pain in my back is no better, but I'm able to stay out of bed a little longer each day.'

He seemed perplexed. 'How is your wife doing?' he inquired.

'Great, thanks,' I assured him.

He scratched the top of his bald cranium and searched for the right words, while I swallowed my Adam's apple.

'I hope you don't mind me asking this question,' he said, with uncharacteristic hesitancy. 'You don't have to answer it.'

'Ask me what you like, Doctor. I'm immune to bad news at this stage.'

'How are you getting along with your wife?'

'Absolutely great. She's the greatest thing that ever happened to me. She has given me a new purpose in life. I honestly believe that only for her I would still be confined to bed or worse. But - what exactly are you driving at, Doctor?'

Embarrassed, he again groped for words. 'I'm sorry - I didn't intend to startle you. But your blood count is very low. I thought something might be bothering you.'

I told him about Andy.

'That explains everything,' he said. 'But you must now concentrate on your own welfare. You may be improving, but you have a long road ahead of you.'

I felt a mighty sense of relief driving away from the hospital. My whole body was still trembling from the shock of those few moments when I thought I was about to be hit with disastrous news.

A few days later I undertook my weekly pilgrimage to see Andy. These visits all followed a pattern. I would first call to the nurses' station to find out the latest news. 'He is feeling rather well today,' I was told.

'Does that mean he's on the mend?' I blurted. She shrugged her shoulders and said nothing.

I hurried to his room and was pleasantly amazed to find him in the bathroom and not on his bed. 'Delighted to see you out of bed and looking so well. The nurse said you were feeling good,' I said.

'So you were doing some checking up on me too,' he replied sternly.

'I'm a glutton for news, particularly good news,' I countered. It was great to see him moving around. I asked him if he would like to take a walk at the rear of the hospital. 'There's a beautiful golf-course immediately behind, the sun is blazing down, and the air is like champagne. If you feel like it, I'll ask a nurse,' I said enthusiastically.

Andy eyes almost popped out of their deep sockets. Clearly, he wanted to be as far as possible from the ward. 'I'd love to,' was his immediate reply.

I rushed to the nurses' station and was told one of them would come with us. 'No,' I insisted, 'we'll travel under our own steam - otherwise he'll feel like an invalid.' I eventually agreed that someone would follow us - but at a discreet distance.

I was as excited as Andy was when the nurse arrived and detached the feeding drip from his arm. I removed the top of his pyjamas and uncovered the emaciated rib-cage of a once-muscular athlete. 'I look like one of those poor starving Biafrans we used to hear about long ago,' he said.

'What do you expect? You haven't eaten in ages. After a walk in the fresh air, you'll have an appetite like a horse.'

It was not easy fitting him with his tracksuit. The motorised suction tube that siphoned his stomach juices through his nose into a bag attached to his side had to be accommodated. And threading his bony arms through his sleeves hurt him cruelly.

Finally, we were on our way. As we passed the glassed-in nurses' station, everyone acted as if nothing unusual was happening. One nurse gave me a sly wink that said they were glad to see Andy being given a taste of normality.

The vibrations of the lift obviously hurt him, but he tried heroically to hide the fact. Outside, a warm evening sun greeted us. 'My God, it's great to be away from that ward even for a short time,' he exclaimed. 'I honestly thought that the next time I would be brought out of there would be on a six-by-two plank.'

Very quickly, he perked up and became positively entranced with his surroundings. 'Look at those flowers! Did you ever see anything so beautiful? And the trees - aren't they magnificent! Do you hear that bird sing? Oh, my God, I've never experienced anything like this before! It's like being in the Garden of Paradise.'

His astonishing rejuvenation moved me as nothing had ever done before. I felt as much in a trance as he. 'Everywhere around us, all the time, is the Garden of Paradise,' I pontificated. 'But we rarely if ever appreciate it. In fact, that very blackbird there could easily be the Good Lord Jesus Himself in disguise, trying to tell us something.'

Andy was tickled pink by my pious outburst. 'I sure never thought I'd see the day when I would hear you speak in tongues, McSweeney,' he smiled.

We walked along soaking up the glorious sunshine and the almost tangible peace and tranquillity. I was absentmindedly watching four golfers approach the green immediately behind the rear fence of the hospital, when I noticed that Andy's jerky stride was quickly becoming puppetry as he fought to stay upright. I suggested he had had enough of his first long excursion in several weeks; he quickly agreed: 'I would love to stay in this peaceful spot for the rest my days, but I think it's best I return to bed.'

As he struggled back toward the hospital entrance he panicked and tried to run, staggered forward like a ghost, and reached the door before me. He threw himself against the wall and waited until I opened the door a few long seconds later. Conveniently, a wheelchair was at hand. 'Can I borrow your chair, please?' I asked the attendant. He acted as if there by coincidence, but his wink confirmed he had been sent to look after Andy.

Back in Andy's room, I remove his tracksuit and dressed him in his hospital attire. 'Never in a million years could you know how grateful I am to you for taking me back to the outside world,' he said. 'Strangely, for the first time, it doesn't seem so bad being back in this room again.'

As I was leaving the hospital, I was beckoned into the nurses' station and asked, 'How did Father Sheahan enjoy his walk?'

I told them how he had relished it, but remarked that he was in overwhelming pain. 'Has he hit rock-bottom yet, or is there any hope for him?' I asked.

'We were delighted to see him get out for a few minutes - he is such a lovely man. But it is amazing that he cannot come to terms with his condition,' was the sympathetic reply.

'Please tell me,' I persisted: 'Is he going to survive?'

'Pray for him and be good to him, and there is always hope,' was the obviously tactful reply. I decided to ask no more questions.

I walked across the car-park feeling miserable. I gazed up at the third floor window and wept inwardly to think that my great friend had possibly made his last journey alive from Room 305.

I phoned Andy a few days later; he told me his friend Fr John Keogh was taking him to Medjugorje, Yugoslavia, for a week. I immediately phoned Fr John and told him the trip would kill Andy. 'I believe you,' he replied. 'But he said it was a dying man's last wish to visit that holy shrine. I was so moved by the way he said it that I had to agree.'

By a coincidence, Jean and I had planned a holiday in Southern Portugal for the same week. It rained incessantly every day while we were there, so we decided to detour to Fatima, another famous Marian shrine, in the north of the country.

Once back in Ireland, I immediately phoned John to ask how was their trip. 'Fulfilling, but the saddest experience of my priestly life. Poor Sheahan had a really tough time - he was constantly in dreadful pain.' John went on to tell me that Andy had concelebrated mass with a large group of priests but had to remain seated during the entire ceremony.

Fr John further revealed to me that not once since becoming ill had Andy ever mentioned the word 'cancer' to him, even though he had visited

Andy in hospital every week. In this context, said Fr John, something notable had happened in Medjugorje: an extrovert American priest said to Andy in John's presence, 'Gee, Father, I believe you have cancer. Tell me, how are you coping with it?' Andy barely answered, but thenceforth seemed more resigned to his illness. John felt that was a significant moment: the small, secretive cancer society of Andy, myself, and perhaps Fr McDowell had been breached.

Jean and I headed directly from the airport to St Vincent's. In the nurses' station, I was told Andy was a changed man since his return from Medjugorje. 'He is much more relaxed and at peace with himself,' a nurse assured me.

When I entered the ward Andy was lying still in bed. As soon as I told him Jean was in the corridor, he perked up, and his voice became noticeably stronger. Jean put on a brave face and said, 'You're looking great for someone who has been through so much. We travelled specially to Fatima to pray for you and brought a little present back from there for you.' She unwrapped a small statue of the Blessed Virgin and handed it to him. His eyes bulged in their sunken sockets as he gazed on the venerated icon. He grasped the plastic and wooden object with such vigour and passion that for a split moment I thought we were about to witness a real life miracle. Andy's deep faith was being publicly revealed for the first time. His response was also graphic evidence that he now accepted he was totally dependent on divine intervention.

He gave us a brief description of his painful but spiritually-rewarding journey. 'It was so peaceful and beautiful. I felt as if I were so much closer to God than ever before. I am very glad to have visited there.'

Jean took a much more confident approach than I and tried to convince him that he was now over the worst. Andy did his utmost to be brave while Jean was present, but soon his strength began to desert him. He still mustered enough energy to ask her mischievously if she had 'any news' after her holiday.

'All I can tell you is, if we should ever be so blessed, we will definitely call it after you - Andy or Andrea,' she said. Andy gave a great big smile of approval. She hugged and kissed him. As we bade him farewell he was nodding off to sleep.

The usual 'post-mortem' took place as we drove home. 'I got the greatest shock of my life when I hugged him,' said Jean. 'It was like holding one of my ten-year-old students. You were as thin once, but somehow I always knew you would pull through. As for poor Andy - I just don't know.'

A couple of days passed, and Andy phoned saying he was about to get more radiotherapy. My heart leapt - this suggested there must at least be some morsel of hope. But when I called the following week, I was told at the nurses' station that he himself had demanded the radiotherapy; he would be receiving no more. I was also asked not to enter his ward until the priest attending him departed. I waited for about half-an-hour until Fr Keogh emerged. 'What's up, John?' I asked.

With tears running down his face he said, 'Andy asked me to help him make out his will. My God, it was heartbreaking! Go in there and do not pretend anything. Just do your best to cheer him up.'

Andy looked much more relaxed than Fr John. 'You just missed the Keogh. Did you see him on your way in?'

'Yes, he told me you were tired after the radiotherapy.'

'He helped me make out my will,' he said, his voice full of resignation.

I looked him straight in the eye: 'Andy, I find it hard to believe that you were the guy who almost single-handedly talked me out of dying. You were the one who convinced me I was going to survive. Now, when you have hit rock-bottom and are on the mend, you do something that must be devastating to your confidence. That's the most stupid thing I ever heard of. You should have waited until your illness was behind you.'

I did not know if I was making any sense, or helping him in any way, or even hurting him. But there was so little I could say.

He was weaker than ever after the exertions of making out the fatal document. The sac attached to his nasal tube and gradually filling with his stomach juices was repulsive, since it clearly showed that his puny frame was being relentlessly siphoned away through his nose. We spoke for a little while, and I did my utmost to cheer him up, but my ill-timed visit had taken its toll.

Two days later Andy phoned me. His voice was pathetically weak. 'When are you calling up this way? I haven't seen you in ages.'

I instantly knew there had to be something amiss. 'I'll see you in a few days,' I replied, but Andy did not seem to respond. All I could hear were intermittent gasps for air followed by exhaling groans. I continued to talk into the receiver, but signalled to Jean to run next door and phone the hospital. It was the most depressing phone conversation of my life. The greatest friend and gentleman I had ever known was pleading for help, but I just did not know what to do. After a few minutes a nurse's voice said, 'Father is going to take a nap now. He is a little tired. Thank you.'

I ran into the bathroom before Jean returned, got down on my knees, and cried like a baby. As I slouched on top of the cool enamel bath, my mind flashed back to the innumerable escapades we had shared. I thought of the hilarious holidays we had spent in various parts of the globe. I recalled the many hundreds of miles we had run in training and his frantic roars of encouragement from trackside during my races. I reflected on the times when, on my piano accordion, I did my best to accompany his powerful and melodious singing voice, which always had the audience yelling for an encore. I thought of our shooting and fishing expeditions, when Andy was at his most daring and adventurous. But above all I thought of Andy the ever-reliable, exuberant, and jovial friend - the man loved by everyone fortunate enough to know him. Now he was silently screaming for a little of the help he had always given in abundance - and I felt so desperately inadequate.

The key in the door signified Jean's return. 'Did you get the message?' she called.

Not wanting her to see my distress, I flushed the cistern and, against the noise of the gushing water, shouted, 'Yeah.' Jean passed into the kitchen, while I gathered my wits. As I stood up, I was startled to see that my tears had flowed from one end of the bath to the other.

When I emerged from the bathroom, Jean ran to me, her eyes filled with tears, and said, 'It's just not fair. May God love poor Andy! No-one should have to endure what he is going through - especially Andy. I pray that God will take him quickly.'

A few days later I called to see him. The nurse told me not to stay long - he was exhausted after visits from the papal nuncio, three bishops, and several priests. When I entered his room I almost collapsed with shock. His wavy locks had turned almost totally grey; his face was skull-like and waxen. Only his pearly white and symmetric teeth were unchanged, as I observed when he smiled in greeting.

He had not eaten in several weeks and was being sustained only by the liquid drip. The motorised suction tube was still taking the redundant juices from his stomach. But his mind was crystal clear.

'Speak to me, but don't ask me any questions,' he said in a barely audible whisper.

Temporarily at a loss, I stupidly asked, 'How are you feeling today?' Fortunately, he thought I was joking, and just smiled. I began relating what news I could think of. He lay there motionless except for the occasional nod of his head to signify he knew what I was saying. Occasionally he would grimace, unable to deny the turmoil going on within his tortured frame. As I spoke, I gazed at his almost unrecognisable face and thought of Jean's words: 'It's just not fair.' All this monstrous suffering was surely not what Andy deserved. How could a loving God inflict such agony and anguish on one of his creatures. Maybe the atheists had a point - surely this was compelling argument against the existence of a benevolent God.

And yet a mysterious aura surrounded Andy - as if God were present in a special way in that room. I felt goose-bumps rise on my kneck and shoulders. My heart began to flutter. I became so scared I wanted to run from the room. I looked around, half-expecting to see some apparition from Heaven - but my very palpable Friend remained invisible. I then looked back quickly at Andy, thinking he might have departed this life at that precise moment. He was still there, and apparently unaware of my close encounter with Divinity. 'Keep talking,' he urged. 'I'm listening to every word you are saying.' Just then one of his Holy Show colleagues entered; I left soon after.

Just before Christmas my father and brother Terry accompanied me to see Andy. Like everyone else, they were stunned by his deterioration. Again Andy put on a brave show. Dad acted as if Andy was in full health, and related stories of himself and Andy's father when they were young, which elicited an occasional, courageous smile.

We were forbidden to stay long. I shook hands with Andy and wished him a happy Christmas. I glanced back at him as I passed out the door and wondered if I was seeing my best friend alive for the last time. To my astonishment, he had raised his head off the pillow and was gazing after me. I walked to my car, wondering if he had been thinking the same thoughts.

These were absolutely heartbreaking moments and hours, when time stood still and I felt I would literally smother with grief.

Back at home my phone rang incessantly. One call was from Scotland and an old seminary classmate of Andy's. When I told Fr Con O'Leary the scenario he said he would fly to Dublin immediately. I urged him not to arrive before Christmas, because Andy had all his mental faculties and might take the timing of such a visit as proof that he was finished.

Con took my advice and called to St Vincent's on St Stephen's Day. He also took my advice to go alone, but to call to the nurses' station and ask a nurse to accompany him. His first reaction on entering the ward was that he was not in Andy's room. He told me later how relieved he was that he had not entered on his own - he would probably have walked out thinking he was in someone else's room.

'To tell you the truth, Fanahan, if we went back to Annakissa grave-yard and exhumed his ninety-seven-year-old dad, I suspect he would look better than poor Andy. We are really depending on miracles.'

The word miracle came back to mind two days later when I heard Andy had sent for the man he believed would one day be pope. 'Any fellow that wears the dog-collar and can sing as well as myself - and has been private secretary to three pontiffs - has all the credentials to be a really great pope,' Andy used to tell me.

Bishop John Magee of Cloyne went straight to Andy's bedside. A nurse gently shook Andy awake. 'Father, there's someone here to see you.'

Andy opened his eyes. 'Is that you, Keogh?'

'No, it's Bishop Magee to see you,' the nurse replied.

Andy clutched the hand of his hero, and in an emotional but very weak voice repeated, 'Thank you so much, Bishop! Thank you so much!'

Andy's deep faith and his respect for the man who had been close to three of Christ's vicars on earth must have persuaded him that this was his final chance of divine intervention. The bishop held my best friend's hand and prayed softly into his ear. He then administered the last sacraments as the exertions of the encounter plunged Andy back into a fitful sleep.

Every hour of every day now became a living nightmare. Each time the phone rang my heart missed a beat. Miracles are rare, but they do occasionally happen. The whole scenario was paradoxical, not least because it was he and not I who now lay so helpless in a hospital bed. Andy was the most indestructible person imaginable - but the Titanic had been indestructible too.

I had intended travelling to see him a few days after Christmas, but everyone advised against it. Close friends were now hinting that I should be prepared to 'let go'. But even when reports reached us that he had lapsed into unconsciousness, I still did not abandon hope. Soon the phone would tell me he was conscious again and saying his prayers.

Very early on the morning of December 30th I reached for the phone. Larry McGuinness's was the forlorn voice at the other end. 'How is Andy doing'? I quickly asked.

His choking voice said, 'I'm sorry to tell you, but he died peacefully at 1.40 this morning -'

I looked at Jean and she was crying too. This moment had to be the lowest of my entire life. Jean clung to me and kept repeating, 'May God rest his soul,' and, 'Thank God all his suffering is over.' My heart was breaking. I did not know what to say or do.

The next few days I spent in an abysmal stupor. A huge crowd travelled to the hospital mortuary. I walked in through the crowded entrance, clutching Jean's arm. Everyone appeared to be crying. It was not easy being brave in that large room which contained the body of my best friend. I looked frantically everywhere but at the coffin. My eyes travelled from face to face - but eventually had to look toward the wooden box. Instantly my body began to shake uncontrollably, and my legs turned to jelly. I then found myself lying on the grass at the rear of the mortuary.

'How near are we to Andy?' I asked Fr Brown.

'He's just inside the wall,' he replied.

'Please take me away to the far side of the car-park,' I pleaded. Soon I was sitting in my car while Andy's friend and fellow-cleric, who had been born and raised next-farm to Andy, sat with me until the cortege departed for the parish church.

I stood with Jean at the rear of the church as the papal nuncio, three bishops, and more then 100 priests sang and prayed for Andy's soul. Several of his priestly friends eulogised the dedicated and hardworking singing priest. It was a beautiful and touching ceremony. Only one speaker struck a discord: 'Even though his extraordinary talent and energy was an inspiration and an example to all of us, he was still not a very spiritual person.'

I knew the remark was well-intentioned, but felt it my duty to reveal a side of Andy which possibly no-one else had been privy to. Later that night, I asked a dazed Fr McDowell if I could say a few words from the altar prior to the burial in Annakissa.

The following day we travelled behind Andy's remains on the long, sad road homeward from Dublin. I felt desperately lost and confused all the way. I wished I had had the courage to look at Andy in his coffin. Now a crazy voice within me was telling me he might still be alive, though the reality was all too obvious. When the cortege stopped at the mid-point of the journey and everyone trooped into the hotel, I sat alone in my car within sight of the hearse. It seemed profoundly cruel to leave my deceased friend on his own.

Having arrived in Annakissa, I sat at the back of the overflowing church as Monsignor Magee delivered a moving oration. Then I rushed home to compose my own tribute for delivery prior to the burial the following day. I took a pencil and began scribbling:

My dear people,

I would like to say a few words about my great and dearly departed friend. My words probably echo the sentiments of many of the lay members of the congregation who had the privilege of knowing Andy. Coming from the same village, I knew him from my youth. To me, more than anything else, he was always a most dependable and trusted friend. I was always aware of the many facets of his various talents. His delightful singing voice gave enjoyment to many and also accumulated millions of pounds for several charities. His laughing voice, his love of sport, his infectious personality, and his ever-giving generosity endeared him to almost everyone that had the good fortune of knowing him.

Never ever did he attempt to indoctrinate me or anyone of his pals with religion or dogma. Still, his obvious lack of constraint strangely had a more salutary and efficacious effect on many of us. But it was in recent years when I myself had contracted cancer - the same disease that eventu-

ally sapped away his life - that, ironically, I really got to know Fr Andrew Sheahan the priest. On the three occasions that he administered the last rites to me - and it seemed apparent that I would be in Heaven long before himself - his incredible faith and especially his astounding devotion to the Mother of God was my single most saving grace. He gave me both a purpose to die and a purpose to endeavour to fight to stay alive. Fortunately for me, my hour had not come. But incredibly, within a few days of my leaving hospital, Andy entered it.

The physical pain and suffering, the mental anguish and distress, which his lucid senses had to endure defy all worldly logic. Still, though he loved life more than most, his departing set an example that will live forever with all of us that were close to him. As his friend Fr Brown said to me outside the mortuary, 'There is really no need now to pray for Andy. All we must do is pray to him.' May God have mercy on his sweet soul.

Before the requiem mass I asked Fr McDowell to beckon me when it was time to approach the altar, because I was still not sure if I could muster the courage to pass near the coffin. I sat with Jean, in a trembling daze, near the rear of the church. A lone piano accordion played the funeral hymn that Andy himself used to sing: *I'm going Home.* Choirs of singers bathed the church in a spiritual, though eerie, atmosphere of which Andy would have been proud. But when it was time for me to speak, my eyes were too filled with tears to even see Fr McDowell on the altar.

All through the reverential rite a strange sensation kept telling me Andy was very much present and enjoying the pomp and ceremony. In my mind's eye I could see him floating high among the lofty rafters of the old church, and passing his own inimitable comments on the rigid solemnity of his final worldly chapter. Through the occasional break in his hearty laughter I could almost hear him say, 'Well, just listen to the Keogh with his sparkling Grecian 2000 hairdo and his doing his utmost to impress. Still, the genuine tone of his voice tells all. And those bishops, whom I scarcely knew, with that sanctimonious look on their faces, and they doing their damnedest to balance those stupid-looking mitres on their heads. And all those hundreds of clerics - half of whom I never met - and of the other half only Gould, Keogh, and Brown took the trouble to come to my twenty-fifth anniversary mass. And all those women crying - that is something I never bargained for. And McSweeney - that surely was a turn-up for the books when I arrived up here before he did. And I once telling him he should be prepared to let go because it was senseless enduring all that torture when the surgeon told him he had malignant cancer. He must be having a good laugh at me now.'

I emerged from my reverie into the overwhelming reality of Andy's finale as the coffin was borne along the short journey to graveside at the rear of the church. When the coffin passed my pew, my teeth rattled and my body shivered as I prayed a silent adieu to my great friend.

Lost in a flood of tears and a sea of people, I slowly followed the elevated casket at a distance. Unable to approach the graveside and temporarily separated from Jean at the perimeter of the crowd, I stood alone for a while. Final prayers were recited, and when the coffin was lowered, the bishops and priests made their usual beeline from centre-stage. As we drove down the hill from the tiny country cemetery, I glanced back, saw the gravediggers cruelly shovelling clay down on top of Andy's coffin, and wondered what this world was all about.

24 A brand new Andy

Life continued. But life without my celestial friend would never be quite the same again. Losing such a close pal under any circumstances is not easy, but to continue battling in my beleagured condition was near impossible.

Jean was now my sole passion in life. My battle for health went on. The numbness in my right leg slowly abated, but my left hardly improved. I began doing gentle exercise and found that a sedate stroll on a level golf-course helped my circulation greatly. Soon I was tinkering with my long-neglected clubs and proving to myself that the old coaching adage about swinging the club slowly produced results better than had my former exuberant lash.

Hospital tests continued for more than a year. I still took mild chemotherapy tablets as a precaution - until the day Dr Con asked me if I had any children. 'Your wife will never conceive while you are on that medication,' he told me. 'I'll take you off them, and we will monitor you with more frequent blood-tests.'

Three months went by, and one day Jean set out on an hour's journey to visit a girlfriend. Fifteen minutes later she phoned me, her words almost indecipherable with excitement. 'I am, I really am!' she kept saying. 'The doctor said the test was positive.' I could scarcely believe my ears. I was to be a father.

We agreed we would drive to both our parents' houses that evening and deliver our great news personally. But a couple of hours later the phone rang again, and this time Jean was crying. My heart sank, but when she told me she had written off two cars by driving hers head-on into another, and that no-one was seriously injured, I had heard the second-greatest news of my life. Jean was fine; so too was little Andy or Andrea.

Five months later my interest in golf had progressed to competition. The satisfaction of carding a respectable score was wonderful. But the sense of accomplishment derived from occasionally out-driving an opponent made me feel as if the word 'cancer' had never been in my vocabulary. Then my sky fell in again.

I was competing in a post-Christmas tournament, and had played the first five holes better than usual, when I attempted to drive the ball the full distance on the par-four sixth at East Cork golf club. My balance seemed perfect as I deliberately described a wide and slow backswing with my metal driver. There was a slight following wind; perhaps I could reach the green. The temptation was too great; I launched myself at the little white orb - but found myself lying on the grass with 20 or more players gaping down on me.

My brother Terry, home on holiday from the USA, took command. Before I knew what was happening, I was rigidly strapped in the back of an ambulance and threading the long and lonely road back to the Mater hospital, while Jean held my head against her six-month bump and kept telling me everything was going to turn out fine.

It wasn't easy lying there paralysed, peering out the rear window at the road along which Andy's body had been carried almost exactly two years before. Nor was it easy knowing that the chances were I would soon be following in his wheeltracks. The thought of leaving Jean and never seeing my unborn baby tormented me every inch of the journey.

An oncology specialist was summoned from his Christmas holiday as the barrage of tests began. Later that night I was taken to St Vincent's ward of the Mater. At 1.40am I looked at my watch and trembled when I remembered that at that precise time two years past, Fr Andy had died in this same city and in a hospital bearing the same name as this ward.

The initial results gave me some hope. After a few days I was taken to my old ward, St Agnes's. It was all too much like old times. The tests and the long hours awaiting the results were as difficult as ever. I could not sit up or get out of bed. Jean stayed with friends and did her utmost to convince me I was going to survive. Then, after two scary weeks, Mr Walsh arrived with the verdict.

'You know my style well by now,' he began. 'The problem has spread to your upper spine - the eighth thoracic or T8 vertebra, to be precise. Dr Paula Cotter and Dr Con C Murphy have expressed a desire to have you transferred back home, where they will treat you.'

Once again, devastating news. But Mr Walsh always made me feel he would find a way. When I asked how the cancer had reappeared when my constant blood-tests revealed nothing sinister, he said, 'It's unusual, but I'm told that in about five percent of cases this is a possibility.'

The journey back to the Regional took almost nine hours on a snow-covered road. I kept thinking of Mr Walsh's 'five percent' comment, and of my brother's advice of more than three years previously: if plasma cytoma progressed to multiple myeloma, my chances of survival were five percent. Those five percents, Jean, and our unborn baby were all I could concentrate on.

When I arrived at the hospital at about six in the morning, Dr Murphy was waiting for me. Con C being a very amiable and gentle man who had looked after my welfare for two years, I felt I could be very direct with him. 'How bad is my situation now that it has apparently spread?'

'Very serious,' was his terse reply. 'We must act immediately. We have no time to do a biopsy. If we leave it any longer, it might be too late.'

'That's fine with me,' I replied almost enthusiastically. 'The last thing I want to do is die.'

My feeble effort to inject a little wit into the proceedings was intended to cheer myself up. Dr Con C ignored it. 'I have discussed your case at length with Dr Seamus O'Cathal of the radiotherapy department. We can give you one direct session of radiotherapy for eight minutes and then put you on an extensive course of chemotherapy, or we can spread the radio-therapy out over several weeks. We feel it's best to begin the eight-minute session immediately.'

While I was being prepared for my journey to the radiotherapy depart-ment, Jean arrived and set about convincing me I had been diagnosed on time and had absolutely nothing to fear. She accompanied me as I was stretchered to the large room with the eight-foot-thick reinforced mass con-crete walls and the two-ton leaded door, the building of which I as resident engineer had supervised ten years previously.

The hissing of Dr O'Cathal's machine brought back old and unwel-come memories. But the painless laser treatment was soon finished, and when I returned to my room I was told I would be on my feet the following day. Events proved rather different.

The physiotherapists arrived the following morning and told me to try getting out on the floor. I could not raise my shoulder even a fraction of an inch; attempts to elevate me onto a pillow failed miserably. Dr Con C was obviously perturbed; he explained to me that bone was living tissue: if direct weight were not quickly put on it, it would collapse. Eventually it was conceded I should be given a respite, and make another effort the following day.

The following day I had not improved one iota; I warned the physiotherapists I could not even move in the bed. Dr Con C caught me by the hand and made to pull me up; I roared in agony. Finally, he said he would return in the evening for another try. But I would simply have to be taken out onto the floor.

Later that morning I asked Dr Dermot Maloney - a young intern and a very promising 400-metre runner - if there was any machine in the physiotherapy department that would elevate me gradually. He answered yes, there was a remote-controlled bed-like contraption; he would personally supervise the process. He also suggested I be transferred onto a bed that could be electrically tilted. This was done, and I could now raise myself almost 45 degrees.

Dr Murphy felt the 45-degree angle was insufficient, and that I should be transferred immediately onto the remote-control bed. The following morning I was transported to the physiotherapy department and moaned and groaned my transfer onto the leather-covered pivotal platform, to which I was secured by four strong straps. With my feet firmly anchored against a protruding step, I began to control my own rate of elevation. Once I passed 45 degrees the weight of my upper body began to exert unbearable pressure on the irradiated vertebrae. I lowered myself quickly, then tried several times to raise myself, but was thwarted each time by a dagger-like pain.

The following day I managed to maintain a slightly steeper angle. Dr Con C insisted I hoist myself to the vertical, but try as I might, I could not.

Early the following morning, as I was being strapped to this pivotal machine, two of the chief physiotherapists hovered ominously nearby. As soon as I had attained the loftiest angle I could tolerate, the two ladies loosened all the shackles and snatched the remote-control unit from my hand. Before I could protest, I was hauled upright and steered by my upper arms away from the machine. I was so stunned and in such pain that, rather than cry out, I had to concentrate all my energies on remaining vertical and conscious. I was more-or-less frogmarched a distance of 50 yards, and all the time I could sense bones being crushed in my upper spine. The pain was beyond words. When finally I was carted back to the ward I summoned Dr

Paula Cotter and told her I was never going through that experience again.

I spent the next two weeks totally immobile in bed, but sitting up, for as much time as I could tolerate, at 45 degrees. I was still in this confined state when the dreaded intravenous chemotherapy began. Dr Murphy set up the drip and inserted a long needle into a vein in my arm. A sachet of saline solution first flushed the veins. Then a larger sachet containing about two pints of murky liquid was attached. While this was dropping into my veins, Dr Con C mixed a yellowish cocktail and injected it into my arm. The burning sensation made me yell. He slowed down the rate of injection, and the hot pain abated. After 30 minutes the plastic container of murky liquid had emptied, and a further saline solution was attached to rinse out my veins.

I had been given my first session of the heaviest possible dose of chemotherapy. Now all I had to do was wait for the sickness to arrive and my hair to fall out. I consoled myself that the look on the faces of my friends when they saw my bald head would make up for the embarrassment and inconvenience.

Three days came and went without undue sickness. Nor was there the expected avalanche of hair on my pillow. Better still, the intense pain had subsided sufficiently for me to roll over on my stomach. Soon I was able to rotate so far as to allow my legs and knees to reach the ground. Then, amazingly, I was able to push myself upright and stand at the side of the bed. The pain was intense, but I was strong enough to bear it. Dr Con C was pleasantly surprised; he told me I could return home as soon as I was confident enough. Later that day I was happily on my way home with my pregnant wife.

It was now almost the end of January, and the baby was due in mid-March. I was confident I would still be above ground by then, and thus be vouchsafed the inconceivable joy of seeing my own and Jean's baby.

Having to be helped to the bathroom at home was an unwelcome embarrassment, but within a week I was able to manoeuvre under my own exertions.

Within days I was back for another chemotherapy session - I was to have one every three weeks. The procedure was the same as before, but the aftermath was very much different. As Jean drove me home, my stomach began to convulse and my head to burn. When I reached home I swallowed an 'anti-sickness' tablet, went to bed, and endured the evening with much difficulty.

The following morning cruelly bore out the classic stories I had heard of chemotherapy sickness. I passed much of the next three days on my knees in the bathroom, my head within safe reach of the toilet bowl. I was taking valium three times a day and doloxine-codeine four times a day to quell the new pain from the collapsed vertebra. This band of inordinate pain encircling my upper rib-cage was the direct result of the large dose of radiation that collapsed that vertebra. After four days the nausea had subsided, but the stinging chest pain persisted.

Three weeks later, the chemotherapy provoked an even more violent hangover. I had been instructed to always eat some food with my anti-nausea tablets, but my ailing intestines made that nearly impossible. Whatever morsel I swallowed usually came back up within minutes. The greater part of the four or five days after chemotherapy I spent laboriously commuting between bathroom and bed.

The following Saturday morning Jean decided to drive herself to the maternity hospital. Not surprisingly - since she was two weeks overdue - they kept her in. I was intending to call to the maternity hospital later that day, but without the constant attention and more-or-less forced feeding that had helped me through the chemotherapy hangover, my entire system began to malfunction within a few hours. I suffered a savage attack of constipation, during which the slightest exertion put unbearable pressure on my spine. I phoned a nurse friend, who reminded me that walking was often nature's best cure for such a log-jam. I rose from the bed, pulled on trousers, shirt, sweater, and slippers, and without really thinking what I was doing, struck out from the safety of my suburban home.

Before long, with the aid of Fr Andy's walking stick, I was hobbling along a quiet narrow road, fighting hard to keep warm against a cold, biting wind. Soon my body temperature began to drop alarmingly. I decided to seek shelter. Beyond a low wall was a clump of bushes, made visible by the illuminated skyline of the city. It was a case of any old port in a storm; I clambered over.

Unfortunately, I failed to notice that the field was much lower than the road. In the dark, I plunged down onto the rough grass. The sudden fright and the impact to my spine left me temporarily paralysed. I tried to rise quickly - but could not move. My first thought was that now I would never see my own little baby; I would be found dead from exposure, probably the following morning, since no-one had a clue where I was gone. That was when I said my first real prayer to 'Saint Andy'.

Aware that I was getting colder by the second, I forced myself to stay calm. After a few minutes my eyes discerned Andy's old walking stick. I grabbed hold of it by the ferrule and began twisting its handle around the thick grass at the base of the bare ditch. My confidence slowly returned as the anchored stick gained leverage.

After an indeterminate period of struggle, I was lying on the side of the road and being awkwardly heaved into a car by some stranger. It turned out I was only a half-mile from my own house, but it was some time before I regained my composure, and it was a while longer before I was safely back in my own bed and devouring the maximum dose of painkillers.

I was awakened the following morning, Easter Sunday, by the phone, and a nurse telling me my wife would have her baby delivered by caesarean section 20 minutes hence. In the sheer euphoria of imminent parenthood, I forgot about my own troubles.

I tossed my pants onto the bedroom floor, and with my specially-adapted aluminium coat-hanger, began dressing myself. Soon I was speeding through the sleeping city, sneaking through every red light, and pondering my unlikely situation. What effect would chemotherapy have on the unborn baby? How great it would be if Jean had a boy! He could be given Fr Andy's name. But a little Andrea would be just as welcome. The gynaecologist had hinted that Jean would have a girl. The ante-natal nurse, Catherine Joyce, who reportedly had a 100 percent prediction record in such matters, was also adamant it would be a little lady - as was every one of Jean's friends, who all happened to be 'experts' on womens' bumps. So Jean's sisters had supplied a veritable wardrobe of pink dresses. For the second time in a few hours, I earnestly prayed to Andy. This time my petition was that the child, whether Andy or Andrea, would be healthy.

I walked as quickly as I could into the hospital and headed toward the labour and delivery area. 'My wife is having a caesarean performed immediately. Someone from the hospital phoned and told me to get here quickly before the delivery,' I said breathlessly to a nurse with a green mask over her mouth. She pointed to a door at the end of the long corridor. I hurried directly in.

The exertions of mounting three flights of stairs, coupled with the complete novelty of being in a delivery room, momentarily confused me. My beautiful brunette was nowhere to be seen. Lying in the bed was a naked lady with flowing blonde locks, who judging by her smile, clearly took me to be the new consultant gynaecologist. Even in my confusion, I was amused to note that, despite her apparent blondness, all her body hair was jet black. I retreated rapidly and decided to ask for Jean by name.

After a quick consultation, I was soon standing in the adjoining ward, still breathless, alongside my smiling wife. Jean appeared totally composed as she eagerly awaited the birth of her little daughter. A doctor advised me to wait in the corridor. I sat in a chair on my own, closed my eyes, rested my head and hands on my knees, and again began fervently praying to Fr Andy for a healthy baby and a safe delivery.

I looked up, and a nurse was standing in front of me holding a baby. She handed the infant to me; it looked straight into my eyes. Once again my world was standing still in a hospital. 'Oh, my God, she's the most beautiful baby I ever saw! She's looking straight at me. Can she see me?'

'It's not a girl - it's a boy,' was the immediate reply.

'Is this Jean Dorgan's baby?' I quickly asked.

'Jesus, I'm terribly sorry! I have the wrong father,' said the startled nurse as she plucked the baby from my twitching arms. 'I was certain it was you was in the preparation ward.' As she disappeared back into the delivery room she turned and said, 'Your baby will be the next to be delivered. I'll be back in about fifteen minutes.'

She returned within minutes. 'This little lad is Jean McSweeney's baby for sure. Your twin is in the next room. Congratulations!'

'Has she had twins?' I gasped.

'No, no!' she laughed. 'I mean the father of that other baby looks just like you.'

The few extra seconds gave me the time to see the brand new human being rather than the vision. For some reason I discreetly glanced to see if he had hand and legs. This happiness was almost too much to comprehend, and it seemed strangely important to assess if the miracle was truly complete. It was and more. Once my speech returned, I said to the nurse, 'Are you positive it's a boy?'

She smiled and pulled back the soft covers: 'See for yourself.'

Ten minutes later I was taken to a room nearby, and Jean and the baby were brought in. We were allowed to stay alone together for 30 magical minutes. Jean was relaxed and calm and, in bed holding our little baby boy, looked more radiant than ever. And this time, for once, I was not the patient. I hugged her head tenderly. Neither of us was able to speak. Eventually I kissed her and whispered into her ear, 'This is the greatest day of my life.'

Jean replied, 'It's my greatest day, too. Isn't the little man a beauty.'

These were truly moments of which dreams are made. It was almost as difficult to comprehend this overwhelming happiness as it had been to believe the awful diagnosis of malignant cancer. I savoured every second, but when the nurse came back for baby Andy, I was ready to return home to bed.

Jean and little Andy spent three more days in hospital. I wanted to spend every minute with them, but it was a huge struggle to drive to the hospital each night; by the time I got there, I was scarcely able to stay ten minutes. So their leaving the hospital and arriving back home was the ultimate joy.

I continued with the dreaded chemotherapy. The baby's awakening in the middle of each night usually coincided with my taking of the painkilling tablets. Fortunately, the pain had abated sufficiently for me to attend his christening when the little fellow reached the grand old age of six weeks.

It was another joy-filled day. Relatives arrived from near and far. Fr Con Twohig, our new local curate, was engaged to perform the honours. His homily contained a pleasant surprise: 'The Good Lord works in strange ways. He gives life and then takes it away in a manner that is often difficult for any of us down here on earth to comprehend. Today we have given a name to this child, the name Andrew or Andy - after, I am told, a friend of your family who was a member of the cloth like myself. I can now reveal - and it surely is some coincidence - that Fr Andy Sheahan and two of his friends stayed with me in Peru less than two years before he died. Today, I'm sure, he is a very proud man up in Heaven knowing that he has someone carrying his name down here on earth.'

Chemotherapy sessions came and were barely tolerated. An X-ray revealed that the T8 vertebra was now no bigger than a penny and that the discs above and below it were squashed beyond recognition. Mr Walsh gave me the Hobson's choice of operating table or chemotherapy and painkillers. The first option was to have two operations very similar to the first ones: an incision through my chest and a graft of bone from my pelvis to the front of the collapsed vertebra. Then a month on the Stryker frame, before the insertion from the rear of another metal plate. The second option was to continue with the valium and painkillers for three or more years and hope the chemotherapy would do its job. Since my ribcage would support my upper torso, even with the collapsed vertebra, I took the second option.

Life, despite the regular horror of chemotherapy, was now the sweetest I had ever tasted - a transcendental scenario beyond my craziest dreams. I had begun fighting the unspeakable foe, cancer, very much on my own. Now I was blessed with the greatest woman in the world and the living miracle of baby Andy.

Life would never, could never, be the same again. All the material riches promised by my civil engineering professors now seemed superfluous and ill-conceived. Even my youthful dreams of Olympic stardom appeared superficial and greedy. Now I found myself much of the time mentally inhabiting that Garden of Paradise that Fr Andy and I had discovered on that apocalyptic stroll in the grounds of St Vincent's. I would sit for hours gazing at our sleeping offspring and tell myself that to duplicate even one hair on his head would be infinitely more difficult than to send a man to the moon, or Mars, or even the farthest star. Watching the sun daily light up the firmament, smelling the heady perfume of flowers, listening to the rapturous music of the birds - every manifestation of nature had taken on a new and intense beauty. Sometimes I wondered if this almost painfully acute sense of God and Nature was entirely compatible with sanity. But the overwhelming evidence was everywhere. Why shouldn't I take the time to ponder and enjoy it?

I often wondered, too, if developing this thing called cancer might not have been a blessing in disguise. I would probably not have met Jean again had I stayed healthy. Nor would little Andy have come into the world. I had so much to marvel at and dream about. My medical battle raged on. But with each passing day, my confidence and hope of survival grew.

Eight chemotherapy sessions cruelly came and more cruelly passed. I was approaching the maximum my body could tolerate. My brother Terry summoned me to the great US of A, where he intended having extensive tests - American style - carried out. I travelled full of hope. Alas, the transatlantic experts deemed my body irradiated and traumatised beyond help. My fate really was in the hands of the gods.

Six o'clock sounded on the first Saturday morning of my visit to the States; Terry and his South African friend Mike Viser were heading for the golf course. I tagged along with the assistance of the golf buggy and found it impossible to keep my hands off the putter while Terry and his four-handicapper friend played the serious stuff. By the ninth hole my confidence had soared to the point where, against all the eminent medical advice present, I decided to attempt the number one wood. Nine holes later, I was elated to have carded a score of 40. In my enthusiasm I persuaded my partners to continue for a further nine holes. This I covered in one shot less with the aid of my new, slow-motion swing. I spent most of the following week recovering in bed from the exertion, but my flirtation with sporting excellence had been a powerful tonic.

Once back in Ireland, I had to face what might be my last chemotherapy session - but was finding it increasingly difficult. The very mention of the dreaded word chemotherapy was enough to make me ill.

The mention of the Cork Regional itself, even the name of the area where the hospital stood, made my stomach churn. I began to concoct in my mind some way of avoiding the terror. But since Jean always took a day off school to drive me to the hospital, my options were limited when the fateful morning arrived. I finally got the courage to face the intravenous poison by promising to buy myself a new set of golf clubs on the way to the hospital, even though all medical advice forbade me to ever again subject my spine to the torsion of the game.

As I reluctantly set out, a surprise letter arrived from Terry's golfing friend Mike Viser: 'Never enjoyed a game of golf so much - especially the last eighteen. Don't forget to maintain the slow, controlled backswing. Remember to always keep the hands over the ball at point of impact. And believe me, even though I am not a doctor, you sure gave me eighteen good reasons why you have beaten your cancer.'

As Jean drove me toward the hospital, I reread the letter and smiled with renewed feelings of determination and optimism.

25 The fight goes on

It was sheer bliss to finally say goodbye to the hated chemotherapy. The worrisome blood-tests were becoming less frequent. And the annual isotope bone-scans were easily endured. Even though Dr Con C always warned of a 50-50 chance of the cancer returning, my confidence was well on the ascendant. Having dealt with the prospect of dying, I was now encountering a new challenge - that of living. Beginning life all over again was something I had hardly considered. But no-one ever had such incentives. I was married to my dream woman; she had given me the living miracle of baby Andy, who before my very eyes was maturing into a splendid little boy; and another baby was on order.

It became apparent to me that if anything good or positive could be said about cancer, it was that it had given me a sublime appreciation of life which I could never have come to otherwise. Life was now for living, and I was about to live life in the best way I knew.

I prayed fervently every day to Fr Andy, knowing that if anyone up there was going to help me beat this cancer, he would. I occasionally prayed, too, to the saintly American Capuchin Fr Solanus Casey, whose birthday I shared. My mother constantly bombarded Padre Pio, the revered stigmatist.

Strangely, though, religious observance began to play a lesser role in my life. Attendance at Sunday mass appeared less obligatory and urgent than it did when I was first stricken. Living each day to the full, seeing beauty in every created thing and every God-given moment, was now much more important. God's presence was tangible everywhere. Reducing it to an hour on Sunday morning's seemed to be sadly limiting. This new and ever-present God was my kind of God.

Two years passed, and the ribs near where the T8 vertebra had collapsed were finally adjusting to the weight of my upper body. My daily intake of valium and painkillers was gradually reduced. Dabbling with the golf clubs became a minor obsession, not least because my performance on fairway and green was a good indicator of physical health. All in all, normality was beckoning.

I was now thinking of how I might help cancer sufferers less fortunate than myself. A fund-raising golf society seemed logical, but how to get it going was not obvious. In this, I was again blessed by a happy quirk of fate.

I was searching for a ball in deep rough beside the third fairway at my local course, Silversprings, when I encountered someone who had hit an equally wayward shot from an adjoining fairway. The face was new to me, but the dulcet voice of the award-winning radio presenter were unmistakable. 'We two should found a golf society and call it The Squirrels,' joked the amiable Steve Bolger.

'The Squirrels?' I echoed.

'Yeah. Then when we spray the ball into the woods we can shout Squirrel! rather than Fore!'

This seemed a providential opening; I briefly explained to this genial character my idea for a golfing society to assist cancer victims. 'I'm with you all the way,' he enthused. 'My beautiful wife, Marion, died from that wretched disease nine years ago, within a year of our first child being born. Let's go for it!'

Now his playing partner arrived on the scene; it was no less a personage than Ger Canning, the television sports commentator. 'This is the first general meeting of the Squirrels Golfing Society,' said Stevie to the surprised Ger. 'You're elected hon sec. I'll be treasurer. And this guy here will be chairman.' The Squirrels were up and running. Later Fr Con Twohig would be co-opted as 'spiritual director'.

My brother Terry, from his base in the USA, constantly monitored my physical condition. Now he wanted me to visit him so he could better plan my return to full fitness. He advised me to bring all my most recent X-rays and tests, because to undergo further X-rays over there would be to expose myself to unwanted radiation.

Before travelling, I decided to pay my annual routine visit to surgeon Walsh. We enjoyed the customary pleasant chat. Then he examined me and seemed pleased with my progress. 'When were you X-rayed last?' he casually asked. When I told him it was more than a year, he said he would like to see how both the L5 vertebra, which he had operated on, and the collapsed T8 were behaving. I had almost neglected to tell him that my only 'new' discomfort was a niggling pain in my right hip. He decided to have that area X-rayed also.

When he emerged with the X-rays, his body language told me something was amiss. 'Your spine looks to have settled as well as could have been hoped for, but your lower right pelvic area is under severe attack.'

He held up the X-ray of my pelvis; it was brutally legible; at one side was a creamy white bone, at the other a series of black bubbles. 'I'm sorry to tell you that you are back in the wars,' he said sympathetically. 'I will inform Dr Paula Cotter. As soon as you return home contact her. You will probably begin radiotherapy immediately. She will advise you as to what further treatment you will require.'

It was heart-breaking bringing such bad news home - and even more painful having to burden Jean with it. But it had to be done; there was no time to waste.

The following day we both went to see Dr Cotter; she had already planned the campaign. 'You will have one intensive session of chemotherapy in a few days and will begin further chemotherapy in a few weeks. You can take your holiday in the USA if you wish.'

Later I called to Dr Con C Murphy's office, hoping he might be able to offer some morsel of comfort. 'All I can advise you is to go and have your will made,' was his uncompromising response.

'Are you really serious, Doctor?'

'Well, with a wife and young baby, and another baby on the way, it's important to have these matters attended to as soon as possible.' Once more my whole world stood still. This was another of those moments that would be indelibly etched in my memory for the rest of my life, be it long or short.

Subsequent X-rays revealed that the three vertebrae in my upper spine were again under attack, as well my arms and ribs. Even in my skull, several semi-transparent holes were visible, some up to half-an-inch in diameter.

Having had a total of eight minutes of hissing radiotherapy in the all-too-familiar room with the eight-foot-thick concrete walls, I headed west. It was great to see Terry again, but it was hard to focus on enjoyment; I felt that the sooner I began chemotherapy the better.

Soon after returning home, I went back to the Regional Hospital. After a routine blood test, I headed for the oncology department with my pregnant wife. Soon a large infusion needle was inserted into a vein in my arm, and the semi-transparent fluid began to flow. Dr Murphy, who by now was a most trusted friend, injected an orange-coloured liquid into the rubberised end of the needle. Later a colourless liquid followed. After about 45 minutes the ordeal was finished.

That evening passed with only minor discomfort. But during the night I awoke to a veritable nightmare. This chemotherapy was clearly much more potent than the previous. Horrific waves of nausea sent me staggering to the bathroom. That was the beginning of an agony that would last exactly four days. I knelt in front of the toilet bowl and, in several violent convulsions, flushed everything from my stomach. The noise woke little Andy, whose crying in turn roused Jean. I stared into the mirror. A froth-like beard covered my jaw; my bloodshot eyes were barely visible; my entire body was trembling. 'Something has gone radically wrong this time, Jean,' I said.

'It's just a reaction to the new chemotherapy,' she replied. 'How about a nice cup of tea? Get a little food inside you, and take another one of those anti-nausea tablets.'

Jean did her utmost to pacify both little Andy and me, but I was terrified to leave the bathroom. My empty stomach continued to retch violently; I was too dizzy to descend the stairs. A weak cup of tea brought brief solace, but soon it too had followed down the toilet. I tried to return to bed, but within minutes was rushing back to the bathroom.

The next day Jean used all her biology-teaching skills as well as some old wives' recipes in trying to ease my plight. Alas, nothing could quell the internal turmoil. It felt as if my throbbing mind and body were detached from one another. Desperate thoughts of ending my misery, by jumping into a river or under a car, flashed through my mind, but the crazy desire to survive kept reasserting itself. Then a tingling sensation would possess me, and I would mentally challenge this thing called Cancer as if I were again an Olympic athlete and it were my most hated foe. 'Damn you, Cancer!' I would repeat over and over through gritted teeth, until I had worked myself into a psychological frenzy, and Cancer, the big coward, was slinking away with its head bowed and its shoulders hunched. Thus I convinced myself that winning would not be impossible after all.

The empty retching left me so exhausted I could hardly resume work the following week. I also had to supplement the chemotherapy with twice-weekly self-administered injections of interferon - Intron A. This had few side-effects, except that my brown locks began to disappear, and the resemblance to my long-dead grandfather grew more marked each time I looked in the mirror.

A fellow engineer I just knew as Tadhg commented one day, 'You look like someone who has seen a ghost.'

'I'll be a ghost myself all too soon,' I replied, then told him briefly about my illness.

'Two years ago I got a brain haemorrhage,' he said, 'and what saved me from certain death was a homeopath and nutritionist named Robyn Smith who lives in a little place called Ballyhooley. You gotta go and see her this very day.'

My parents lived within three or four miles of Ballyhooley, but hocus-pocus medicine did not impress me; I privately dismissed Tadhg's advice. A few days later, still unable to concentrate on my work, I collected little Andy from the babysitter and headed for my parents' home. Without any prompting from me, my mother mentioned Robyn Smith: 'All I know about her is that she is originally from New Zealand, and many people around here think very highly of her. Come on, let's go for a spin. What have you got to lose?' Just to humour her, I agreed.

Within minutes of meeting this slim, pretty lady with flowing blonde hair, I was converted. She acknowledged the efficacy of modern medicine, but felt that since this was my third time on chemotherapy and the cancer was widespread a new approach would help. 'Your immune system needs to be boosted as much as possible,' she said. 'Since nearly everything we eat and drink is chemically contaminated, it is imperative that from now on you consume only organic foods.'

When I realised that 'organic' essentially meant wholesome or 'old-fashioned' foods grown without the dubious benefits of chemicals or artificial insecticides, I was sold on the idea.

'What do you ordinarily eat for breakfast?' she asked.

'Cornflakes, rice crispies, the usual - with plenty of milk.'

'Those are nutritious, but what you need most of all is food that rids your body of all the toxins from the previous day.'

'How do I achieve that?'

'Organic baby oatlets with goats milk,' was the unequivocal reply. She proceeded to tell me that for dinner and supper my staples should be either free-range chicken, venison, unfarmed sea-fish, occasional lamb - all served with organic potatoes and, of course, organic vegetables. She then specified several organic food supplements I should take at set times each day. All alcohol was forbidden; ordinary tea must give way to a special decaffeinated type; even regular drinking-water had to go through a purifier.

Amidst all this advice, I kept harking back to a recent conversation with my farmer brother-in-law. While Liam was gloating over his huge new John Deere tractor, I wondered why the extendible metal arms of the attached sprayer had rusted to the point of collapse. 'The sprays are so corrosive that the metal doesn't just rust - for some reason it simply disappears wherever the spray is not washed off completely,' he said. 'What these chemicals must be doing to the poor cows, and all of us ultimately, is frightening to say the least.'

Two hours flew as I chatted to the charming Robyn Smith. I left with several sheets of handwritten instructions. The following day my taste buds were sampling items they never knew existed. I could eat as much as I wished, but it was obvious this new regimen would take some getting used to.

The prospect of returning to hospital for a second session of chemotherapy was still unthinkable. I had the utmost respect for and confidence in Dr Cotter and Dr Con C, but decided a 'fresh' opinion might help. A friend, Dr Colm Quigley, made an appointment for me with an oncologist in another hospital. Dr Donald McCarthy was a relatively young man with impressive credentials.

'It is extremely difficult,' he told me, 'to tolerate VAD chemotherapy every two weeks. The alternative is to have the chemotherapy once a month by staying in hospital and having the drip in your arm for four days. An anti-nausea drip in the other arm makes the procedure more tolerable. Perhaps, though, they are trying to push you to the limit, which may not be such a bad idea.'

Wanting to elicit as much information as possible from this fresh intellect, I asked, 'What if the chemotherapy fails to kill the cancer?'

He did not answer immediately, but picked up the telephone on his desk. 'This guy is a world expert in this field,' he said as he dialled the number of a London hospital.

After a short wait, he asked, 'What's the most up-to-date information on bone-marrow transplant for a young man with multiple myeloma?' As soon as he put the phone down, he said, 'One-third, one-third, one-third - but less than a hundred patients throughout all Europe have had the operation. And it hasn't yet been tried out in the USA. Of course, the bone marrow harvested from yourself a couple of years ago was discarded because it was too irradiated. So you would have to get a compatible donor. No - I don't think this is a realistic option, Fanahan.'

'What's all this 'one-third' business?'

'Oh, a third improve, a third remain as they were, and a third die during the operation.' I was too scared to press the matter further. But that triple one-third was another chilling statistic indelibly etched in my mind.

As soon as I returned home I got in touch with Dr Con C and insisted on staying in hospital for the four-day treatment as described by Dr McCarthy. Dr Con C was glad to oblige, particularly when he learned how ill the first dose had made me.

The following Wednesday Jean took her usual day's leave from school to drive me to the hospital. This time I had toothbrush, pyjamas, and four days' supply of organic food in my suitcase. After the usual blood tests we headed for the oncology department. In my inattentive state, I took a while to notice that the same chemotherapy sachet as before was attached. When Dr Con C arrived he decided to continue with the prepared concoction, because the four-day sojourn in hospital would greatly diminish the hangover. The drips were removed, and Dr Con C escorted me to my room. 'The bear does not really jump on my back until tomorrow,' I remarked.

The genial doctor quickly got my meaning. 'If you want Jean to drive you home and back in again tomorrow morning, then you're free to go home.'

Little Andy came to with his usual shout the following morning. The dawn was breaking - but there was no sign of the dreaded fever. The morning turned into the afternoon, and I began to wonder if the crafty Dr Murphy had given me some innocuous placebo.

After another two weeks I duly returned for the third chemotherapy session and entertained Dr Con C with the story of my organic diet and its apparent connection with my post-chemotherapy well-being.

A further eight sessions of the alien treatment came and went, and incredibly, there was no adverse reaction whatever. It was truly a great day for me that Tadhg and my mother persuaded me to go to Ballyhooley.

Dr Cotter recommended I supplement the chemotherapy with twice-weekly self-administered subcutaneous injections of interferon - Intron A. This had few side-effects other than the thinning out of my cherished brown locks. After a few sessions, I was taking a shower when I noticed I was up to my ankles in warm soapy water; the drain-hole had been clogged by the falling hair.

Friends, particularly ones with sparse thatches themselves, began offering comments - as if I could not see in the mirror. 'Christ, your hair is falling out at a fierce rate,' was the general gist.

Eamon Kehoe was the chief offender. A good friend, he apparently felt it his duty to give me a weekly bulletin on the status of my head. But the the tide turned; having shed half my mane, I began to regain it even thicker than before - and certainly thicker than Eamon's. The bold Eamon was perplexed. I got deep satisfaction when, after grudgingly admiring my shining tresses one day, he asked rhetorically, 'Tell me, is that interferon very expensive?'

Gradually my confidence and belief in this wonder drug grew, and I came to view it as yet another indispensable tool in my survival kit.

But the trauma, and the miracles too, continued. The scrutiny for unusual lumps or suspicious symptoms never ends. All too often this would lead to X-rays or scans and the consequent zapping of some life-threatening 'hot spot' by Dr O'Cathal and his radiotherapy laser beams.

It was a sobering experience when I witnessed the birth of our second son; the agony that Jean endured for 12 hours made me think that perhaps chemotherapy wasn't the most painful thing in the world after all. But taking the manly little Andy to the hospital to see his baby brother was a tremendous joy.

Having spent the equivalent of two years of the past eight incarcerated in seven hospitals, and having still to visit the Cork Regional at least twice monthly, I have every reason to respect and admire orthodox medicine. But for all its wonderful practitioners and awe-inspiring technology, my faith in it remains qualified. There is still a place - and an important one - for what I might call supplementary paramedicine, and even for informed personal experience.

Dr Con C and Dr Cotter have gone way beyond the call of duty in monitoring my condition; and their expertise in systemic chemotherapy has helped keep the dreaded disease at bay. Dr O'Cathal and his laser-beam have been on hand to burn out potentially-lethal 'hot spots'. And surgeon Walsh has used, and may even again use, his enormous skills to repair structural collapse.

And yet I am convinced that the organic foods and complementary vitamins prescribed by Robyn Smith have been just as vital to me in recent times. Without them, I doubt I could have coped long with the harrowing chemotherapy sickness, not to mention the four painkilling tablets and two valium I have to take each day.

Exploring every avenue of possible cure or remission has became an obsession. My athletic training taught me that moderate activity is a life-saver. The natural environment, the wind, the rain, the green grass, God's infinitely varied sky, are a daily therapy. My energies may fluctuate from day to day, but the effort is always worth it. Sometimes, Jean will have to help me from the bed; on other days I will play golf almost like a seasoned pro.

Every medical journal I can lay hands on is studiously scrutinised for physical treatments or psychological ploys. When such medical data is scarce, I delve into animal biology.

'It's amazing the effect that stress has on premium quality pigs, especially if it occurs in the hours before slaughter. It changes the colour of the meat and makes it virtually unusable,' said one veterinary inspector to another during the meal at a relation's christening party.

'It's the identical situation in my department with cattle,' said his companion. 'The meat even changes texture. "Blood-spattering" is how we refer to it.'

This bizarre conversation over dinner induced me to return to the library. The volume of scientifically documented evidence was mind-boggling. The lesson to be learned from our four-legged friends had to be heeded: excessive stress is a killer. My destiny, I conclude, is very much in my own hands.

In this context, I just have to be the luckiest guy that ever lived. Jean is the only girl I ever wanted to marry; she continues to be my greatest joy and inspiration. Both of my treasured little boys enrich each day beyond words. I have everything to live for.

Despite the greatest incentives in the world, however, there is an enduring trepidation that relentlessly haunts the cancer patient, driving him or her sometimes to desperation. Whether alone, in the midst of good friends, on the golf course, the self-monitoring never ends. While the workaday world carries on regardless, the cancer victim is furtively scrutinising his own physical responses for fear of new and terrible symptoms.

Sometimes, the spectre of the disease raises its ugly head in the unlikeliest of situations, as happened not long ago. I was innocently surveying a building site, when I noticed smoke billowing from a nearby building. I rushed to the nearest house to phone the fire-brigade. There was no response from the front door; I hurried to the back window. My timing could hardly have been worse; there on the sofa, in a highly compromising position, were the woman of the house and one of my doctors - whose name I have been careful to omit from this narrative.

I laughed inwardly as I made the urgent phonecall. But before I left, my good humour was brutally punctured by the cuckolding medic. Having buttoned his trousers and recovered his professional poise, he asked, 'How are you feeling these days?' When I told him I felt I was on the mend, he shook his head: 'It's really unbelievable. Every test and X-ray said you would not survive to last Christmas.' Then he asked if my wife had had a second baby.

'Another Fanahan - a beautiful, healthy boy who's exactly six months old,' I said proudly.

'Truly amazing. You were never supposed to see that baby,' he replied authoritatively.

My heart and stomach sank. In unfamiliar surroundings, the familiar feeling of imminent death once again engulfed me. The gravity of my condition could not have been more succinctly summed up. The trip back home was a blur.

Jean and my two little men were absent; I headed directly for bed. But the thought of burdening her on her return with my depressing story seemed unfair; I dragged myself out of the bed and headed for the most tranquil spot I could think of - my local golf course. I walked along the perimeter of the course, my eyes brimming with tears, wondering what future I might have.

A robust shout shattered my reverie. It was my sometime golfing partner and great friend Willie Murphy; he wanted me to join him. I did my utmost to conceal my funereal news, but Willie knew me too well. When I related what I had been told, he took a number of deep breaths and stared through me for several long seconds. Then he began to shake his head, while viciously throwing an iron into his golf-bag.

'God rest poor Fr Andy's soul! He always said not to heed a word from those doctors who like to play God. Do you know what, Fanahan - I wouldn't believe one damn word that sonofabitch told you. What the hell did you expect? You walked into someone's house and caught him with his pants down. What else could the hypocrite do but try to scare the daylights out of you. Forget you ever met the bastard. Come on, grab a club and a ball. Let's play golf!'

The author gratefully acknowledges the support of Waterford Crystal